THE WISE MEN

of the WEST

VOLUME I: THE WEST

THE
WISE MEN
of the WEST

A *Successful* SEARCH FOR THE PROMISED ONE

IN THE LATTER DAYS

a novel by

JAY TYSON

The Wise Men of the West © Copyright 2019 by James E. Tyson.
ISBN 13: 978-1-7324511-5-5
   Library of Congress Control Number: 2019953102

Printed in the United States of America
Second Printing: 2021
18 17 16 15 14   5 4 3 2 1
Edited by Mark Heinz
 Illustrations by Michael Gellatly
Cover design by Glen Edelstein

SOMETHING
OR **OTHER**
PUBLISHING

Info@SOOPLLC.com
For bulk orders, e-mail: Orders@SOOPLLC.com

If in the uttermost corners of the East
the sweet savors of God be wafted,
he will assuredly recognize
and inhale their fragrance,
even though he be dwelling
in the uttermost ends of the West.

– FROM THE *TABLET OF A TRUE SEEKER IN THE BOOK OF CERTITUDE*

I believe in the Father
I believe in the Son
I believe in the coming
of the Promised One
Who calls to all people:
Now the time has come—
One fold and one Shepherd,
the healing has begun.

– FROM *"THE HEALING HAS BEGUN," A SONG BY DAVID NOLL (2001)*

To everyone who has humbly hoped to see,
or prayed to witness,
the coming of the Promised One,
and to those who have longed to be
among the first generation of His followers,
this book is dedicated.

Contents

VOLUME I: THE WEST

MAPS

A Few Notes for the Reader

OCCASIONAL NOTES OF GENERAL INTEREST have been added at the bottom of the page on which they occur. Additionally, for those readers interested in a more complete understanding of the historical facts upon which the story is based, please note that when the names of historical events or people first appear in the text, I have placed these names in italics. Details about them can usually be found in an online encyclopedia under the name thus provided. In cases where further sources of information might be helpful, I have provided an endnote leading to additional information and a bibliography at the back of the book. As to the cities, towns, and historic places mentioned, all of them are real, although a few might have changed names since 1843. The maps provided at the start of Chapters 9 and 12 will help the reader follow along.

Quotations from the Bible are taken almost entirely from the King James Version; direct quotes from Scripture are in italics. This was, by far, the most widely accepted English version of the Bible in the 1840s and remains one of the most widely used. In addition, when referring to a specific biblical quote, the narrative often provides only the chapter, not the verse. Anyone who is inclined to look up the quote is thereby encouraged to read the whole chapter and thus to understand the quote in greater context.

Similarly, quotes from the Quran, also in italics, are generally taken from George Sale's version, translated in 1734. This was the first version to be translated directly from the Arabic into English and one of only two

English versions available in the 1840s. It remains one of the few versions that attempt to translate every word into English rather that leaving several transliterated Arabic words in place. It also provides a wealth of explanatory notes helpful to the Western reader.

I have striven to the best of my ability to provide an accurate description of the times, places, and people. I trust that the scholar who focuses on the particular details of the history of any of these places will indulge occasional inaccuracies I might have inadvertently included. This is, necessarily, my own individual understanding of history. As such, it can never be authoritative nor is it intended to be. Although many of the ideas are rooted in the teachings of the Baha'i Faith, some of my own extrapolations may also be found. I hope the reader will take all of them as an opportunity for reflection and discussion, and as a doorway to a more detailed study of the history of these times, rather than as an end in themselves.

Many first names in the Middle Eastern world are simply Arabic versions of biblical names. Where this occurs, I have typically added the Western version in parentheses upon the introduction of the character to assist the Western reader.

The reader will note that I have adopted the convention that pronouns that refer to any of the Messengers of God will normally be capitalized out of respect and also as a way to distinguish references to Him from references to others. Two exceptions to this rule are noted: (a) pronouns among the words or thoughts of someone who does not recognize the validity of the Messenger are not capitalized and (b) when discussing the messenger in relation to God, his pronouns are not capitalized as he exists in the state of utmost humility in that relationship.

As in most historical fiction, I have refrained wherever possible from introducing direct interactions between historical characters and fictional characters. In the few instances where this necessarily occurs, I have made every effort to keep these interactions as historically plausible as possible.

A Note of Gratitude

No ONE CAN SPEND SIX YEARS writing a book without obtaining significant insights and help from many he finds along the path. Space does not permit me to list all that was done by those of you who helped me, but you know.

First, I thank my wonderful wife for all her patience and wise advice. For perspectives from various religious traditions: Susan Maneck, Soheil Sohrab, Habib Hosseiny, Joel Smith, John Vincent, Craig Shere, Bhabani Pattanayak, William Collins, Paula Drewek, Wade Fransson, and Betti and Robert Knickerbocker. For pointers, ideas, encouragement and general help: Emily Goshey, Scott Duncan, Peter Murphy, Rodney Richards, Jim Traub, Robert Stockman, and Julie Geredien.

And finally to all reviewers who assisted in checking the manuscript, the authors of the wonderful sources I've used (listed in the bibliography), and the publisher's talented team, I am deeply grateful.

Foreword

SOMETIMES THE DIVINE COMES in the guise of unanticipated and even seemingly unfortunate circumstances. And often God answers our longings and prayers in ways counter to our aspirations and expectations as the deepest lessons are revealed in the most jarring parts of our journey.

Thus are the similarities between the path that inspired Jay Tyson to write this book and that taken by its two main protagonists, Zach Thompson and James Lawrence. Zach, the son of a pious and successful American shipping company owner, and James, a scholarly British Orientalist, are typical nineteenth century gentlemen on an atypical journey. Setting out upon the inspiration of an idea, they soon find that idea shifting in ways they couldn't have imagined.

Tyson's journey toward writing *The Wise Men of the West* began with a modern mechanical mishap in 2013, but its roots trace back to the previous autumn, when he visited the lovingly preserved farmhouse of William Miller in Low Hampton, New York, and conversed with some of its Christian Adventist caretakers.

Miller, a nineteenth century military veteran and farmer, also found his life's journey taking unexpected turns when his personal study of the Bible led him to the conclusion Christ's return was imminent, and he was called to preach accordingly. The resulting "Great Disappointment"—when Christ didn't descend to Earth from the clouds in 1844—was regarded by many as Miller's great failure.

But what if he wasn't so wrong after all?

Tyson's visit to Miller's farmhouse was inspired by his belief that there was much to be learned from this dramatic turn of events.

Eight months later, after selling the old family home, Tyson was making his way along the Ohio Turnpike in a rented truck carrying three large pieces of old family furniture back to his current home in New Jersey. He began reflecting on his earlier visit to Miller's farm and the implications of Miller's insights.

"A thought came to me that it might be possible to write of a couple of Christian Adventists who were willing to travel in search of the return of Christ, people who expected a more conventional return rather than the mega-miraculous one from the sky," Tyson recalls. "Within a few minutes of thinking this thought, the truck I was driving started to shake violently."

He pulled over and contacted the rental agency, and the truck was soon in a shop. But the repairs would take an entire day.

"So I suddenly had twenty-four hours with nothing to do," Tyson states. "But I had a pad of paper and a pencil, so I started my exploration of how such a story might unfold. That was six years ago. It is wonderful to be finally bringing this to a conclusion!"

And now we as readers can benefit from the conclusion of Tyson's work. We can begin our own journey, traveling alongside Zach and James as they move toward and through the Holy Land, an ancient region in which they find new hope. It is as much a profound inward spiritual quest as it is a physical trek. Tyson's deep knowledge of religion, geography, and history create a rich and immersive reading experience. *Wise Men* is a trip well worth taking. My hope is you enjoy and appreciate it as much as I have.

– Mark Heinz, Editor

List of Fictional Characters

	Name	Relationship/Role	1st Ref
1	Zach Thompson	Main character—a true seeker	Prologue
2	Gabriel Robinson	Nephew of Zach	Prologue
3	Sarah Thompson Robinson	Sister of Zach/Mother of Gabriel	Prologue
4	Isaiah Robinson	Husband of Sarah/Father of Gabriel	Prologue
5	Josiah Thompson	Father of Zach	Prologue
6	Daniel Thompson	Brother of Zach	Prologue
7	Clara Thompson	Wife of Daniel	Prologue
8	Jeremy	Zach's assistant & traveling companion	Chap 2
9	Hezekiah Mulligan	Traveling acquaintance on Hudson River	Chap 2
10	Elijah Goodman	A follower of William Miller in England	Chap 3
11	Rev. Wilson	Adventist minister	Chap 5
12	Rev. Woolworth	Anglican priest	Chap 6
13	James Lawrence	Orientalist & traveling companion	Chap 7
14	Father Timothy	Catholic priest	Chap 8
15	Father Alexi Kallistos	Greek Orthodox priest	Chap 10
16	Shaykh Hakim	Muslim Shaykh from Akka	Chap 10
17	Siyyid Youssef	Traveling companion—Akka to Jerusalem to Tiberias	Chap 11
18	Moshe	Jewish keeper of the Cave of Elijah	Chap 12
19	Suleiman	Host in Jerusalem	Chap 15
20	Musa	Traveling companion—Tiberias to Karbila	Chap 16

Historic (non-fictional) characters: There are many figures from the nineteenth century (or earlier) who appear in the book. They are introduced in *italics* in the text to distinguish them from the fictional characters listed above.

THE WISE MEN
of the WEST

Introduction

THIS BOOK IS AN INVITATION. It is an invitation to revisit and re-evaluate a question people began asking two centuries ago: "Are we living in the 'latter days' as described in both the Old and the New Testaments?"

And the people of those days had good reason to ask. Granted, a few have asked this question in every age, but in the early 1800s there were some particularly good reasons to raise this question more earnestly. When the disciples asked Jesus for a sign of the time of His return, He gave them a very clear one, stating the gospel would be *"preached in all the world for a witness unto all nations"* followed immediately by His words *"then shall the end come"* (Matt. 24:14). With the development of ocean-crossing ships, European explorers and missionaries had carried the gospel to all nations across the globe and borne witness to His truth to the entire world by that time.

There was also a sense that old ways were ending and something new was stirring. The Dark Ages of Europe had ended with the Renaissance, or rebirth, of the quest for knowledge and understanding. This led to the Age of Discovery, the Age of Reason, and the birth of America as the first major modern republic. The careful study of science in those days was beginning to yield its first fruits of technology, whether for good or ill, in the form of the steam engine and the cotton gin in the late 1700s and steam-powered riverboats and engines pulling wagons on short railroads in the early 1800s. For many people, it indeed seemed to be at least "the close of the age" if not "the end of the world."*

---

* The phrase translated in the King James Bible as "end of the world" has been more accurately rendered in more recent translations as the "close of the age" (or "eon," which was the actual word found in the earliest Greek manuscripts.)

1

So people began to wonder, to ask about, and to investigate the question. Several religious movements were born, particularly in the northeastern part of the United States, including the Church of Jesus Christ of Latter-day Saints. Its very title reflected the belief of its founder, *Joseph Smith*, that the biblical "latter days" had indeed arrived. Others included many of the Adventist churches, whose belief in the second coming (or advent) of Jesus can be traced primarily to the teachings of a preacher named *William Miller* of Low Hampton, New York. In 2012 I visited his farmhouse there, which has been lovingly preserved by the members of the Seventh-day Adventist Church. From them, I learned more of his story. The dialogue started back then has led, however indirectly, to the writing of this book.

Mr. Miller found solid biblical reasons to believe the latter days were near at hand. He followed Jesus' instruction to look to a particular part of the Book of Daniel in order to understand the time of His return. Tens of thousands gathered in great camp meetings to listen and prepare for the great event. But when the predicted date arrived in 1844, nothing happened (or so it appeared). Although Mr. Miller remained convinced his understanding was essentially correct, most of his followers were downcast and disillusioned, while scoffers loudly ridiculed them. Ever since, the date has been known in Christian circles as *"The Great Disappointment."*

Some returned to their Bibles to see how they might recalculate the date and wait again. Some decided that a spiritual event must have occurred in heaven and that the promised return of Christ on Earth would have to wait until some unspecified time in the future. And some decided to abandon any attempt to understand biblical prophecy or even to understand religion itself.

But apparently no one stopped to consider the possibility that they might have correctly understood the *timing* while misunderstanding the *manner* in which Christ would return. No one seems to have learned a lesson from the Wise Men of the East, who traveled from ancient Persia to find Jesus at the time of His birth and who understood not only the timing of His arrival but also the manner. They were not dissuaded when they found a recently-married couple – a carpenter and his wife, who had recently given birth. These were people of such humble means, that on the night of the babe's birth, they were unable to find room at an inn, and thus had to place Him in a manger where animals fed.

In spite of the physical appearances, those Wise Men were somehow able to recognize the future spiritual King and Savior. They were wise indeed.

Alas, in the mid-1800s, during this period of intense anticipation about the coming of the Promised One, it seems that there was no one in the West wise enough to undertake a similar search. But it leads us to wonder: What if such men had existed? What would they have found if, at that time, they had put aside the common, literal understanding of how Christ would return, pursuing instead the notion that Christ might return in a manner similar to His original appearance? What if they sought a return similar to that of Elijah, who arose in the form of John the Baptist, as Jesus Himself had explained (Matt. 17:10–13)? What would some nineteenth century wise men have found if they were looking for someone who would go forth in the spirit and power of Jesus in the same way that John the Baptist went forth "in the spirit and power of Elijah" (Luke 1:17)? If He returned in the same manner as Jesus' first arrival—as someone who was physically normal but who had super-human spiritual power, knowledge, understanding, and compassion—would they have been able to find Him?

This book is an exploration of what they could have found. For even in the mid-nineteenth century, there were clues scattered across humanity's scriptures and collective consciousness—clues that could have been gathered and connected by anyone sufficiently detached from preconceived ideas and dedicated to a far-reaching search.

*   *   *

THE EXPECTATIONS OF THE imminent return of Christ did not end in the West when He failed to materialize from the literal clouds in 1844. While the recalculations pushed the date forward, the evidence of the closing of the past age continued to mount as new inventions and the Industrial Revolution created an ever-more-rapid rate of change. The vast destruction of the American Civil War was also seen by many in apocalyptical terms ("Mine eyes have seen the glory of the coming of the Lord" is the opening line of the "Battle Hymn of the Republic"), with American losses far greater than any other war the country has endured, before or since.

And from the Jewish perspective, the evidence was even stronger. In many Old Testament prophecies, both the "latter days" and the coming of the Messiah are closely associated with the return of the Jewish people to the Holy Land. The Jewish return movement started in the early 1800s and continued through World War I, when the British abruptly ended centuries of Islamic control over the region. Then, through an astonishing chain of events (including the horrific and genocidal Nazi attack on the Jews of Europe) and against all imaginable odds, the state of Israel was reborn in 1947 and was able to stand against neighboring nations bent on its destruction.

Thus, the many Old Testament prophecies of the return of the Jewish people to the Holy Land in the "latter days" were fulfilled. However, since those prophecies also predicted the coming of the Messiah in the latter days, Jews, Christians, and even Muslims were left to ponder anew the question: Where is the missing Messiah? How could God have dramatically fulfilled this half of the promise of the latter days without fulfilling the other half?[†]

Most of the literature on both Christian and Jewish expectations of the 1840s covers not only the expectations that people had but also how God failed to meet their expectations. This story is different. Although it touches on the failure of some prophetic expectations, it is focused on the one substantial success now known to history.

So this book is an invitation to explore, or perhaps re-explore, these questions.

It is also a tapestry woven of both fiction and history. It's a story that seeks to convey a feeling of the experience of historical events through fictional characters without changing history itself. We will witness it through the eyes of a pair of fictional wise men, who were both capable of connecting the dots of the prophecies of the Old and New Testaments and had the means to pursue this question on a journey eastward.

---

† To this day, some Jewish groups refuse to recognize the legitimacy of the state of Israel because the biblical prophecies are so clear that the return to Israel can only happen in association with the coming of the Messiah.

The Wise Men of the West are explorers, both physically and spiritually, who, much like the Wise Men of the East in Jesus' age, set out in search of the Promised One of their religion. Their journey provides us with the opportunity to explore many of the ideas of their time as we travel from America to London, then on to Rome, then to the Holy Land, and, from there, yet farther east, ultimately to the land of the original Wise Men of the East, the land of Persia, where the prophet Daniel had his visions of the latter days, the visions that Jesus Himself cited as holding the key to answering the question of the time of His return. Along their route, they will discover that their search for the return of Jesus is just a part of a far larger story—a story that bridges and connects all the prophetic religions of humanity.

In John 14:2, Jesus explained that He was going ahead to heaven to prepare a mansion for His followers. But He also said that in His Father's house, there are many mansions, thus suggesting that there could be many legitimate religions. A careful inspection of their scriptures shows that each of the former religions has prophecies that are fulfilled in the latter ones and that can serve as tunnels linking these mansions. This book is an exploration of some of those tunnels and the connections they imply.

Like all good explorers, we must be prepared to learn something new. And like all good explorers, we must choose our route carefully. Lessons learned at the early stages of this journey are vital as they become the foundations for further lessons that will become understandable only at a later stage of the journey.

So come, let us join our explorers now on their two-year saga in search of the Promised One to learn of their discoveries, which can transform the present cacophony of human religious experience into the most marvelous melodies and the most heavenly harmonies the world has ever known.

VOLUME I

THE WEST

The Adoration of the Magi

Prologue:

ON THE TWELFTH DAY OF CHRISTMAS...

"An epiphany," explained Zach to his inquisitive young nephew, Gabriel, "is the sudden realization of a truth, as if revealed by God. And God showed the Wise Men how to find the infant Jesus. That's why we call this night our commemoration of the *Epiphany*."

It was evening on January 5, 1843, and Zachary Thompson was returning from the Epiphany church service with his sister, Sarah; Sarah's husband, Isaiah Robinson; and their son, Gabriel, who was nearly nine years old. The twelfth and final day of Christmas would be celebrated tomorrow, and they were all looking forward to gathering with the rest of the family at the family home in the port city of Perth Amboy, New Jersey.

Walking along the frozen mud ruts in the street at this time of year was daunting. Horses and the carriages, carts, and wagons they pulled had churned up the muddy street by day, and the cold night air had frozen it. A dearth of streetlamps did not make the trek any easier. But the stars were shining brightly, like glittering jewels in the crisp, clear night sky, which reminded them all of that magnificent night so long ago.

"I've always enjoyed the Epiphany story," remarked Zach wistfully. "The coming of the Wise Men from the East to find Jesus at His birth... there is something almost magical about it."

Traditionally, most of the churches believed the Wise Men arrived on the twelfth night after Jesus was born, which is why the Epiphany service was held on that evening.

"I really like the story too," offered young Gabriel.

"Ah, I reckon you do," replied his father with a smile, "especially the part about the gifts that the Wise Men brought. Why, just think: If the Wise Men had not appeared with their gifts, we might not have the tradition of giving gifts at Christmas!"

He reached down to tickle his son a bit.

Everyone chuckled. But for Gabriel, it was more than the gifts. He, too, loved the magic of the story.

"Uncle Zach," he inquired, "how did the Wise Men know that they should look for a bright star? And how did they know that they should travel to Jerusalem to look for the baby Jesus? And where did they come from?"

"This son of mine is always asking questions," Sarah said wearily. She had grown tired of trying to answer them all.

"It is good to ask questions," replied Zach with a smile. "Let us see if we can find some answers." He patted the boy on the back and said, "The Wise Men, or '*Magi*' as they were called in the earliest versions of the Bible, came from the priestly class of far-off Persia, east of the Holy Land. They traveled a long time, crossing the wide desert on camels in search of the newborn Jesus. But I don't really know much more about it than that. Perhaps when we are together with your grandfather tomorrow, you can ask him yourself. He has studied many things."

*   *   *

ZACH'S FATHER, JOSIAH THOMPSON, was sixty-eight, a considerably advanced age for that time, and had not been feeling well. He remained at home in the care of Zach's older brother, Daniel, and his wife, Clara, along with Gabriel's three-year-old brother, Timothy.

By the following day, Josiah was feeling a little better, and so they enjoyed their traditional family gathering, took down the Christmas wreath, and shared the dried fruits, nuts, and other edibles that had adorned it, along with a big family meal.

Josiah had founded and run the family's shipping business, although he had recently turned most of the control of it over to Daniel and Zach. He was a Quaker, of the Orthodox branch. They believed in studying the Bible and quietly reflecting upon it. They participated in the more traditional "programmed" services.

Josiah had long ago taken an active interest in Bible studies for himself. Zach shared this interest with his father, more than his brother and sister or their spouses. Josiah and Zach were particularly interested in understanding the Bible's prophecies, from both the Old and the New Testaments, and how these might pertain to the current age—a topic that was much discussed during those days.

At dinner, Zach said to his father, "Yesterday, Gabriel asked some questions about the story of the Wise Men, which I was unable to answer."

He asked Gabriel to repeat them.

"Hmmm," Josiah replied ponderingly. "Those are excellent and deep questions and not so easily answered. Indeed, how would some priests from a foreign country with a foreign religion know of the signs of Jesus' birth? Even the Jewish priests were uncertain of the time of the coming of their Messiah. We know that the Wise Men were guided by a bright star, but who told them to look for a bright star at that time? And who told them that they should make the dangerous, thousand-mile journey across the desert to reach Jerusalem in order to search for the Holy Child? We know they came from the East—and Persia was the vast empire that dominated all of the lands east of the Holy Land in those days. In Persia, there was a class of wise men, called magi, who studied all the sciences and the prophetic books of their religion, which was the ancient religion of Persia. It had been taught about a thousand years earlier by a prophet of those days, whose name was *Zoroaster*."

Gabriel was enthralled as his grandfather continued, "This prophet, Zoroaster, taught that there was only one God, just as Abraham and Moses had. And so, in those days, when most of the world believed in many gods—a god of the thunder, a god of the sea, a god of crop growth, and so on—there were two nations that believed there was only one God. One was the nation of Israel in the west. The other was the nation of Persia in the

11

east. And between them lay the vast desert of Arabia. So for centuries, they did not have much contact with each other.

"A few centuries after Zoroaster's life, when the leaders of the Israelites were misbehaving and not following the laws of God, God sent them various prophets to warn these kings that they must change their ways or God would stop protecting them. Alas! Those kings were so arrogant that they did *not* change their ways. And soon enough, a strong army arose from Babylon, which is near Persia. It rode across the Arabian desert, conquering cities and kingdoms and taking their people as prisoners back to Babylon to work as slaves for their king. When this army reached the Holy Land, they did so again. And so, the Israelites were conquered. Everyone and everything of importance was taken away to Babylon."

Gabriel's mind turned to harrowing imaginations as he struggled to fathom God's wrath in the form of Babylonian armies as Josiah continued his tale.

"But then, while they were captives in Babylon, a mightier monarch, *King Cyrus* of Persia, sent his armies to subdue Babylon. So both the Jewish people and the Babylonians became captives of King Cyrus. Now, when the King discovered that his Jewish captives were also believers in one God, just as he and the rest of the Zoroastrians of Persia were, he recognized that the Jewish people were special. With the help of some miracles you may have heard of in the Bible stories, he was eventually convinced to allow the Jewish people to return to Jerusalem to rebuild it. So even though there were the vast Arabian deserts between these two peoples, there was a connection because they both believed that there was only one God.

"And just as the prophets of the Old Testament heard the words of God and thus were able to predict many things that would come true, so also apparently God must have spoken to Zoroaster, who taught many things to the people. According to the records of some of the earliest Christians, one of the things God taught Zoroaster was that another Messenger would come after about a thousand years and that his people should look for a bright star at that time. That would be a sign that it was time to search for the one who would be called 'the king of the Jews.' It was this teaching of Zoroaster that started the Wise Men on their search for Jesus. When they found Jesus, their joy was not simply in finding Him but also in realizing that the ancient prophecy of their own prophet had indeed come true."

Josiah sat back, feeling that this was an adequate, if somewhat simplified, explanation of the things he himself had learned, mostly from his readings of stories of the Old Testament and from the *Syriac Infancy Gospel*, a translation that he had acquired in recent years.[1]

Gabriel had been watching his grandfather with searching eyes. He was pleased to have some answers to his questions and fascinated by the new possibilities those answers presented. But he was not completely satisfied.

"Thank you, Grandfather, for telling me all of these things, but I have one more question."

"And just what would that be, young man?" replied Josiah with a jovial smile.

"Well, since Zoroaster gave his people the right teachings—there was only one God—and also the right teachings about how to find the baby Jesus, why is there no Book of Zoroaster in the Bible? There is a Book of Zechariah and a Book of Zephaniah, but there is no Book of Zoroaster."

Josiah was surprised at the penetrating depth of this question. He looked at Zach, and then they both looked at Sarah. She rolled her eyes and shrugged. "As I've told you, he likes to ask questions."

After a thoughtful pause, Josiah replied, "Well, I can see you have been studying the names of the books of the Bible from A to Z. It's wonderful indeed that you know them all so well. And your question is a superb one too. I can only say that the books of the Old Testament are about the revelations that God gave to the prophets and Messengers of the Jewish people, which is to say, Moses and the other descendants of Jacob. As Christians, we have inherited the Jewish scriptures and traditions but not those of Zoroaster."

He turned to the others at the table and mused, "It is indeed strange, though, as I think about it. We have been celebrating the success of the Magi's search for more than 18 centuries now, and yet during almost all of that time, no one from the West has bothered to inquire about the background and details of the prophet whose remarkable prophecy started those wise men on that wonderful search. I've heard tell that the holy book of the Zoroastrians was first translated into a European language by a Frenchman named *Anquatil-Duperron* just a few years before I was born, and the first small parts were translated into English only about 20 years ago. English-speaking scholars have known for nearly 150 years that the Wise Men were led by a prophecy of Zoroaster, yet no one seems to be interested in going to the sources of that prophecy. Perhaps..." Josiah paused, looking at each person around the table, and then said, "perhaps someday one of you may help to discover more about Zoroaster and the Wise Men yourself."

The other adults dutifully returned the patriarch's glance, but Josiah's idea seemed to strike a deep chord with Zach; his eyes glinted with enthusiasm.

Gabriel also smiled broadly at this notion and seemed pleased with the answer. But his curiosity was still not satisfied.

"Grandfather," he continued, "some of my friends tell me that someday soon, Jesus will come down to us from heaven and return to visit us here again. Some say He will take us all up to heaven. They tell me of all sorts of amazing and frightening things that will happen when He comes back. Is that true? If He could do that, I asked my friends, why didn't He do that when He came the first time?"

Josiah thought this question over for a moment. Then he replied in a careful, measured tone, "People have many different expectations about how Jesus could return. But they often fail to understand that God does not need to act according to people's expectations. His knowledge, power, and wisdom stand far above any human expectations. When Jesus, the Messiah, was in the Holy Land 1,800 years ago, the Jewish people had many expectations that God would send a strong, military Messiah who would lead the Jewish people to overthrow their Roman oppressors. But instead, God sent a seemingly powerless teacher who taught about loving your enemy and praying for those who persecute you. A few centuries later, the world saw how these humble teachings did indeed conquer the whole Roman Empire. But those who had clung to their old expectations had already been left behind—cast out of Jerusalem and out of the Holy Land.

"Jesus may return again soon, in any one of many ways. It is my dearest hope that you will not allow your attachment to any particular expectation, or the expectations of any friends," Josiah nodded toward Gabriel, "to cloud your thinking and to cause you to make a mistake like the one made by some when Jesus came the first time.

"Your friends have raised an interesting point. But I would ask you to remind them that Jesus *did* come down from heaven when He came long ago. He showed us that the real Jesus was not a body but a spirit. And although there were miracles accompanying His birth, His greatest miracles were His teachings, which gradually spread until they overcame the entire Roman Empire. In truth, the spirit of Jesus came down from heaven. But His body appeared first as that of an infant—a unique infant indeed, who was found by some very wise men. Should we expect that His return would be any different?"

The Great Meteor Storm of 1833

Chapter 1

THE QUEST BEGINS

"ZACH!" YELLED CLARA. "ZACH, come quickly!"

Zach dropped the tools he had been using to repair the cabin inside one of his father's schooners and scrambled up onto the deck to find out what the commotion was all about.

"It's your father," she yelled in a distressed tone from the shore-end of the pier. "You need to get home *now!* I don't know how much longer he will last."

Clara had been caring for Josiah for several weeks. He had been unable to completely shake off the illness he had developed over the Christmas period.

Zach threw on his overcoat and quickly wrapped his scarf around his mouth and nose to protect against the cold air of late January as he hustled toward Clara. "What happened?" he inquired as he reached the end of the pier.

"I don't know for certain, but his fever seems to be up again, and he's asked that you and Dan and Sarah come to his bedside. He wants to have a talk with all of you." She paused and then added grimly, "Maybe a *final* talk."

Zach and Clara moved quickly past the wagons and horses at the end of the pier, over the frozen ground, up the hill on Smith Street, then to the left for a short distance on Water Street. The Thompson home sat at the top of a small ridge, overlooking the Arthur Kull Sound and Raritan Bay. The winter sun was already beginning to set over the low hills to the southwest.

As they hurried along, Zach was thinking of the special bond he felt with his father due to their shared interest in Bible studies. It had started for them one clear night almost a decade ago, on the deck of one of their ships returning from England, when a huge display of falling stars, later known as the *Great Meteor Storm of 1833*, was witnessed by all on board. It prompted a sense of foreboding among many of their first-class passengers, who knew from the Bible that the falling of the stars from heaven was one of the signs of "the end of the world."

But one passenger—a young Greek priest on his way to start a ministry in the small Greek-American community of St. Augustine—explained that "the end of the world" was a mistranslated term. He noted that in the original New Testament—which was written in Greek—the term that was used was "eon." Thus, the phrase was more accurately understood as "the end of the eon" or "the end of the age" rather than the end of the physical world. He assured the passengers that although there might be good reason to worry about the many changes that this new age might bring, the world itself would not end.

This insight led Josiah to a long train of thoughts, during his daily practice of silent reflection, concerning the best manner in which to understand the other prophecies of the Bible, particularly those that refer to the "latter days." After careful study and much pondering, he and Zach reached the conclusion that many of the references to the outwardly miraculous return of Christ at the end of the age were meant to be taken metaphorically, or spiritually, rather than physically. With this in mind, Josiah had begun to realize that just as with the close of the Jewish age some eighteen centuries earlier, the greatest miracles associated with Christ's return would be *spiritual* in nature.

Several preachers in America and England had reached the conclusion that the "latter days" spoken of by many of the prophets of the Old Testament had arrived because by now the gospel had been preached in all nations. Jesus Himself had said, in Matthew 24:14, that this would be the sign. Some, including *William Miller*, the famous preacher from Upstate New York, had done specific calculations based on clues found in the New Testament Book of Matthew and the Old Testament Book of Daniel and concluded that Christ would return in 1843 or 1844. Both Josiah and Zach found these explanations compelling.

Thus, by 1842, he and his father had both concluded that Christ would return not from the sky, as many believed, but initially as a child, just as He had appeared previously; that He would come from the East, most likely from the Holy Land; and that He would make Himself known in some way within the next two years. Josiah had also expressed the hope that he and Zach would be able to sail to the Holy Land in order to be among the first people to find Him. But now, as Zach hurried toward his family's home, he wondered if his father's poor health had put an end to this hope.

Clara and Zach ran up the front steps leading to the high porch overlooking the bay, hastily entering the house and then dashing up to Josiah's room. They found Dan already there, along with Sarah, Isaiah, and young Gabriel, who had managed to follow along with his parents.

Josiah was propped up by a pillow, but he was looking pale and gaunt.

"I'm glad to see you all here now," said Josiah in a slow and somewhat strained voice, "and I want you to all listen carefully to what I have to say so you will all understand me clearly and remember everything after I am gone." He paused to catch his breath while everyone stood in hushed silence, teary-eyed and keenly aware of the gravity of the present moment.

"I am very pleased with you all. You have all done well during these past several years, helping your mother during her final years and now helping me since I've been on my own. But I'm not sure how much longer I'll be here, so I want to tell you plainly what I want you to do once I'm gone."

He turned first to Daniel and said, "Daniel, you've been managing the shipping business I started nearly 25 years ago, and you've been doing a very fine job of it, so I want you to continue to manage it. 'Tis a fine and growing business, and I expect it will stay that way if you manage it right. And I know you can do it; you seem to have a knack for it."

"Yes, Father," replied Dan. "I'll do my very best to keep it going strong."

"I'm sure you'll do it well. But I won't allow you to keep all of the profit for yourself, do you hear? You'll need to share as much of the profit as Zach needs, and up to a third of the assets as well, for I have a special task for him.

19

"And also for Sarah. Although she and Isaiah are prospering lately, I want you to set aside some of the funds to ensure against any misfortunes that may come their way in the future. Also to ensure that their children are properly educated so that they may always be able to thrive."

"Yes, Father, I will certainly do so."

"Do you solemnly promise?"

"Yes, indeed, Father...I solemnly promise."

"Very well then," Josiah replied.

Daniel and Clara had been unable to have children, and Zach had never married, so Sarah and Isaiah's children were Josiah's only grandchildren.

Turning now to Sarah, he said, "You make sure to take good care of young Gabriel and young Timothy as well, and any others that you and Isaiah bring along. You'll bring them up strong in their character and strong in their faith. Do you solemnly promise?"

"Oh, yes," replied Sarah with tears in her eyes, "of course, you may rest certain that Isaiah and I will do our very best to see them raised properly."

"Very well," he replied.

Then turning, he said, "And now to Zach, with whom I have had such a wonderful bond over these past many years. For he, most of all, has shared my particular interest in the Scriptures, and through our study of them together, we have learned many a wondrous thing. All of you know of our studies and of our special interest and expectations concerning the times in which we live based on what Jesus taught about the prophecies of Daniel. You no doubt have heard me express my hope of traveling to the Holy Land this year or next and my hope of being among the first to witness His appearance there. And Zach has spoken of his desire to join me in that journey.

"Alas!" continued Josiah. "It looks as if God will not allow me to reach that Promised Land. I may not be with you much longer. And even if I recover from this, I will be far too frail to undertake such a journey.

"But Zach is young and strong, bright and brave," he added, looking admiringly at his younger son.

At nearly thirty-five years of age, he was at the height of his manhood, having developed his strength from the chores of the shipping business and his intelligence from the many people he met while sailing, in addition to his penchant for reading. He sported a broad moustache, which added intensity to his brown eyes, and dark brown hair.

"He shares my interest and has no family responsibilities," Josiah continued. "Therefore, Zach, I ask you to travel to the Holy Land this year on my behalf and to search there for any clues regarding His appearance until you find Him, if you can. If nothing can be found by the end of next year, then return here to help your brother." He paused, and then added slowly, "But if you should find anything, send home news of the Glad Tidings, and then do whatsoever He commands you to do. You've heard your brother solemnly promise to cover the costs you may incur. I know you will not be wasteful in your use of this money. Now will you solemnly promise to undertake this journey?"

Without thinking much about the implications, Zach simply said, "Yes, Father, I solemnly promise."

"Wonderful! We have all heard the vows you have taken concerning how you must carry on after I am gone. Now I can rest peacefully knowing that you will carry them out. And remember, after I am gone, I will still be watching over you, helping you, to the utmost extent possible, to carry out your promises."

Darkness was falling, so Clara lit the lanterns and candles to provide some much needed light for the room.

Josiah said he was feeling better now, so Clara ladled out some soup for him from the large kettle that remained warm as it hung over the main fireplace. He sipped a little, but then said he was feeling tired and bid them to go about their normal business so he could sleep.

Clara made him as comfortable as possible and reminded him to call out to her if he needed anything during the night. The siblings spoke in hushed tones about what their father had said. They agreed that his spirits seemed lifted after he had said it, and they hoped that he would recover from the illness soon. Sarah and Isaiah returned to their home nearby.

Josiah did not call out at all that night, and everyone rested peacefully. However, in the morning, when Zach went to look in on his father, he came out with a grim expression and summoned Dan and Clara.

"Yes, he seemed to be in good spirits after speaking with us last night," Zach said, "but apparently it was his final rally.... It looks as though he passed away quietly in his sleep sometime during the night." Clara gasped. Dan hugged her and said how sorry he was to hear the news.

Then he said he'd go down to Sarah and Isaiah's home to let them know, while Zach said he'd begin arranging plans for the funeral.

*　　　*　　　*

THE FUNERAL CAME AND went, with a great number of family friends and well-wishers stopping by to give their condolences and offers of help.

Dan had lost his great mentor, but there would be no major changes in his daily life. He had effectively been running the shipping business since their mother had passed away two years earlier.

For Clara, her caretaking role was now lighter, and she would be able to focus on helping Sarah more with her children.

And for Sarah and Isaiah and their family, little would change as they were already raising the children as Josiah had instructed.

But for Zach, adhering to his father's wishes meant a big change was coming—for his immediate future at least.

Not that he objected. He was a natural adventurer and relished the opportunity to travel. He had sailed with his father to England a couple of times and several times on his own on business matters.

But to go all the way to the Holy Land! That was some serious traveling. His father had spoken truly: Zach was fascinated with their studies of the Bible and particularly with the preaching of William Miller, the self-taught minister from Upstate New York who had followed Jesus' guidance regarding prophecies from the Book of Daniel, which were clearly pointing to the return of Christ, possibly as soon as that very year—1843. So his father's assignment fired his imagination. But after a few days, it settled down, and he began to think of the practical difficulties of the task.

About a week after the funeral, while running some errands, Sarah stopped by at the Thompson family home and found Zach there. After inquiring how he was doing after the departure of their father, she asked, "Zach, are you *really* planning to sail to the Holy Land? It is such a far, distant place, and I should think the journey would be fraught with much danger.

"And besides, if Christ should return next year, as Father and you seem to believe, we will all hear about it soon enough, I suppose, even if we don't see it as instantly as many expect. Isaiah and I could really use your help here, and I'm certain Daniel and Clara would appreciate your assistance in managing the shipping work."

But Zach replied firmly, "Sarah, I *must* go, first and foremost because it was the dying wish of our father. You were there—you heard it. I promised him that I'd go. But beyond that, it is an event of *enormous* importance. The whole Christian world has been waiting for this for more than eighteen centuries. Besides, I do not have any legitimate reason *not* to go—I am a sailor, so travel upon the sea is no difficulty for me. If I had a wife and children to look after, I might have some excuse."

Zach thought momentarily about Ruth, the only woman he had seriously courted. She was soft-spoken, was very kind, and had a tender heart. Alas, while they were courting, her uncle perished in a storm at sea. This alerted her to the dangers of a sailor's life, and her interest in Zach waned. Her decision, not long thereafter, to marry a different suitor had wounded his heart so deeply that he lost all interest in courtship and began to regard himself as being married to the sea and the sails.

"But as you know," he continued, "it seems that neither luck nor God's beneficence have favored me in this respect. Perhaps He has other tasks in store for me. And although I don't have sufficient money of my own for this journey, Father has provided for that through his instructions to Dan. Who else has such an opportunity?

"Those alone are sufficient reasons for me to go. But beyond that, Father was right in saying that I shared his interest in understanding the prophecies of the Bible, and particularly in understanding all about Mr. Miller's study of the prophet Daniel. The coming two years are not just any years. They offer an opportunity of a lifetime...nay, the opportunity of nearly two millennia. I would have loved to travel there with Father, as he had contemplated, but I am still happy to travel there on my own and to discover whatever I can, as he has requested of me at the last."

23

Sarah sighed and rolled her eyes.

"I don't know why so much attention should be paid to this particular prophecy over all of the many prophets in the Bible. There must be a thousand prophecies in the Bible. So out of all those, your William Miller has selected one from Daniel and has tried to demonstrate that it points to the return of Christ this year or next."

"Sarah," Zach said ardently, "perhaps you have not heard the whole of it from Father or me previously. It was not Mr. Miller who selected that particular prophecy. It was Jesus Himself. He pointed to it directly when the disciples asked Him concerning the time of His return. Do you remember your Bible studies? Do you remember chapter 24 of Matthew? *'Tell us, when shall these things be?'* the disciples asked, *'and what shall be the sign of thy coming, and of the end of the world?'* Jesus described that it would be after a long time—that wars would pass, and rumors of wars and earthquakes and various other problems, *'but the end is not yet.'* He went on to describe many conditions to look for. Various religious leaders may debate the meaning of those descriptions, but in some respects, it doesn't really matter, because in addition to describing the conditions, He also gave us *the time* He would return."

"He did?" Sarah objected. "I don't remember reading that."

Zach continued, "Well, when they were speaking in 34 AD, He did not say, 'I will return 1,810 years from now.' That would no doubt have been too long a time for His followers to bear. So He answered with a somewhat hidden reference. Instead of saying it explicitly, He simply told us to look at two visions of the future, which the archangel Gabriel gave to the prophet Daniel and which Daniel recorded in his book, in chapters 8 and 9. Clearly, it would take some pondering to understand exactly what was meant by those prophecies. I'm not even certain that Matthew himself understood since he added a parenthetical note after Jesus cited these prophecies, saying, *'whoso readeth, let him understand.'*

"And it seems clear that Daniel himself did not understand the exact meaning of the visions he had witnessed, for when he asked the angel, near the end of his book, how to understand their meaning, he was told not to worry, *'for the words are closed up and sealed till the time of the end.'*

"But now the gospel has been preached to all nations, so we *have* reached the time of the end. We, as the readers, *have* understood. Here, let me show you."

Zach took out a sheet of paper and a pen and sketched a sideways-looking V. At the junction on the left, he wrote 457 BC. "Both prophecies are dated from the year that the king of Persia directed the Jewish people to rebuild Jerusalem after its destruction by the Babylonians." Then he added two references:

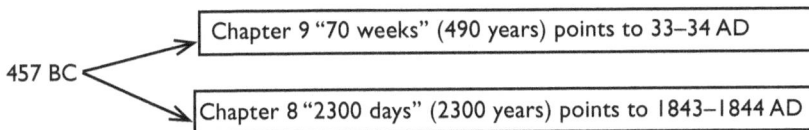

```
                      ┌─────────────────────────────────────────────────┐
                   ┌─►│ Chapter 9 "70 weeks" (490 years) points to 33–34 AD │
457 BC ◄──────────┤   └─────────────────────────────────────────────────┘
                   └─►┌─────────────────────────────────────────────────────┐
                      │ Chapter 8 "2300 days" (2300 years) points to 1843–1844 AD │
                      └─────────────────────────────────────────────────────┘
```

"One of these two prophecies from Daniel—the one from Chapter 9—clearly points to the crucifixion of our Lord. And it was perfectly accurate—a prophecy undeniably fulfilled exactly 490 years after the starting date. Now, if we use the very same method and the very same starting date for Gabriel's other prophecy, it brings us directly to 1843–1844. It would make absolutely no sense for one of these to be perfectly correct and the other one to be all wrong.

"So to summarize, it is *very* clear: The disciples asked Jesus when He would return. Jesus gave a description of the conditions to expect and then gave a date by referring to Daniel: 2,300 years from the year that the edict was given to rebuild Jerusalem—a date known to historians. That, then, is either this year or next. Depending on how you count the year zero, it is either 1843 or 1844."

"I see," replied Sarah cautiously, recognizing that Zach would not be dissuaded. "And I recall Father's unusual belief that Jesus would return in much the same way as He had appeared the first time—first as a child with innate knowledge and only later as a great teacher."

"Exactly," Zach said. "The belief is less common but *not* unheard of. Some of his thinking was inspired by the teachings of the *Reverend George Bush* in New York, whose careful analysis of the original Greek and Hebrew words pointed us away from the more commonly accepted understandings.

Perhaps we can go into these in detail at another time. But suffice it to say that our father was not content to wait here for the news of Christ's new teachings to reach America. Instead, he dearly wanted to search in the Holy Land for himself. And *that*," concluded Zach, "is why I must go."

Sarah was gazing out the large front window of the house, which provided a magnificent view of the southern tip of Staten Island and the northern side of the Atlantic Highlands, which together formed the Raritan Bay on which Perth Amboy was located. As she watched a sailing ship that was gradually disappearing below the far horizon, she thought about the long journey. "You will be on your own, and it is so very far away. If you must travel, you should find someone to travel with you, for your own safety at least."

"I greatly appreciate your concern, Sarah," Zach replied sincerely, "and I clearly would have preferred to have the companionship of our father as we traveled. I, too, have been thinking about how much better it would be to travel with a companion. And with that in mind, I have been planning to write to Mr. Miller himself to inquire if I could meet with him to discuss my plans and to find a willing travel companion."

"Do you think he would go with you?" Sarah asked with surprise.

Zach chuckled. "No indeed. He is no doubt too old to make the journey—you know he is nearly as old as Father was. And besides, from his talks and writings, he seems quite fixed on the idea that Jesus will return from the sky rather than appearing in a manner similar to His original appearance. But...perhaps he has heard of others who would entertain the notion and who would be willing to join me in my travels."

"Well, for your own sake, I hope you are successful in finding someone."

"Thank you. But, of course, I do already have someone who will be with me."

"Oh? And just who might that be?"

"Do you remember how, just before Father passed, he assured us that he would do his best to watch over and guide us? I do believe he will be with me."

"No doubt," replied Sarah with a note of skepticism. "I just hope he will be able to deflect the swords of the pirates or the pistols of the highwaymen you are likely to encounter."

As she turned, she noticed the longcase clock in the corner. "Oh! I must get to the fish market before it closes. I appreciate your sharing of your thoughts about all of this. I'm not certain if I agree, but at least I understand a little better now. And I do hope you will succeed in finding a fellow traveler." She bade him farewell and was off to complete her errands.

*   *   *

ON A RAINY DAY about a week later, Zach started the melancholy task of sorting through his father's papers and other belongings. He wanted to save anything that pertained to his father's study of the Scriptures while at the same time separating out the things that Daniel would need to continue to effectively run the shipping business.

The process called to Zach's memory almost everything he had known about his father. Josiah Thompson had been a member of the Quaker community of Perth Amboy, which was originally the capital of the province of East Jersey. Born in 1775, he had some early recollections of the latter part of the Revolutionary War, but he was far too young to play any role. In 1790 he apprenticed himself as a sailor on the merchant boats that plied the inland waterways of the Raritan and Hudson Rivers, both of which terminated at or near Perth Amboy. Some years later, he was hired as a hand on one of the great sailing ships that crossed the Atlantic for ports in Europe. With the expanding volume of trans-Atlantic trade, he rose quickly through the ranks on the ships, becoming a captain by 1804. This enabled him to have a share in the profitable trade. Shortly thereafter, he married Dorothy, a devoted young woman from their Quaker Meeting. Daniel arrived on the scene in October 1806, while Zach was born in April 1808. After a couple of miscarriages and a sister who died as an infant, Sarah was born in 1814. In those days, there was frequent harassment by the British Navy, but after the War of 1812 ended, the outlook for American trading looked promising; by 1816 Josiah had done well enough to become the owner of his ship. He soon added a few river sloops and barges that would collect goods from ports on the Raritan, the Hudson, and Long Island Sound for transshipment to Europe. Thus, he started his own shipping company, and it had prospered handsomely.

Zach mused at how fortunate or foresighted his father had been in choosing Perth Amboy as a location and in choosing shipping as a trade. The new country was growing rapidly, and the expansion of its trade was facilitated by a host of canals that were opening large areas to commerce. Even before the canals, the tonnage of shipping on the Raritan and Hudson Rivers was among the highest in the nation. The canal linking the Hudson River to Lake Champlain was completed in 1819, providing access through the north end of the lake all the way to the southern edge of Canada.

The Erie Canal opened in 1825, expanding the reach of shipping to the west end of New York, and through its connection to the Great Lakes, its reach had expanded along a route of well over a thousand miles into the heart of the continent. Many of the Erie Canal workers were even now working on a new canal to connect the small town of Chicago, at the end of the Great Lakes, to the mighty Mississippi River. These, together with a network of other recently opened canals, funneled food and products from almost the entire northeast, as well as parts of Canada and the Great Lakes region, down to the ports of New York and Perth Amboy for shipment abroad. It was no surprise to Zach that the years had been so busy and so profitable.

Among the Quakers, many believed the return of Christ referred to a spiritual event. However, the Quaker practice of quiet reflection upon Scripture led Josiah to notice, in the prophetic books, references to future events that seemed too specific to be understood in spiritual terms alone. He could not escape the conclusion that a Christ-like figure would appear once again to mankind, just as Jesus had appeared eighteen centuries earlier and as Moses and Abraham had appeared many centuries before that.

Like much of the Orthodox Quaker community at that time, he had been giving more attention to the Scriptures than the earlier generations of Quakers had. But unlike many of his fellow Quakers, he believed God would once again speak to humanity through a Messenger who would have the same "spirit and power" as Jesus, just as John the Baptist had appeared with the same "spirit and power" as Elijah, according to the opening chapter of Luke's gospel.

Had not Jesus Himself confirmed to His disciples that John was the return of Elijah? Josiah felt certain that in a similar manner, the spirit and power of Jesus would return as a new Messenger but not necessarily bearing the name "Jesus," in the same way that John did not bear the name "Elijah."

He used to ask, "Does not even the Book of Revelation tell us that He will bear a new name? Go, look at chapter 3 verse 12 and see for yourselves."

He believed that the new Messenger would not descend from the physical sky, contrary to what Mr. Miller's followers generally believed. "Nay!" he used to say. "That kind of thinking is what caused the Jewish people to miss Jesus 1,800 years ago. Nay indeed! We shan't make that mistake again."

So it was fair to say that his perspective on this question was not the usual one—neither by Quaker standards nor by Mr. Miller's.

Since the descriptions of the *conditions* for the return of Christ were so open to interpretation, Josiah was not inclined to put too much weight on those prophecies. But the one thing that seemed most clear to him was the reference to a specific *time* of the fulfillment. It was back in 1834, while he was studying these time-related prophecies and shortly after his discussions with that Greek priest about the "end of the age," that he first read of the teachings of William Miller. He found much of Miller's understanding of the time prophecies to be thoroughly sound.

Josiah's wife, as well as their older son and their daughter, had taken little interest in such thoughts. But Zach was of a similar mind, and they had spent many a wonderful evening pondering various biblical passages together and sharing their understandings of what these must mean. They had gone together to hear Mr. Miller speak in New York City in 1840 and again in nearby Newark as recently as last May.

Among his father's papers, Zach found a set of notes that Josiah had taken from Mr. Miller's talks and publications that seemed to summarize Miller's teachings, or at least the parts that Josiah could agree with. It was dated from the previous June, a month after the Newark talk, so it was unclear as to how much of this came directly from Mr. Miller and how much was Josiah's own thoughts. But Zach found it to be a useful summary that he wanted to review, so he added it to his collection of the papers to be saved.

*   *   *

ZACH HAD BEEN CONTEMPLATING the prospects of his travels to the Holy Land for a few weeks, trying to anticipate the difficulties that might arise. Sarah was not the only skeptic. His neighbors and many of his family's friends tried to emphasize the dangers involved, without seeing its importance. He himself was beginning to have his own doubts. But then something occurred that established in him an unyielding determination to undertake the journey, while silencing the objections of family, friends, and neighbors. It was a sign in the sky.

Walking home shortly after sundown in mid-February, he noticed a comet low in the southwestern sky. This was not entirely unusual; he had seen Halley's Comet while on one of his Atlantic crossings to England with his father in 1835. But during the course of the next few weeks, this comet grew brighter and brighter, reaching such brilliance it could be seen clearly even during the daytime.

Soon excited talk of it was on everyone's lips. No one could remember ever having seen or heard of such a spectacularly bright comet. Many recalled the Great Meteor Storm ten years earlier. Many, including Zach, also remembered the famine of 1816 during the *"year without a summer,"* which afflicted both North America and northern Europe. They wondered if these were the signs of the times, as given in Luke 21:11: "...famines, and pestilences; and fearful sights and great signs shall there be from heaven."

And combined with the widespread discussions about Christ's return, many were asking if this was "the sign of the Son of man in heaven," of which Matthew had written in chapter 24 of his gospel. It seemed clear that something portentous was happening, causing worry in some quarters and near panic in others.

The brilliance of the comet continued to grow during the first week of March. At that point, the comet had a two-pronged tail, with a length that spanned a quarter of the sky. It remained as long and as bright until March 21, when it started to gradually decline. When people checked the records, they all acknowledged that there had never been such a brilliant and long-tailed comet. ‡

For the Christian world, it was impossible to ignore the connection to the story in Matthew of how a similar comet or bright star had signaled the Wise Men from the East to start their journey in search of Him who *"is born*

‡ The comet would come to be known as ***"The Great Comet of 1843."***

the King of the Jews." And so it became the cause of great discussion in all of the newspapers, as well as among a great many people, as to what might be the significance of this startling sign at this particular time. Was this indeed a sign of the things that Mr. Miller and other Adventists had foretold?

To Zach, it was an undeniable signal that now was the time to begin once again the search for the coming of the Christ, just as the Magi had done.

At this point, he resolved to put aside any reservations or nagging concerns from friends and neighbors and to dispatch a letter to Mr. Miller himself, requesting permission to visit him at his home in order to discuss in greater detail his understandings of Daniel's prophecies and his own plans for traveling to the Holy Land to search for additional signs or indications of the coming of the Promised One until, God willing, He was found.

He posted his letter on March 21 and was anxiously hoping to hear back within a couple of weeks. But early April arrived with no return letter. So he wrote again, with a bit more urgency in his tone, explaining his intent to leave for England early in the summer. A letter came back after a fortnight from Lucy Miller, Mr. Miller's wife, who apologized on her husband's behalf for the delay and explained that he had suffered from a serious attack of a skin disease, erysipelas, while preaching near Sarasota Springs in mid-March and how he had spent two weeks there just to recover enough strength to make the journey home. He was still recovering, and she would send word when he had recovered sufficiently to receive visitors.[2]

While waiting, Zach proceeded with other plans for his travels. He considered how he might carry the money he needed to pay for all of the costs of such an extended journey. Paper money might be difficult to exchange, at least at a fair price, in such faraway places. Coinage—even gold—would likely weigh too much to constantly carry. (And he knew the only way to make sure it was safe was to keep it on himself always.)

Then he recalled a story he had read as a youngster from *The Travels of Marco Polo.* It described how they had purchased fine jewels, which they had sewed into undergarments that they wore at almost every point and how they kept a diligent eye on them whenever they took the opportunity to bathe. When they were in a sizable city, they would remove a single jewel and exchange it for local currency, which would carry them a long way.

Thus they traveled safely all the way to China and back. So Zach had the local tailor make such a garment, having an inner lining with many small pockets, without explaining its purpose. He estimated the cost of travel for almost two years since he wanted to be able to remain in the Holy Land until the end of 1844, if necessary. His father's account had sufficient funds, and so he set to work gradually converting the funds into gemstones and secretly sewing them, one by one, into the pockets of this unusual undergarment.

He prepared a list of all the things he would need for the journey, but the thing he needed most was a well-seasoned traveling companion. He hoped Mr. Miller might have some suggestions.

Chapter 2

DISCUSSIONS ON AN UPSTREAM JOURNEY

IN MID-MAY, ZACH RECEIVED another letter from Lucy Miller stating that her husband's health was gradually improving and that he could receive visitors so long as their stay was not protracted or stressful. Zach responded immediately, advising her of his itinerary.

Zach planned to ride one of the Thompson schooners scheduled to head up the Hudson with the next load of goods for farmers in the Albany area. From there, he knew he could find other boats that could carry him through the locks around the rapids and then up to the canal at Fort Edward. Canal boats were in service now, and they reached up to Whitehall, which, according to Lucy, was but six miles from the Miller farm.

Zach loved sailing, so having a water path from his home to Mr. Miller's suited him just fine. The overland routes by horse or carriage were jarring on public roads, and the turnpikes were not much better, there being virtually no paved roads. A few short railroads had been built but none through the countryside along the route to Whitehall.

He preferred to not travel alone, so he asked one of the company hands, Jeremy, to join him on the journey. He was a bright lad of eighteen years who had recently started with the company. He had also shown some interest in religious issues.

By the following Thursday, May 25, the schooner was fully loaded with its wares for sale, and so they set out up the Hudson River early the next day.

The Hudson was a long, flat river—virtually at sea level for the 150-mile journey from Staten Island to Albany. It was easy sailing with warm spring breezes and dramatic views of the Palisade cliffs of northern New Jersey and the Catskill Mountains farther north. Beyond these, there were many pleasant hills, woodlands, and farms on both sides of the river, all in full springtime bloom.

Many other boats were making their journeys, including the occasional steamboat, which had been plying these waters since Robert Fulton launched the first one—*The Clermont*—on this river, a year before Zach was born. Some travelers liked the reliability of the steamboats, but Zach disliked their noise and black smoke. He preferred the quietude and the fresh air of sailing. It provided him with plenty of time for reflection, and he was in a mood for reflection about his upcoming journey.

Zach had been thinking about the comet that had shone so brilliantly in the March sky and the story of the Wise Men of the East, who had also seen some brilliant star—perhaps a comet—that had prompted their journey to the Holy Land. How fascinating a story that was! He thought back to the explanation that his father had provided at the end of the past Christmas season and the questions that Gabriel had raised.

"Hey, Jeremy," he asked as they sat on the deck watching the scenery, "do you know anything about the story of the Wise Men of the East?"

"The Magi?" Jeremy replied. "Well, we hear the story every year at Christmas service. They were from somewhere in the east and saw a bright star and followed it until they found the newborn Jesus."

"Yes," replied Zach, "but there is much more than that. Comets or other bright stars appear in the sky from time to time, and people, especially wise people, don't just get on a camel and start a thousand-mile journey every time this happens. They were wise men, who had read their own scriptures. And there must have been something in their scriptures that told them at least approximately when Jesus was to be born, which country to travel to, and to look for a star as a sign that it was time to commence the search."

Jeremy considered this all for a moment and said, "Perhaps so. I'd never really thought about that."

34

So Zach continued, "My father read that the Magi came from the land of Persia. The people there followed a religion started by their prophet, named Zoroaster, who wrote their scriptures a long time ago—almost as long ago as the days of Moses. He learned that it was a prophecy of Zoroaster that led the Wise Men to the infant Jesus."

"So..."

"So here's my question: If Zoroaster was able to accurately prophesy of the time and country of Jesus' birth, was he a true prophet like the prophets of the Old Testament? Or was he a false prophet?"

Jeremy puzzled over this a bit. If Zoroaster had been a false prophet, he wondered, how could he have accurately foretold the coming of Jesus? But if he was a true prophet, why was it that no one in the West seemed to pay any attention to his religion?

Finally, he said, "Maybe he was a false prophet who was very clever and somehow figured it out, or he maybe was inspired by Satan."

"I've thought about that answer myself," said Zach, "but then I came across Jesus' own explanation of how to tell a false prophet from a real one. Do you remember it? It's in chapter 7 of Matthew, where, after warning us to beware of false prophets, He says, '*Ye shall know them by their fruits... A good tree cannot bring forth evil fruit, neither can a corrupt tree bring forth good fruit. Every tree that bringeth not forth good fruit is hewn down, and cast into the fire. Wherefore by their fruits ye shall know them.*'

"So Jesus Himself is telling us that if the prophecy was accurately fulfilled, that is, if the fruit was good, it must come from a true prophet. Jesus said false prophets *cannot* bear good fruit. Moreover, if it had been a bad tree, it would not have endured from the time of Moses to the time of Jesus. It would have been '*hewn down, and cast into the fire*' a long time ago.

"But as to why the scriptures of Zoroaster are not included in the Bible and why no one seems to read or learn about His teachings, I really have no idea. Every year at Christmastime, we celebrate the birth of Jesus, and 12 days later we celebrate the Epiphany—when the Wise Men successfully concluded their search—a search that was initiated by an ancient Zoroastrian prophecy. And yet we never seem to stop to inquire about its source or what its accuracy should imply.

"All Christians will readily explain that they believe in the truth of two religions, Christianity and Judaism. But I myself have no idea why they ignore the third religion when the evidence of its truth is recalled every year at Christmas."

Jeremy was puzzled. "Maybe they figured that there were enough prophets in the Old Testament already and they really didn't need any more," he offered. "Or maybe they just didn't want to include any that were from so far away as Persia was."

"Yes," replied Zach, "that's what my father thought. Yet if they had included Zoroaster's prophecies, perhaps the Jewish people would have had more success at recognizing Jesus, at least at the time of His birth.

"Also, the Jews weren't always far away from Persia. Do you recall the story in the Old Testament of how the Jewish people were conquered by the Babylonians and taken away from Jerusalem, living in captivity in Babylon?"

"Yes indeed."

"And how, after a few years there, Babylon itself was captured by the Persians and thus both the Babylonians and the Jews became part of the Persian Empire?"

"Yes, I remember the story of the mysterious hand, which wrote on the wall, and how Daniel was the only one who could read the writing on the wall and understand it."

"Well," Zach explained, "at the beginning of the Book of Ezra, it says that God inspired the Persian king, Cyrus, to allow the Jews to return to Jerusalem and to decree that the temple of the Jews should be rebuilt. It is entirely different from the story of the struggle in Egypt between Moses and the Pharaoh. The relations between the Jews and the Persians were good in that they both recognized there was a single God who guided them both. Also, Isaiah says, in chapter 45 of his book, that the Lord called Cyrus His 'anointed,' which is a term that is reserved for a king who was supported by God.

"So in both the story of the rebuilding of Jerusalem and in the story of the Magi, that is, in both the Old and New Testaments, we find the beliefs of the Persians treated as if they were a true revelation. And yet no one today seems to acknowledge it."

"Well, that's an interesting thought," Jeremy said. "I guess the preachers I've heard have just bypassed this lesson."

They sat quietly for a moment, watching the passing hills in the afternoon sun and thinking.

Then Zach added, "One other lesson that my father learned from the story of the Wise Men: Don't expect major miracles and don't have preconceived ideas about how He will appear. Think about this: The Wise Men were looking for '*He that is born King of the Jews*,' right?"

Jeremy nodded. "So the Bible says."

"And yet they were willing to leave Jerusalem—the royal city of the Israelites where the outward kings would be—and go instead to Bethlehem, a city without a single palace! They did not restrict their search to young princes nor to royalty. They were willing to look even among humble people in the most humble of places.

"The Jewish people had many prophecies about the coming of the Messiah. But when these referred to a 'king,' the religious leaders imagined He would be an earthly king with weapons and armies instead of the spiritual king that He was. It was no wonder Jesus later referred to such leaders as 'blind.' They did not seem to be able to understand the spiritual dimension of any of the prophecies. But the Wise Men had eyes that were spiritually open. They did not allow outward appearances to fool them. And my father was determined that we should approach our journey to the Holy Land in the same way."

Jeremy knew all about the plans for the journey—it was much discussed among the family and staff of their shipping company. He asked, "Do you think you might find some new wise men from the East when you get there? I mean, if they had a prophecy of the coming of Jesus 1,800 years ago, perhaps they have another one for His coming now. And besides, the comet we all saw was so large that I suppose everyone in the entire world saw that sign. How could anyone miss it? Perhaps they are even now planning their own travels."

"Now that's a fascinating thought," Zach replied. "I hadn't considered it before, but yes, I suppose it is entirely possible that others from Persia or elsewhere may be preparing to make the same journey. I'll have to keep my eyes open for them as well."

"I have no doubt that you are well qualified to make the journey, and you're more likely to succeed than anyone I know," offered Jeremy confidently.

"Thanks," Zach replied with a smile. "If God is willing, I will succeed, and if not, at least I'll have carried out my father's wish."

*   *   *

ALTHOUGH THE SCHOONER COULD sail at night, they anchored that evening at Saugerties to drop off some passengers and take on a few others. The following day, Zach was chatting with one of the new passengers, Hezekiah Mulligan, an older gentleman who apparently sailed the Hudson often. Zach mentioned that he was traveling to Whitehall to meet with Mr. Miller, and Hezekiah noted that he was familiar with the Millerites.

"Why, just a couple of months ago, as I was making the trip up to Albany, I had a long conversation with a group of them. They were returning from a trip to Illinois to meet with *Joseph Smith*, of Mormon fame."[3]

Zach had read of Mr. Smith and the Church of Jesus Christ of Latter-day Saints. Mr. Smith claimed to have been directed by an angel to find several golden plates in a hillside near where he lived in Upstate New York and then was guided by the angel to translate these into the Book of Mormon, which had been published in March of 1830.

Mr. Miller's spiritual quest, although less miraculous and more methodical, was happening at the same time; he first made his views public in the summer of 1831. Both presentations had been preceded by over a dozen years of preparatory experiences, study, and reflection. Both of them had their early religious awakenings in the years of 1816–17.

One of the things that attracted Josiah and Zach to Mr. Miller's teachings was that he was not a self-promoter. He had never desired to start his own denomination but rather to open the eyes of people in many existing churches.

After several years of self-study of the Bible, Mr. Miller had come to his conclusions about the imminent coming of Christ, but he was not inclined to share them publicly. Although a part of his conscience was urging him to share his findings with the rest of the world, he promised God that he would

38

speak only if someone asked him to speak. And as it happened, someone came by later—on the very same day he had made his promise—and asked him to speak at a nearby church. He kicked himself for making such a promise, but how could he now refuse? Thus William Miller's preaching career was launched.

As to Mr. Smith, although he attracted many followers early on, some of his teachings about angels bearing golden plates had been too strange for many of his fellow residents in Upstate New York to tolerate, and so some persecutions began. Thus, he and his followers migrated, following the path of some of their successful missions, first to Ohio, then Missouri, and then western Illinois.

Zach asked Hezekiah, "What did Miller's followers have to say concerning Mr. Smith?"

"Well, they were a bit disgruntled, I must say. They had traveled all the way to the Mormon town *Nauvoo*, in western Illinois, on a mission to share Mr. Miller's teachings, especially those concerning the timing of Christ's return, to see if they could reach some mutual understanding. Yet they didn't achieve their goal, as Mr. Smith was quite fixed on the particulars of his own understandings. So they returned empty-handed."

"So what do you think of Mr. Smith and his followers?" Zach inquired.

"Me? Well, I really don't know what to make of them. One of my cousins heard Mr. Smith's preaching early on, and he was so impressed that he headed west to join them. They're very dedicated—I'll give you that. But I'm not so sure about those plates of gold buried in a hillside in Palmyra... seems a little odd to me."

Zach agreed. "Perhaps Mr. Smith received some teachings that were golden. I mean, we speak of gold to describe things that never deteriorate—things that last forever—like the 'Golden Rule.' That's a kind of golden tablet I could understand as coming from an angel. But if he was talking about the actual metal from the ground, that doesn't sound like the kind of thing that angels carry around."

"Well, who knows?" replied Hezekiah. "And who knows what will become of Mr. Smith and his followers? But one thing I'll say for him. He has warned us about the slavery question, that it may lead us to a terrible war, and I have no doubt of that."

"Are you an abolitionist?"

"I am," replied Hezekiah firmly, "and I'm not afraid to say so. I was mighty pleased when our state of New York outlawed the practice 16 years ago. It should've been sooner."

"Most of the slaves in New Jersey have been set free," offered Zach rather sheepishly, "although I'm afraid it hasn't been fully outlawed in our state yet."

As Quakers, his family had opposed the practice of slavery for several generations. "Some are called 'indentured servants for life,' but it amounts to just about the same thing, I'd reckon."

*   *   *

UPON REACHING ALBANY, ZACH heard a whistle and then the screech of brakes as a steam train arrived in Greenbush, on the opposite shore. He shot a quizzical look at a fellow passenger on the deck. "I didn't realize that they'd completed the eastbound line," Zach said.

"Yes sir," the passenger replied. Zach could tell he was a local. "Completed it just last fall. Now you can leave those bumpy wagons or carriages behind and ride in smooth comfort all the way to Boston—and on a regular schedule too."

Zach wasn't much more enthusiastic about the steam engines belching smoke along the railroad lines than he was about the steamboats belching smoke on the rivers. Still, he had to concede the benefits of routes that ran east to west, such as the Boston–Albany one. These routes didn't lend themselves to river or canal travel, since the rivers ran mostly north to south.

It was late on Saturday when they reached the dock. They remained on board the following day as work was forbidden by law on the Lord's Day, including the work of operating the canal.

Zach had started a diary to record the events of his travels. While he was sitting on the deck in the morning sun, Jeremy pulled up a chair.

"I was thinking about our talk yesterday, as well as other ideas I had heard from your father—about how most people, if they are inclined to consider the topic at all, speak of Christ's return as the end of the world, when the most extreme things will be happening."

"Yes," Zach acknowledged, "that's very often what they think. The prophetic parts of the Bible are written with spiritual language, in a way that fires the imagination and demands attention. Yet when people read them in such a material age as ours, they are easily mistaken to predict material events instead of spiritual ones."

Jeremy explained how some of his friends pointed to several passages in Matthew in which Jesus speaks of the "end of the world."

"My father taught me about that," replied Zach. "In every place He used that phrase, the actual word He used was 'eon,' at least according to the oldest versions of the text, which are in Greek. Thus, He was speaking of the end of the eon, or age, not the end of the physical world.

"Moreover, in chapter 9 of Paul's letter to the Hebrews, he refers to Jesus' sacrifice of His life as having happened 'now, once in the end of the world.' Clearly, the physical world did not end after the crucifixion of Jesus. But it certainly was the end of their eon—that is to say, it was the end of the Jewish age.

"So we believe that Christ's spirit will return next year, in the person of a new Messenger, and this will mark the end of the age in which we have been living but not the end of the physical world."

"Well, that's quite different from what most people say," Jeremy answered, "but it does make sense. However, one of the other quotes that my friends sometime cite comes from Matthew 24. It is the one about how the sun and the moon would be darkened and the stars would fall from heaven. They think that this would destroy the earth entirely."

"That's an excellent example of the spiritual language I mentioned," replied Zach. "Most of those listening in the pews hear this description and think of it as something new. Yet if they read their Bibles carefully, they would understand that this kind of description was used by many of the Old Testament prophets—Isaiah in chapters 13, 24, and 60; Jeremiah in chapter 31; Ezekiel in chapter 32; Joel in chapters 2 and 3; and Micah chapter 3, at least. When Jesus' disciples heard these words, they no doubt thought of the similar language that these Old Testament prophets had used. But in Acts 2, Peter clearly explained that the reference from Joel was already fulfilled with the coming of Jesus and the Pentecost.

"If the physical sun were actually darkened and if the moon turned into blood back then, as Peter said, then why were such extreme events never recorded by any of the historians of those times? Surely everyone would have noticed it. And again, the physical world did not end at that time.

"So it seems very clear to me that Peter, as well as the Old Testament prophets, are using these terms spiritually, not materially. The people of Jesus' time were living in a spiritually darkened age, when the spiritual light—which religious leaders are supposed to supply—had been lost and the reflection of that light had been eclipsed, much as the light of the moon is eclipsed when it passes through the earth's shadow, sometimes turning it blood red.

"And in the same manner that the stars serve as reliable guides when we wander, across deserts or seas, so also the religious leaders are supposed to provide mankind with reliable guidance for our spiritual lives. Yet in the time of Jesus, as well as today, most of these guides are lost—which is to say that these stars have fallen."

"We do live in an age of great darkness," Jeremy concurred. "There are so many different religious denominations, and they don't seem to agree on much. I think some of the leaders spend as much time denouncing each other as they spend on providing spiritual guidance. Even many of the founding fathers of our country seemed to think that God created the world and then left us alone. How can we know what to follow when we are being led in so many different directions?

"Like Mr. Mulligan, I, too, see the evil of slavery, and yet so many preachers, especially in the South, seem to condone it. I also see the terrible problem of drunkenness and how many of our workers can't do their work much of the time because they love their drink."§

"So," Zach replied, "you can begin to see how when the prophets use the term 'darkness,' it has little to do with the absence of physical light and everything to do with the absence of spiritual guidance."

"Yes, I can see that," Jeremy replied. "But one of my workmates cites Luke, where it says in chapter 21 that *'heaven and earth shall pass away.'"*

---

§ Historical note: Per capita alcohol consumption reached an all-time high in the U.S. in the 1820s, which sparked the creation of the American Temperance Society in 1826. They worked for many decades to educate Americans on the problems of excessive alcohol consumption.

"Well, that can be understood in a couple of ways," Zach said. "Certainly the disciples, and indeed all of the Jewish people, had a very limited understanding of life in the afterworld and how it was related to life in this world. Jesus' crucifixion and His triumph over death created a whole new way of thinking of the spiritual heaven and earth for Christians. The limited Jewish concepts have indeed passed away.

"But even if we are thinking on a more physical level, we have to acknowledge that Copernicus has transformed our understanding of the physical heavens by placing the sun in the center of it. And likewise, our original understanding of the physical earth—that it is a flat disk extending outward to some unknown edge—has passed away. So the 'passing away' of heaven and earth could also be understood as the passing away of old conceptions rather than the physical heaven and earth.

"And so it goes with every one of those references to the amazing things that are to happen upon Christ's return. People's minds easily jump to the physical understanding. They do not usually stop long enough to ponder the spiritual meaning. They are unacquainted with the other parts of the Bible that could shed some illumination on these inner meanings. And though they may have had, in former ages, guides that could help them understand the spiritual meanings, those stars are now fallen, and we live in an age of spiritual darkness.

"I dare say that even if some of the knowledgeable religious leaders might be inclined to consider spiritual alternatives, others are keenly aware that the material interpretation draws crowds to the pews and inspires them to empty their pockets into the collection plate. I mean, if the physical world will end soon, you aren't going to need your money anymore, are you?"

Zach had his doubts about the sincerity of some of the preachers he had heard.

He continued, "In Matthew 24 and 25, where we find most of Jesus' prophecies, He gave us many signs of what to look for as an indication of the coming of the latter days. He described a long period of history, with its persecutions, wars, pestilence, and earthquakes as well as false prophets and divisions in the church so that Christians would betray and hate one another. And because of this iniquity, 'the love of many will wax cold.' Surely we have seen these divisions as various denominations have broken away during the Reformation and as millions that have died in the resulting wars since Martin Luther's days.

"But He gave us a simple sign to look for: He said that the gospel of the kingdom would be preached '*unto all nations; and then shall the end come.*' And as I said, this is *not* the end of the physical world but the end of the *age*, when we can expect His return to open up a new age.

"Surely with the explorations of the world during the last three centuries, the gospel of Jesus has been preached to all nations. I've read Madagascar—the last nation to receive Christian missionaries—received them in 1818. And even areas that aren't nations, such as the interior of Africa, were opened to the gospel just last year. It is abundantly clear that we are living at the end of the age as Jesus Himself described it.

"He tells us to count the years according to the prophecy of Daniel, which is exactly what Mr. Miller has done, and this clearly points to 1844 as the year of fulfillment.

"In Matt 24:16–20, He speaks of it as a time of great testing requiring the greatest detachment both from the things you own and from family ties. I have felt this during these past few months as many people have questioned why I should leave my life of comfort in Perth Amboy. But Jesus has warned us to be ready to let go of such attachments, so I will not look back.

"As to verse 21 and the 'great tribulations' that are to be expected, most people understand these to be tribulations that will be visited upon the unbelievers. But I am not so sure."

Jeremy raised an eyebrow, but Zach continued: "Remember that in the days of Jesus, there were many people—most of the Jews in fact—who hoped to see the Messiah. Yet their leaders all had particular expectations of the manner of His appearance. Many imagined He would lead an army that would put the Romans to flight and would sit on the throne of King David. Others imagined that He would be able to part the sea, as Moses had done. Certainly He would exalt the Jewish religion and not allow Gentiles to be followers.

"So His appearance caused much tribulation among the Jews. Some were humble enough to recognize that their former expectations might be incorrect and that God, in His all-knowing wisdom, might have a greater plan in store. Thus, they were able to recognize the truth of Jesus' teachings.

"But others, perhaps misled by their own religious leaders—whom Jesus Himself denounced as 'blind guides'—clung to their own pre-determined views and ignored or even persecuted Jesus' early followers. Those leaders seemed to be telling God, 'Unless you send a Messiah according to my expectations, I will not believe!' Spiritually, they were lost.

"But there is another tribulation. That first spiritual tribulation begets an outward tribulation: Since people are, in large part, spiritually lost, they make decisions out of ignorance or from a material perspective, and these decisions lead to outward problems for their whole society.

"When the majority of the Jewish people turned away from Jesus, they put their trust in political and religious leaders who were ready to rise up against the Romans. But that approach led the Romans, less than 40 years later, to destroy Jerusalem and not too long thereafter to banish the Jewish people from the Holy Land—a great tribulation that they continue to suffer to this very day.

"So I wonder whether we will follow the same pattern in this age. Most of our religious leaders insist that their own particular expectations must be fulfilled. Yet their expectations differ. It is impossible that all of them could be correct. How much tribulation must occur in peoples' manner of thinking before they are willing to recognize that God's fulfillment may be different from what they were expecting?"

Jeremy sighed. "I suppose that is true. Most people, perhaps all, will have to go through the anguish of letting go of *something* if all are going to come to a common recognition of the new Messiah."

Then he added, "And what about you, Zach? Have you thought about the fact that you, too, might have some misunderstandings and might have to change something about your own expectations?"

This caught Zach off-guard, and the notion made him uneasy.

After a pause, he replied, "Yes, the thought has crossed my mind. I can't rightfully ask others to approach the task of seeking the Messiah with humility unless I do the same myself. I don't know what things I might tend to cling to, but I pray that I'll have the humility to let go of my own misconceptions when the time comes."

He paused again, as if trying to envision it, and then continued his review of the twenty-fourth chapter of Matthew: "In verses 23–25, Jesus warned the disciples about false prophets, whom we can know by their fruits, as we discussed the other day. He warned that some of these would call themselves 'Christ.' My father and I agreed that this indicates that the Promised One—the return of Christ—will not actually use the same name. Rather, He will be called by a 'new name,' as mentioned in Revelation 2 and 3 and again in Isaiah 62.

"But as to where He would appear, Jesus simply said it would be 'out of the east' as lightning, which apparently comes typically from the east and travels to the west. That is why I am traveling to the east—to the Holy Land.

"He spoke of the sun being darkened and the moon not giving forth her light, as we discussed earlier. And as I previously noted, my father and I believe that His coming on the clouds with great glory is a metaphor for His spiritual greatness, just as He arrived before with enormous spiritual power even though the spiritually blind could not perceive it at that time."

By this point, Jeremy had opened Zach's Bible and was following along in Matthew 24 as Zach explained their understanding of the verses.

"It says here, '*But of that day and hour, knoweth no man...*'" pointed out Jeremy.

"True. And I have no doubt that we will not be able to predict the exact *day or hour*," replied Zach. "But Jesus and Daniel gave us a way to determine at least the *year*. And perhaps Jesus was referring to the men of His time. After all, why would God have provided Daniel with the prophecies of the time of the end if He did not intend for the people of that time to understand them?

"Still, it is certainly true that many will not understand. He compares it to the days of Noah. Most people laughed at him until it was too late. And He compares it to a thief in the night, who comes quietly and leaves before the owner of the house realizes what has happened."

"That sounds quite different," Jeremy noted, "from the Christ who descends with a trumpet blast."

"Exactly my point!" declared Zach. "The spiritual coming is with a trumpet blast, as in verse 31, but the physical coming is quietly, as a thief, as in verse 43.

"In short, every one of the verses of prophecy can be understood in a spiritual sense. Yet there are many people who think only of the material sense and thus become lost."

"Well, you've certainly given me a lot to ponder," said Jeremy.

Zach replied, "I am grateful for your questions. They cause me to think further as well."

By now the sun was setting over the western horizon, and it was time to find a meal and some rest in preparation for tomorrow's journey.

*   *   *

ON MONDAY THEY BOOKED passage on the *Pocahontas*, scheduled to depart on the following day. It was one of the newly built sailing canal boats specially designed to carry goods and passengers not only on lakes and rivers but also through the locks on the Champlain Canal. It had masts that could be lowered for passage under the low canal bridges and keels that could be raised to allow passage through the shallow locks. These boats could reach the north end of Lake Champlain in Canada. And up there, the *Chambly Canal* was scheduled to open the following week.

The captain had a load that would be among the first to be delivered from Albany directly to Montreal on the St. Lawrence River. The boat would pass through 12 sets of locks: six going up the Hudson and another six in the canal leading from Fort Edward to Whitehall and Lake Champlain. The captain, crew, and cargo would continue from there descending again through the new locks almost to sea level near Montreal. "Such a marvelous feat of engineering!" thought Zach.

As they sailed upriver toward Fort Edward, Zach was thinking about his father and what his father might have said when meeting Mr. Miller. He recalled the notes from Mr. Miller's talks he had found

among his father's papers and got them out of his sack to review.
They read:

> Read the Bible for yourself so that you will not be led astray!
> The question of 'When?' is not so difficult. Jesus' disciples asked
> Him in Matthew 24.
> 'Tell us, when shall these things be?' (v3) i.e., When shall You
> return?
> First described what sounds like a long period of time. But says
> that the end is not yet (v6).
> Also certain signs of times & the increase in wickedness & lack
> of love for God.
> Then says, "_gospel of the kingdom shall be preached in all the_
> _world for a witness unto all nations; AND THEN SHALL THE_
> _END COME._"
> Today, the gospel is preached in all nations, so we _know_ that the
> end is at hand!

Josiah noted many ideas given about the meaning and exact interpretation of the signs and how they might apply and continued:

> But, besides signs, there is a single verse that points to the
> number of years. v15
> He tells us to look at the prophecy of the "abomination of desola-
> tion, spoken of by Daniel the prophet." (Also in Mark 13:14)
> In the whole Old Testament, one thing about all the prophecies:
> They are descriptions of future events; almost never call out the
> exact year these events will happen.
> _The only exception to this rule is Daniel._ Several key numbers
> are found in his visions.
> This is why Jesus pointed us to a few particular chapters in
> that book.
> Book of Daniel—comprised of 12 chapters. 1st six are history
> of miraculous things that happened to him. How he, with most of

the people of Judah, were taken into captivity by the Babylonians. Through his ability to interpret king's dreams, he rose to prominence & won the king's favor.

He read the mysterious writing that appeared on the wall in the king's palace. Interpreted it, accurately forecasting downfall of the Babylonian king at the hand of neighboring Persia.

Daniel rose to prominence in the Persian court when king's hungry lions refused to destroy him while confined overnight in their den.

Last six chapters of Daniel cease to be narrative. Describing series of dreams and visions Daniel had. References found here to "abomination of desolation" & "transgression of desolation"—only in Chapters 8, 9, 11 and 12—nowhere else in the entire Bible!

So we know exactly where Jesus was pointing.

Chapter 8: One saint asked another how long until the desolating sacrifice would end. The other says, "Unto 2,300 days; then shall the sanctuary be cleansed."

In sum, we have from both Matthew 24 and Mark 13, Jesus' clear statement that He will return will be at the time of the end & that it is associated with the end of the transgression of desolation, which is at the end of 2,300 days.

God, speaking to Daniel through Gabriel, was saying something very specific here. This number is not one that might have been mistranslated & not a rounded number, like 2,000, which could have originally been "thousands." It was not even like 2,400, as in as a couple dozen hundreds. A very specific number, found nowhere else in the entire Bible. It seemed to be pointing to a very specific point in the future.

But even Daniel could not understand the vision back then. And apparently it was intended that he would __not__ understand it. Gabriel said "Understand, O son of man: for at the time of the end shall be the vision" (v17). At the end of the chapter: "shut thou up the vision; for it shall be for many days." Even Daniel, the great interpreter of the king's dreams, confessed that he was astonished and "none understood it" (v27).

We would be lost were it not of God's grace.

We had a number, but we knew not what it meant nor the starting point from which to count. How could we understand something that even Daniel could not?

But here & in Chapter 12, Daniel says we will understand it later, for the visions are 'closed up and sealed <u>till the time of the end</u>' (12:9).

Now we are living at that time of the end—that time when the gospel of the kingdom is being preached in all the world, just as Jesus said. Now is the day in which that vision can be unsealed! (This gave him courage & cause for hope.)

A "day" in the realm of the saints refers to a year in our world (for there are other references in the Old Testament where the term "day" is used for a year —Num 14:34 & Ezek 4:5).

2,300 normal human days is a little more than 6 years, and clearly, nothing significant happened 6 years after Daniel had seen this vision.

But even when we know it is 2,300 years, how shall we find the starting point of those years?

Many were perplexed by this. By God's grace, he realized: The revelation Gabriel brought in Chapter 8 was linked to the revelation Gabriel brought to Daniel in the latter half of Chapter 9. These are the only 2 revelations brought by Gabriel in the entire Old Testament!

Here he again spoke of the abomination of desolation & here he referred to the crucifixion of our Lord, Jesus Christ. This vision served as the key, which removed all doubt about the first vision. For though it was a vision of the future from Daniel's perspective, from our perspective, we know it was clearly fulfilled in 33–34 AD.

8:25: Gabriel describes "cutting off" of the Messiah during the 70th "week" after issuance of the commandment to rebuild Jerusalem, that is, before the end of 490 years in human terms.

The "cutting off" of the Messiah is a clear reference to the crucifixion of our Lord. A clearer reference could scarcely be imagined! Isaiah used the same term in chapter 53 of his book, describing how the Savior would be "cut off out of the land of the living."

We know exactly when that happened. If we measure the "week" & "days" described going backward from the crucifixion, again taking a year for a day, we come to the year 457 BC. And when we check all of the known records, we find that, yes indeed, Artaxerxes, the king of the Persian empire at the time of the Jewish captivity there, issued a commandment to rebuild Jerusalem in that very same year! (See Ezra 7:11)

Now it becomes clear & certain that these two visions from Gabriel are correctly measured from 457 BC. The vision of Chapter 9 describes 70 weeks, that is, 490 days in the Lord's terms—490 years in ours. Sometime during the last "week" (7-year period), the Messiah, Jesus Christ, would be "cut off." This happened exactly as foretold!

Now we are certain of two things:

1. The term "day" in the Bible's prophecy means a year in human terms AND
2. we should start out counting from 457 BC.

Understanding both & returning to the vision of the 2,300 days from Chapter 8, we are certain now that transgression of desolation should end 2,300 years after 457 BC.

That brings us to the year 1843.

The Book of Ezra even gives us the day from which the time is counted: "first day of the first month of the year." In the calendar of Persia, this is the spring equinox, or March 21.

At the bottom was a parenthetical note, with questions that Josiah had added:

51

(Does he know that there is no year zero in the calendar, so 2,300 years after 457 BC is actually 1844 AD? And what of the 1260? What of the return of Elijah as John the Baptist? Will that occur again?)

It was unclear to Zach how many of these ideas were directly from Mr. Miller and how many were from Josiah's own thinking. But he found the notes to be a fairly accurate summary of his own discussions of the prophecies with his father.

It was perfectly clear to him: Daniel's chapter 9 prophecy of the crucifixion of Jesus was unquestionably fulfilled. Using the same "day for a year" principle and the same starting date, Daniel's chapter 8 prophecy of "the cleansing of the sanctuary" would certainly be fulfilled in the coming year or two. Jesus Himself had equated this prophecy with His return when He answered His disciples' questions about this in Matthew 24.

Zach recalled from conversations with his father that the last three parenthetical questions were things he wanted to ask Mr. Miller. Zach was glad to have this summary and several other useful notes that his father had left. He recalled his father's final promise to help him as much as he could, and he felt that these notes would certainly do so.

The sun was nearly set by the time he finished reviewing the notes. After a modest meal with Jeremy, it was time for them to retire to their cabin below deck in the boat, which continued sailing through the night until it reached the next lock.

The boat reached Fort Edward on the following afternoon, the last day of May, and stopped for the night to discharge and pick up some passengers as well as some goods.

Fort Edward marked the spot where the Champlain Canal branched away from the Hudson River. The muleteers, whose animals pulled the canal boats, adhered to the speed limit of four miles per hour, so the 25-mile trip, including passage through the six sets of locks, made for a long day's travel. But by dusk they arrived at the village of Whitehall, where they soon found the local inn and enjoyed the relatively spacious quarters, a welcome relief from the cramped cabins of the boats.

The William Miller House
Low Hampton, New York

Chapter 3

MEETING WITH WILLIAM MILLER

Zach and Jeremy were up early, and before the sun had risen above Skene Mountain on the east side of town, they began their six-mile trek to William Miller's farm on the cusp of the Vermont border, north of Low Hampton. The fine spring day energized their steps as they gazed over the well-kept farmlands and rolling hills of this most pleasant landscape.

Arriving shortly after noon, they were greeted by Mr. Miller's wife, *Lucy*, who apologized for the delay but explained that it was unavoidable because of his continued recovery from the erysipelas, which had occurred during his strenuous travels. Upon his return, his condition had improved slightly then worsened again, and he was still too weak to travel.

She requested that they allow him plenty of time for rest. Zach assured her that they would not stay long. She and their son, *William S. Miller*, then assisted William Miller down the stairs and into the parlor.

They greeted him, and Zach explained how his father and he had attended Mr. Miller's lectures in New York City and more recently in Newark, near their home, and how intensely his father had hoped to see the great day—but sadly, he had passed away in January. Mr. Miller acknowledged the mortality of all who live and how he himself felt exhausted by all the work of the past couple of years. But he was recuperating and hoped to begin lecturing again soon.

Zach reflected on what an interesting man sat before him. For this was not your typical preacher, trained in the seminaries, too often proud or arrogant, and searching for the largest crowd of followers.

He was originally a farmer and a deist, believing in a Creator who did not interfere in the world. An experience during the War of 1812, which nearly killed him, and the early loss of several family members had transformed him into a believer by 1816. He had studied the Bible for himself rather than adopting the interpretations of any particular church. And he had never intended to become a preacher; he was resistant to the idea for many years. When he was finally called to share his ideas from the pulpit, he was surprised to find so many people responding. An unceasing string of invitations from many denominations soon arose.

Zach requested, for his own benefit as well as Jeremy's, that the preacher provide a basic explanation of how they could be certain of the accuracy of the prophecies pointing to the imminent return of Christ.

They listened in rapt attention as he explained the basic outline: the question the disciples asked Jesus, His explanation to look to the prophecies of Daniel, and how they had now come to understand that both prophecies should be dated from the same starting date. One of them led directly to the crucifixion of Jesus, while the other led directly to the current year.

Zach sat back for a moment, absorbing the particulars of Mr. Miller's explanation. For although it was quite similar to the notes his father had taken from the lecture, it seemed so much better when heard directly from the preacher.

"That is absolutely clear," said Zach as he thanked him heartily for the explanation. Then he added, "My father wanted me to ask about a couple of things."

Mr. Miller said he would be pleased to consider them.

"My father knew a bit about the numbers used in Roman times—the Roman numerals, as they are called—I for 1, V for 5, X for 10, and so on. He noted that they had no zero. And he said he remembered learning that the Romans did not even think of zero as a number."

Mr. Miller acknowledged this.

"So that being the case, the year that came after what we now call 1 BC was not the year "zero" but the year we now call 1 AD. Therefore, although on the mathematical timeline, the distance from the beginning of 1 BC to the beginning of 1 AD might appear to be two years, in practice, it was only one year. Inasmuch as one year is missing here, it must be added to the end of the period. Thus, the end of the 2,300 years should be in the year 1844, not 1843."

Mr. Miller sat back and thought for a bit. He acknowledged that others had brought this point to his attention. He noted that it was because of such considerations he was disinclined to try predicting the exact date. But he said the time was well-nigh—most likely sometime this year or possibly next. "So we must be watchful."

He glanced to the window in the parlor. From it, he could see the eastern sky. He noted that he expected to see Jesus coming from the east, citing Jesus' description in Matthew 24: "For as the lightning cometh out of the east, and shineth even unto the west; so shall also the coming of the Son of man be."

"So I have heard," continued Zach. "Now, if I may, my father had two additional questions he wanted me to ask of you."

"Certainly," replied the preacher.

"The first concerns the references that are found in Daniel's final vision—the one described in chapters 11 and 12. At the end of that vision, Daniel describes a period of "a time, times and an half." With each 'time' being a year, we understand this to be 3-1/2 years, or 42 months, or counting each month as 30 days, this comes to 1,260 days in the language of scripture, that is, 1,260 years in the language of men. And at the very end of the chapter, he refers to another period of 1,290 days and again to yet another of 1,335 days. If specific numbers have a clear and definitive meaning, what do these numbers refer to?

"Moreover, we have studied the Revelation of St. John—the vision that Christ gave to John of what would happen in the future. In many ways, it seems similar to the vision of Daniel, and no doubt they both saw some of the same things. Like Daniel, the Book of Revelation seems to convey some of its meaning through particular numbers. We found several references to the 1,260 days, or the 42 months, or to the 3-1/2 years, or the 'time, times and the dividing of time,' and all seemed to be references to this period. But counting forward from 457 BC, 1,260 years brings us to 804 AD, and we knew of no major event that occurred at that time.

"And more curious still: While John saw many things in his revelation that were also seen by Daniel in his visions, nowhere in John's revelation is there any mention of the 2,300 days or the 70 weeks. Yet the reference to the 1,260 days is found in both books, so it must be very significant. Do you know what its significance is?"

Mr. Miller thought for a moment. He said that, clearly, there was no longer any need to refer to the 70 weeks because by the time of John's revelation, that prophecy had already been fulfilled. As to the absence of reference to the 2,300-year prophecy, he suggested that perhaps it was not used because it dates from the Jewish period, which had passed by the time of John's book.

But as to the 1,260 years, Mr. Miller went into an extended explanation of a 475-year period after the crucifixion ending in 508 AD followed by 30 years and then the 1,260 years ending in 1798 AD followed by a 45-year period, which seemed to be there to fill the gap between 1798 and 1843.[4]

Zach paused and thought about this for a moment. It seemed to him that this convoluted explanation and calculation had none of the clarity of the 2,300-year prophecy. "Why," he wondered to himself, "was this 1,260 number given such prominence in both Daniel and the Book of Revelation, while in Mr. Miller's explanation, it is just one piece of a long calculation?"

While he granted that Mr. Miller's explanation might possibly be correct, he felt he should keep his mind open to other possibilities here. So rather than raising an objection, after the thoughtful pause, he simply said, "Interesting..." and then he moved on.

"Now, my father's final question is not about the *time* of Christ's return but rather it concerns the *nature* of His return."

He had been hesitant to ask this question knowing that both he and his father held an uncommon view on this matter. Yet they had reached it after much careful study.

The preacher said that the nature of Christ's return seemed obvious to him. He cited the first chapter of the Book of the Acts of the Apostles, where it is said that the disciples saw Jesus taken up into heaven. And two men, standing among the disciples, told them that Jesus will return from heaven in the same way.

"Yes," said Zach, "I know that this is what is commonly believed. And my father understood why so many people might believe that way. But he wondered if it was the only possible interpretation."

Many highly educated clergy at this point might have dismissed the possibility that a shipmaster like Josiah, who had no formal education from a seminary, might be able to come to any worthwhile independent interpretation of matters relating to the Bible.

But Mr. Miller was not such a person. He himself had been a farmer for most of his life and at one time a military man while, at another, a local politician. He never had formal religious training but acquired most of his knowledge of the Bible by studying it for himself, and he had a certain respect for others who had done likewise. So he listened with the ear of a fellow student of the Bible and inquired as to what other possible interpretation there might be.

"I know from reading your book," Zach continued, "that you recognize the role of metaphor in prophetic language. As I recall, you stated in your book, 'Prophetical scripture is very much of it communicated to us by figures and highly and richly adorned metaphors.'[5]

"My father was, likewise, inclined to think of the spiritual meanings behind the words themselves. He, like you, knew that the use of parables and metaphors was a common method of conveying spiritual truths in Jesus' time. He asked me once whether I thought Christ ascended into the physical heaven or the spiritual heaven. When I said I had always assumed He meant the physical heaven, he referred me to John 3:13.

"There, Jesus explained to Nicodemus that He had already come down from heaven, and He stated that He was in heaven even as He was speaking to Nicodemus. Again, in 6:38, Jesus clearly said that He had 'come down from heaven.' And yet we know from the Christmas stories that He was born and grew up in a manner that was, in many respects, similar to other people.

"So what does it really mean to 'come down from heaven'? Jesus gave us another explanation a few verses later in the same chapter of John when

He said, 'I am the living bread that came down from heaven.' We know, of course, that Jesus was not physical bread that came down from the sky, but rather, in the same way that bread sustains our physical life, Jesus' teachings sustain our spiritual lives.

"Although the physical bread will sustain our physical lives for a time, ultimately our bodies will die. But Jesus made it clear that the spiritual teachings He gave would keep us spiritually alive forever, both in this world and in the life hereafter.

"Since Jesus had taught that His 'descent from heaven' was, in reality, the descent of those spiritual teachings from the heavenly world, should we not also consider that His return from heaven could mean that further teachings would again flow through a special person in our times, whom we must find? As my father said, perhaps He will come down from heaven again the same way He came down from heaven before—initially as an infant."

Mr. Miller looked startled. He had preached long and often about Christ's return and about all of the miraculous things that would occur— how the believers would be lifted up into the sky and how the unbelievers would be damned to torment as they met their destruction. The idea that Jesus might appear in a manner similar to the way He came the first time— outwardly as a humble carpenter's son but spiritually with great glory— seemed out of the question.

Moreover, the great miraculous appearance of Christ's second coming would offer clear and undeniable proof that the ministers were right in what they taught. And the possibility that such clear proof was near at hand had motivated many to attend his sermons and to join the churches where he and so many others preached. "Well," he started, "that would be an *entirely* different understanding...."

As he paused, Zach continued, "My father also directed my attention to the return of Elijah. As you know, the second chapter of Second Kings tells us that Elijah did not die. No, rather, he was taken up into heaven in a whirlwind—disappeared, as it were, into a cloud of sorts. And we know from the very end of the Book of Malachi that Elijah was promised to return before the coming of the Messiah.

"The scribes of Jesus' time certainly expected that Elijah would come before the Messiah. For this very reason, the disciples asked Jesus as to whether Elijah was to come first. You may recall both from chapter 11 and again from chapter 17 of Matthew how Jesus explained that Elijah had already come in the person of John the Baptist. Moreover, at the beginning of Luke, the angel Gabriel explained to John's father prior to John's birth that John would go forth with 'the spirit and power of Elijah.'

"So my father's question was that if the return of Elijah can mean the return of the same spirit and power in the vessel of a new person with a different name, might we not also expect the return of Christ to come in a similar manner?"

This was clearly a line of reasoning that Mr. Miller had not previously given much consideration. He replied that he could see that Zach's father had studied the Bible for himself, and he would find no fault with that since it was exactly what he himself had done.

But he noted that there were many, many other references to the coming of Jesus that suggested all manner of miracles that would accompany Him when He returns.

"I know," said Zach. "My father and I spent much of our spare time during the past several years studying them. And we found that every last one could be understood to have a spiritual meaning as well as the material one.

"To take one more example: In several places in the gospels, Jesus says that He will return from heaven on the clouds. Now, if He is coming from the spiritual heaven, what are the clouds? Are they not those things that block out the light of the spiritual sun? So when Jesus returns and is old enough to start teaching, many people will certainly have some clouds of misunderstanding, which will initially block the light of His teachings. But His teachings will be so brilliant that they will shine through these clouds and dissipate them."

"Perhaps..." said Mr. Miller cautiously. But he then asked Zach about a quote from the first chapter of the Revelation of St. John, which states when Christ returns, '*every eye shall see Him.*' He wondered how, if Christ were to return in His original manner, could every eye see Him?

61

Even if He was welcomed everywhere, it would probably take more than a lifetime to travel, by conventional means, to all the places on the earth where people live. So if He came in the conventional manner, some eyes would not see Him, he reasoned.

Zach leaned forward and said, "Yes, but in addition to our physical eyes, do we not also possess spiritual eyes? Didn't Jesus repeatedly refer to the scribes and the Pharisees as 'blind guides'? Yet their physical eyes were perfectly good. Do not our spiritual eyes give us the ability to see the truth of spiritual teachings? Even more, in chapter 13 of Matthew, Jesus clearly explains how having eyes and ears means having spiritual understanding. So might this not mean that everyone will have the spiritual ability to understand Christ's teachings when He returns?

"And yet in spite of this, it also says in Matthew 24 and in Luke 12, and again in Revelation 3, that He will come 'as a thief,' and He warns that we must stay watchful for His coming, unlike most, who will have fallen asleep spiritually. So how can we understand something that 'every eye shall see' while, at the same time, most will be blind or asleep and thus not seeing?

"And if Jesus returned from the physical sky—and everyone saw Him with their physical eyes—who would refuse to believe in Him at that point? Everyone would be compelled to become a believer. But if God had wanted to compel us to believe in Him, my father felt certain that He would have done that a long time ago. Instead, He always offers us the choice, and in making the right choice, we grow in the spirit.

"My father concluded that we all have the spiritual capacity to recognize Him when He returns, if we will open our eyes to the idea and not allow the things of this world to blind us to His truth."

And then, with a far-off look, Zach added slowly, "And it seems to me that even now, in the past twenty-five years or so, more and more people have a general awareness that something *is* happening. Something *is* changing. And so they are looking. It is such an awareness that draws them to you and to others who preach of the return.

"It draws them as well to Joseph Smith and his Latter-day Saints and to *Charles Finney, Alexander Campbell*, and a host of others. Even in my father and me—we have both sensed that something is happening, although we don't yet see it with our physical eyes."

Mr. Miller acknowledged that this understanding might be possible but cited the one practical problem it would create: If Christ might return in a conventional manner, one would need to know where to look for Him.

"*That*," said Zach, "is *exactly* the conclusion my father reached. And he felt that the right place was none other than the Holy Land. He was hoping that he and I could travel and remain there during the whole of the year 1844 so that he might have a chance to witness this most momentous event in modern history.

"But alas, as I mentioned, he died during the winter past. On his deathbed, though, he asked that I should travel to the Holy Land in his stead. And this I intend to do."

Mr. Miller took a long look at Zach. Zach was a young man—strong and hearty-looking—but the preacher noted how arduous such a journey would be.

Zach said, "You forget that my father was a sailor before starting his shipping company. And I myself have made the journey to Europe on behalf of my father several times already. Now, I will admit that I'm not one of those Nantucket boys, who will sail halfway round the world in search of whale oil for our lamps. A journey to the Holy Land is no small thing, but for one who has sailed to Europe time and again, it is not as daunting as a landlubber might think."

He smiled.

The preacher was also curious as to whether they expected to find the Messiah as an infant or as a grown man.

"My father and I had pondered this for a good while. And though we did not reach a firm conclusion, we had some thoughts. We know that the Wise Men from the East found Jesus as an infant, and they seemed to know from their own prophecies that the star would signal His *birth*.

"But in our case, the 2,300-year prophecy from Daniel states, '*then shall the sanctuary be cleansed*.' Again, thinking in the spiritual sense, we were inclined to believe that the sanctuary is the place of religion in man's heart and that it has become defiled by other things—whether lust for power, fame, wealth, or ease. True religion has become sullied in men's hearts, so the cleansing of the sanctuary is the sweeping away of the old religious norms that focus on power, fame, and wealth. This is not done by an infant but rather by a grown teacher. However, inasmuch as this is just our conjecture, I will keep my eyes open for both the teacher and the infant."

Although Mr. Miller had not changed his mind on the question of how Jesus would return, he realized that it didn't matter whether Zach was traveling, since people would see Christ's return from the heavens regardless of where they were on Earth.

But allowing for the small possibility that the return might not occur until 1847, as some of his fellow Adventists had claimed, he considered that there was a chance he might see Zach again. So he asked Zach to promise, if he discovered anything in the Holy Land, he would bring the news back to him so that he would be among the first to know.

"Yes sir!" exclaimed Zach. "You can depend upon it."

Then, sensing a small measure of encouragement in Mr. Miller's face, he said, "May I be so bold as to inquire whether you have any followers who might be inclined to join me in my quest?"

The preacher said he would have to give some thought to that question, but most were overwhelmed with various aspects of the preaching work.

Lucy entered the room to say that her husband would need to rest for the remainder of the afternoon but invited Zach and Jeremy to stay for dinner and the night so that they might be well rested before their departure in the morning.

After dinner, they spent a bit more time discussing Zach's father's understanding of some of the prophecies in both the New Testament and the Old. "One of my father's questions was whether Daniel's prophecy of the 2,300 years refers more exactly to the return of Elijah, who is to appear 'before the great and dreadful day of the Lord,' according to Malachi 4:5. He wondered if, once again, someone would return with 'the spirit and power of Elijah' to cleanse the sanctuary of the human heart and thus prepare people for the return of Christ, even as John the Baptist had used baptism as a symbolic cleansing process to spiritually prepare the people of his time."

Mr. Miller noted that opinions varied on this question. But he questioned why Daniel did not then provide another date—the date for the coming of Jesus Himself.

Zach commented, "He did, actually, provide not one but two additional dates, at the very end of his book—which I'm sure you recall. Not simply the '1,260 days' but also the '1,290 days' and 'the 1,335 days.'"

But Mr. Miller had an alternative understanding of these two dates.

"Well," offered Zach, "if Elijah returns and the world is not destroyed, then surely he will guide us directly to the return of Christ."

On that much they could agree.

In the morning, as Zach was packing his bag, Mr. Miller called him to his room. He had an envelope in his hand. He inquired as to whether Zach had been in correspondence with a man from London by the name of Elijah Goodman.

"I've never heard of him," replied Zach. "Why do you ask?"

Mr. Miller explained that he had considered Zach's request for a traveling companion but did not know of anyone locally who might be so inclined and could be spared from the intense work of preaching the news. But upon awakening, he recalled a letter from a follower in England who seemed to share many ideas similar to those of Zach and his father. He found it among his papers in the morning.

He explained he'd been too busy to reply and wondered if Zach could write on his behalf. He figured that since Zach would likely be stopping in London, they might be able to meet face to face and perhaps even travel together.

"I'm much obliged," said Zach. "I shall certainly be most interested to review it as I return to Perth Amboy. And I'll write to him and dispatch it straight away."

And with that, he tucked the envelope into his bag, and both he and Jeremy bid the preacher farewell.

Chapter 4

WHY NOT MAKE IT EASY?

ZACH AND JEREMY STARTED their trek down to Whitehall to catch another canal boat and head back home. The day was again warm and sunny, and the air was invigorating. The countryside was flourishing with the growth of the new season. As they hiked, Zach was thinking of his discussions with Mr. Miller when Jeremy offered some ideas of his own.

Jeremy wasn't well trained in the Bible, but he had a natural curiosity about religious matters and had been sitting quietly in the parlor, listening respectfully as Zach and Mr. Miller had their discussions.

"I hope you don't mind my listening," offered Jeremy.

"Not at all," replied Zach. "Our thoughts and discussions are open to all who will hear."

"Well, I'm not all so educated in these matters," said Jeremy, "but there is one thing I really don't understand. Maybe I'm just too simple, but I wonder why it is all so complicated—figuring all this out about the ancient prophecies from Daniel and all. I mean, when the disciples asked Jesus about the time of His return, why did He not simply say that it would be 1,844 years after His birth?

"And if He is to come in the same manner as He came before, why didn't He simply tell us where He would be born? You know, we make appointments all the time. Why couldn't He just do the same thing, even if it was over a much longer time? Why do so many of the prophecies of Jesus and the prophets seem to be given in a hidden language? Preachers may study these things, but how is the simple man to know? Must we wait for the decision of the preachers? Are we not supposed to be ever watchful too?"

"I think there are a couple of reasons for this," replied Zach. "The first comes from just knowing human nature.... When you were a child, did your parents ever leave you and your brothers and sisters unattended?"

"Well, not often, but on occasion at home for a few hours."

"And did you ever think of doing some mischief while they were gone?" asked Zach.

"That was my brother's specialty. He was always thinking of mischievous things to do." Jeremy chuckled. "And sometimes he'd get us to go along with his plans."

"But I suppose you knew things would have to look normal by the time your parents returned."

"Absolutely. Otherwise, there'd be hell to pay from my father."

"And your parents no doubt knew of your inclination to go astray—or at least your brother's inclination. And they no doubt knew that the longer they were away, the greater the mischief would be."

"Very likely."

"So, if they were wise, they might let you think that they would be back soon, or at least let you think that they might return at any moment. As long as you were thinking that they would soon return, you would be disinclined toward any major mischief."

"Hmm..." Jeremy recollected. "Yes, I suppose that's likely true."

"Do you think that as the Lord's children, we are so different?" said Zach. "On a larger scale, are we not inclined to go astray over several generations? If Jesus had told us, 'I go away and will return after eighteen centuries,' how would the people of those days have acted? No need for them to behave well—they didn't need to worry about Him returning in their lifetimes. Even though it was essential for people to heed the teachings of Christ for the development of their souls and the development of civilization, many would have said, 'Why worry? I'll let my descendants of that age worry about heeding Christ's teachings.'

"But in the Lord's wisdom, He no doubt knew it was better for us to be ever uncertain about the time of His return and thus be ever watchful. So even though the visions were given to the prophet Daniel, the meaning of the visions was 'shut' to Daniel. He himself testified that 'none understood it.' Its fulfillment would occur at some unknown time in the future.

"When Jesus spoke of His return in chapter 21 of Luke, He said, '*This generation shall not pass away till all be fulfilled.*' Many of His followers understood that to mean He would return before they died, or at least before their children died."

"Yes," Jeremy interjected, "that's probably why early Christians were left with the expectation that He would return soon."

"Exactly. And the expectation of His possible return continued for a long time. Jesus warned His followers to be ever watchful. This state of uncertainty helped keep the followers on course.

"But as to the verse itself, we now understand it meant that the same generation who see the signs that Jesus described would also see His return. These are the signs we spoke of on our trip up from Albany."

"Yes, I remember," said Jeremy.

"I, too, have thought about the questions you raise. I think there is a second reason that the meaning of the prophecies was '*closed up and sealed till the time of the end,*' as Daniel said."

"And what is that?" Jeremy asked.

"Well, when I look at the long arc of the life of religion, what I see is that it starts with God's message to His chosen Prophet, be that Abraham or Moses or Jesus. At first it is in a pristine state since there are few followers and much opposition, sometimes even persecution. Only those who are detached from the cares of normal life are willing to accept it.

"Gradually, more people come to the realization of the truths it teaches, and it grows. No doubt God helps it grow, but also within each new generation, a greater number of people are able to see its truth, and it becomes easier for people to let go of the old ideas that blocked previous generations from accepting it.

"Eventually, it reaches the point where it is not persecuted but is more readily accepted. The general society around it is affected by God's message, and as people understand the wisdom of these teachings, the whole society prospers and flourishes. This happened in Christianity after the emperor, Constantine, became a Christian.

"But when it reaches such a stage of success, the religion also enters a stage in which an unseen danger lurks. Now those who join the religion no longer need to be detached from worldly concerns in order to be members. Now it becomes the norm. Now people follow the religion because their forefathers have followed it, or because the rest of their friends are members, or perhaps because it will improve their social standing, their political position, or their business concerns.

"They are doing the right thing, no doubt, but not entirely for the right reason. Still, the truths taught by the new religion are benefitting society and are helping hold it together. But as the religion has become a big part of society, its organization must grow, and its leaders necessarily become more powerful.

"At first, these leaders, having understood the true spirit of the religion, may not be affected by any concern for their positions. They understand rightly their relation to God and the people they serve. But as the generations pass, occasionally people enter whose motives are less pure. Some have a hidden lust for power; some are attracted to the wealth that the religion controls. Others arise who have their own interpretations of some of the teachings of their Messenger.

"In the early days, when the followers are threatened by outside forces, they realize that they cannot afford to bicker or become seriously divided over small theological points. But as that threat wanes, some feel that there is room to promote new interpretations. And while they may be right, the arguments tend to divide the religion into different schools of thought.

"Over time, these divisions become solidified into different denominations. People in positions of authority and power cling to their positions. Eventually, they become more dedicated to preserving their interpretations and their positions, and the wealth that comes from those positions, than striving to preserve the simple truths that God's Messenger originally taught. Eventually, we reach the stage of having scribes and Pharisees."

Jeremy listened with rapt attention. He thought not only of the decline of the Judaism in the days of Jesus but also of the decline of Christianity from its earlier days. How many were the wars that had been fought between Christian nations and how many the denominations into which it

70

had devolved! How many had died as a result of the Inquisition or as a result of the wars between Protestants and Catholics in Ireland alone—the home country of his parents.

He recalled how, after several centuries, the Spanish Inquisition had finally come to an end just nine years ago. He, for one, was glad to be living in a country that protected everyone's right to believe as they saw fit, where they could practice their religion without hindrance.

"Yes," he said, "I have often wondered whether we have reached such a stage again."

"Indeed," said Zach. "It is as if religion has a springtime, when it is new and verdant, followed by a summer of growth and an autumn of harvest. But then it enters a winter of decline, when '*the love of many shall wax cold*,' as the Lord has said.

"After we've reached this stage, it is time for the renewal of religion, the time for a new springtime. And then the 'anointed One'—that is, the 'Christ' in Greek or the 'Messiah' in Hebrew—that special Being will appear to teach us once again, bringing a new revelation of God's guidance to a world that has become lost in its disputes and impure motives. And that's exactly the stage that, I feel, we've reached. And some people can sense it, even without scriptural or prophetic proofs.

"But to return to your question about why the predictions of Christ's return are not written more explicitly, let us suppose for a moment that the prophecies of the time and place of Jesus' coming, together with a description of Him, had been written perfectly explicitly so that no one could have any doubts when He arose to start His teachings. What would have happened?"

"Well," said Jeremy, "I suppose the scribes and Pharisees of that day, along with everyone else, would have felt obligated to accept Him."

"Yes, but would they have accepted Him in their inmost hearts and been willing to change anything according to His new revelation? Or would they have retained their desire to remain in their position of leadership? Would they have expected to become the leaders of the new religion?"

"No doubt since everyone saw them as the legitimate leaders of the old religion, they would have seen themselves as the ones best qualified to be leaders of the new religion," answered Jeremy.

"Absolutely correct!" exclaimed Zach. "And although Jesus would not have been crucified, He would have eventually ascended to His Father in His older age, as did Moses. Then the new religion would have been led by the leaders of the old one. And although having listened to His new teachings, they would have inevitably brought many of the problems and flaws of the old religion over into the new one."

"Yes, unavoidably so."

"Thus, in order to ensure that the religion remains pure and true to the teachings of the Christ during its crucial early stages, a purification process is absolutely essential—a process that screens out all of the mistaken elements of the past religion as well as screening out the love of position, wealth, and authority. Isn't this what John the Baptist spoke of when he described how Jesus would separate the wheat from the chaff? I believe that this separation—this cleansing—is what the angel meant when he told Daniel that after 2,300 years the sanctuary would be cleansed."

As they were walking down the wooded lane, Zach paused to pick up an acorn. As he held it in his outstretched hand, he said, "Consider the germ of the oak tree. God has wrapped it in a hard shell to protect it from easy destruction by all sorts of attacks from animals and elements till it finds its opportunity to extend its root into the ground and starts to become a mighty tree.

"I believe the new revelation is similarly wrapped in a protective shell. That shell is the language of metaphor, parable, and especially prophecy. These require reflection, insight, and a measure of humility to be understood.

"The prophecies, in particular, are difficult for all to unravel and impossible for the prideful leaders of the old religion to understand. It prevents them from entering into and destroying the newborn life—the precious seed—of the new religion until the seed has had the chance to take root and grow. The new springtime brings with it new life. The old may pass away."

"Yes," said Jeremy, "I see your point. There is a great wisdom in the way the Lord has wrapped the prophecies of His coming in veils that are not easily removed by the insincere."

Zach paused a while, recalling the original question. "You also asked about how the simple man was to know and whether he had to wait for the priests and preachers to study and decide on these things. My answer to that is no. Often it is actually *easier* for the simple man to recognize Christ. Do you remember the disciples?"

"Of course."

"Was there a scribe or rabbi among them who had studied all of the books of the prophets?"

"No. As I recall, they were all fisherman, tax collectors, or common people."

"And yet they recognized Jesus as the Messiah," continued Zach. "How did those men, who were uneducated, manage to recognize the Messiah when those trained and educated scribes failed to see Him? Did they study the prophecies of the Old Testament?"

"No, I'm sure they didn't—most of them probably couldn't read. I guess they just somehow saw the Lord and heard His teachings, and they just *knew*."

"Exactly so," said Zach. "The simple and pure in heart do not worry about what others think. They do not think about how a change might affect their position or their standing in their family or community. Those who have little wealth do not need to worry about how accepting God's Messenger will affect their wealth. Therefore, Jesus said, '*Blessed are the pure in heart, for they shall see God.*'

"I believe we all have a deep, hidden ability to recognize Christ. It is not with our outward eyes nor is it with our book-learning. I think there is something that is built into each of us. Indeed, how could God expect us to be watchful for the return of His Promised One if He had not given us the ability to spiritually see?

"The study of prophecy will serve as a guide to some. But it can be an obstacle too. Moreover, by itself, it is insufficient. Ultimately, we must each hear the words of a possible prophet and search our own souls to determine whether it is the Word of God.

"But the problem is that we so easily let other things get in the way—especially as we become more knowledgeable, or have more authority, or gain more wealth. All too often these things become a hindrance to our spiritual eyes. We lose our humility and our detachment, and with it, we lose our ability to see spiritually. In Matthew 18, Jesus said that His followers must become 'as little children' in order to enter the kingdom of heaven.

"So perhaps the simple man has an easier task than the learned scholar. But for the sake of the learned ones, there are mysteries to unravel. And indeed, in Jesus' time there were learned men who did *not* allow their own interpretations to make them prideful, and thus they were able to find Jesus at the very start."

"Yes," said Jeremy, "the Wise Men of the East, as we discussed on our boat ride coming here—the Magi of the Christmas story."

"Indeed. They were the scholars of their day. As I mentioned, they had traveled all the way from Persia because the prophecies of their own religion had foretold the coming of the new Messenger. Although they were looking for '*he that is born King of the Jews*,' they did not confine their search to palaces. And when they found Him, they were not put off by His humble birthplace. So it *is* possible to use the prophecies successfully."

"And you and your traveling companion, if you find him, are hoping to do the same thing next year when Jesus returns," said Jeremy.

"I don't know if we shall be as fortunate as they were or if God will bless my efforts as richly as He blessed theirs," replied Zach, "but as you've heard, I've promised my father that I would try."

Jeremy replied, "I have no doubt that you will succeed. And when you do, you will be called the 'Wise Men of the West.'"

Zach chuckled. "If anyone is wise, it would be Mr. Miller, who clearly figured out *when* Christ will return, and perhaps my father, who understood *how* He will return."

"But," interjected Jeremy, "if you are able to figure out exactly *where* He will return, you will surely be counted as one of the Wise Men."

"Well, figuring out the 'where' should be the easiest part. And in any case, fame is certainly not my goal. But we will leave everything in God's hands."

A wagon was approaching, and soon they had a ride for the remaining distance to Whitehall. At the shipping office, they booked their passage on a sailing canal boat scheduled to leave on Monday morning.

On Sunday they rested in Whitehall and attended the Quaker meeting. Here the "unprogrammed" form of worship was practiced—silent meditation interrupted only if and when the Friends were moved by the Holy Spirit to speak. Zach's thoughts initially turned to his gratitude to William Penn and the early Quakers for establishing the idea of religious freedom so strongly in the state that now bore his name, a century and a half earlier. He silently thanked God that this precious principle had been successfully incorporated into the founding of America. It was a new way of life, suitable to the New World that was developing here, where religious differences would lead to discussions rather than to warfare. He could see its potential for serving as a pattern for resolving many of the world's problems. He wondered whether this might not all be a part of God's plan for the "healing of the nations" in the latter days, as described in the last chapter of the Bible.

As his thoughts then turned to his discussion with Mr. Miller, the question of the nature of Christ's return came back to his mind. Mr. Miller's view was certainly the commonly held one. Some of the descriptions written by the disciples and other early Christians were so vivid that the consideration of other alternatives had initially required a strong effort on Zach's part.

But the lessons from his father came back to him, reminding him of how the Jewish leaders had also been expecting a Messiah capable of doing vast miracles to overwhelm the pagan Gentiles who surrounded them. Those who were able to let go of such expectations became Christians. Those who could not let go suffered as Jerusalem was destroyed by the Romans about thirty-five years after Jesus' crucifixion. And another sixty-five years later, the Jewish people themselves were banished from the Holy Land. By that time, a quiet Christian conquest of the Greco-Roman world—unbeknownst to almost everyone—was well underway.

"Personal attachment to particular expectations," Zach thought silently as he shook his head, "while God has something else in mind." He prayed that he might be able to avoid a similar fate. As he prayed, Matthew 7:7 came to him: *"Ask, and it shall be given you; seek, and ye shall find; knock, and it shall be opened unto you."*

"Clearly," thought Zach, "Jesus knew that we must *make an effort* to search for Him at the time of His return. He cannot return in a manner that requires no asking, no seeking, no knocking. Yes indeed, an effort to search is essential."

He arose, exhilarated from his meditations, and returned to his room. He wanted to update his diary. In response to Jeremy's comment as well as his own meditation, he added a title: *The Wise Men of the West? A Search for the Promised One in the Latter Days.*

Chapter 5

THE LETTER OF
ELIJAH GOODMAN

Zach eagerly anticipated reading the letter from Mr. Goodman of London. He wondered what views they held in common. Sitting on the deck of the boat on Monday morning, he pulled out the letter and began to read.

Elijah Goodman was of the Methodist church—an offshoot of the Church of England that had been initiated there by *Charles and John Wesley* about a hundred years earlier. One of the church's tenets he found appealing was that man should use reason in understanding the teachings of the Bible. This, then, was not so far removed from Zach's Quaker beliefs regarding Scripture.

So it came as no surprise to Zach that Elijah Goodman had read Mr. Miller's teachings and was compelled by his arguments concerning the time of Christ's return.

"As you so rightly explain," he wrote, *"the accuracy of Daniel's prophecy concerning the crucifixion of Jesus was fully demonstrated to be perfect. Surely Daniel's other prophecy, which points to our time, should not be expected to be any less accurate."*

Like Zach and his father, Mr. Goodman understood that the Jews of Jesus' time failed to recognize that the Messiah's power was essentially spiritual, not political or military. Moreover, he shared Zach and Josiah's concern that Christians of their own time might repeat the mistake of taking prophecy only literally.

Elijah explained: *We know that Christ has existed 'before Abraham was' (John 8:58) and we know that He 'came down from heaven' (John 6:38). Yet no one saw the physical body of Christ descending from the sky. No indeed! The gospel affirms that He was born as a child and grew into manhood. So why should His return from heaven be any different today from the way He came down to us eighteen centuries ago? Some say this contradicts the prophetic testimony of the New Testament. But I say it contradicts only a particular understanding of the prophecies—a misunderstanding as serious as the misunderstanding of the Jews at the time of Jesus. The reality of Christ is His spirit, or His 'spiritual body' as Paul called it in I Corinthians 15, which has existed from the beginning of time and which is distinct from His natural body."*

Zach could see by this point why Mr. Miller had given him the letter. He was ecstatic to find someone whose reasoning and reflections were so similar to those of his father and him.

Elijah went further in the exploration of this theme: *"We know that God lives in that spiritually exalted place we call 'heaven.' And Christ is there with Him, according to the Apostles' Creed. But this is not somewhere in the upper atmosphere, which is a physical place. Were I to climb a tall mountain or harness a flock of birds to take me to the upper atmosphere, though I travel through each and every cloud, my search for the Christ would be in vain. Yet He will appear to whomsoever He wills, even though they lock their doors and shutter their windows, as John described in chapter 20 of his gospel.*

"If you are unsure on this point, you should speak with the Rev. George Bush¶ when you next travel to New York City. I have read his writings, and he provides clear evidence and compelling reasons that the body of Christ that arose after His crucifixion was a spiritual body, not a material one."

Zach sat up when he read this; he remembered his father speaking of Rev. Bush, whom he had heard giving a lecture during one of his visits to

---

¶ Reverend George Bush, Professor of Hebrew at New York University, summarized his teachings of this subject in *The Resurrection of Christ: In Answer to the Question, Whether He Rose in a Spiritual and Celestial, or in a Material and Earthly Body,* published in 1845. His insights, guided by his familiarity with both Hebrew and Greek, provided a compelling argument that Christ's spiritual body, not His physical one, was the intended meaning in the resurrection accounts.

New York, just across the river from Perth Amboy. Now he could see why Mr. Goodman's ideas seemed so similar to those of his father. He remembered hearing from his father about Rev. Bush's careful investigation of the original meaning of several key words, such as "to see," and how, in the original tongue, the version of the Greek word that was chosen to describe Christ's appearances after the crucifixion clearly implied a spiritual vision rather than seeing with one's physical eyes.

Mr. Goodman's letter continued: *"John said that he was 'in the Spirit' when he saw the vision of the Christ and all that was recorded in his Book of Revelation. And Saul, likewise, saw a vision on the road to Damascus, which was so real that he ceased persecuting the Christians and became Paul, the apostle. Yet those who were with him, though they heard the words of the Lord, said they saw nothing.*

"Now you will say that the disciples saw Christ taken up into a cloud in heaven and that He will return 'in like manner,' according to the first chapter of the Acts of the Apostles. But I say unto you that as the frequency of the visions and the immediacy of His presence gradually departed from His followers so, in like manner, upon His return, the awareness of His presence will gradually appear to us. The 'cloud' that obscures our vision will be pierced by the dawning light of His teachings.

"And you will ask, 'After Christ's crucifixion, did the disciples see visions of the risen Christ or did they see His body?' We say, 'The visions that they saw were very real. They were so real that they were thoroughly convinced of the truth of eternal life in the heavenly realm—so much so that they were happy to sacrifice their lives in this world. And thus, the body of His followers arose from the death of doubt and unbelief that had enveloped them upon Jesus' arrest. And this body became alive to the reality of eternal life. They became fearless in the face of every manner of threat that the Jewish and Roman leaders could attempt to use. Thus it was that this body of Christ—the body of His followers, that is, the nascent church—arose to life after He sacrificed His physical body. It was as if His very spirit, having left its physical body, had entered into His followers and inspired them to act in a manner that was unconquerable.'

"Now, if you will read the Scriptures carefully, in the four gospels and the Book of Acts, you will find fourteen times in which the disciples and Mary

and Saul are reported to have seen the risen Christ. Seven of these have characteristics to suggest that this was a vision, or a 'celestial body' as Paul says. Four seem to suggest it was both a vision and a physical appearance. Two give no indication one way or the other. And only one suggests Christ's appearance was solely physical—the one in Matthew that says that Mary Magdalene and the other Mary 'held Him by the feet.' Or was this simply a literary expression indicating their begging Him to stay?

"Which way shall we judge it? The overwhelming indication is that these were visions—very real and seemingly tangible—but not physical."

Zach paused for a moment as he recalled his father's description of Rev. Bush's lecture, which was remarkably similar to Mr. Goodman's letter.

"And then you will ask, 'Was not Jesus' tomb empty?' I say, Yes, indeed it was empty on Sunday morning. And Jesus' body had been placed in it on the Friday before sunset. Matthew says that Joseph of Arimathea rolled a stone over the entrance. But if one man can roll such a stone into place, then I suppose another man can roll it aside also.

"Matthew says the Romans sealed the stone and placed a guard there sometime on Saturday—the Jewish Sabbath. But what happened between Joseph's placement of the stone on that Friday evening and the sealing sometime on Saturday is anyone's guess. There were, no doubt, several who either saw or heard about the placement of the body into the tomb. Whether they were driven by the emotion of being a member of His family, or the devotion of some of His followers, or even perhaps the action of one who was inspired by a vision of Jesus Himself, it is impossible to say.

"But there were several who had both a reason and the means to remove His physical body. Any suggestion as to the final location of the resting place of those sacred remains would be pure speculation on my part.

"Consider also this: Fewer than ten verses prior to Joseph's placement of the stone, Matthew tells us that immediately after Jesus' crucifixion, 'the graves were opened; and many bodies of the saints which slept arose, and came out of their graves after His resurrection, and went into the holy city, and appeared unto many.' Yet none of the other gospels affirm this extraordinary event, which would have been astounding, at the least, if it were physically true. Nor do any historians of those times recount such an amazing occurrence. But most

people simply understand that Matthew was willing to use terms like 'graves' and 'bodies' and 'slept' and 'appeared' in an allegorical or spiritual manner here. I say, if he speaks allegorically here, why would he not speak allegorically a few verses later?

"If the disappearance of the material body initially uplifted the dispirited disciples, it was surely the appearances of the visions of the reality of Christ that gave them the unshakable conviction that He was triumphant over the death of the body and that they need have no fear.

"For they now understood that they, too, would be triumphant no matter how much the world might try to defeat them or even kill them. It was this belief, this Spirit, which quickened them and brought new life to the 'body' of Christ's followers. It was this body of the faithful followers (a term that Paul uses on several occasions) that had 'died' amidst its fears and doubts on that terrible Thursday night and which was then raised to a new life of unwavering faith within three days—that is, by Sunday evening after the crucifixion. It was this temple—the temple of the faith of His followers—that had been destroyed but which Jesus was able to rebuild within three days, as John recorded in the second chapter of his gospel."

Zach put the letter down for a few moments to absorb it all. He had not previously thought through the full details of how the nature of Christ's resurrection had a direct bearing on an understanding of the manner of His return, linked as these two are by that passage in Acts 1:11.

He knew a large part of the Christian world believed Jesus' material body had been physically raised from the dead and physically lifted up into heaven. He also knew many were bound to have great difficulty letting go of that idea.

But when Zach took out his Bible and began to carefully review each of the fourteen instances of Christ's appearance after His crucifixion, he became convinced that the approach of both Elijah Goodman and Rev. Bush was sound and well-reasoned. The letter continued:

"Please, my good fellow, do not misunderstand me! I hold that Christ was indeed raised from the dead. But hear the words of Peter and Paul, the two earliest Christian writers: Peter made it clear, in his first epistle, that Christ was 'put to death in the flesh, but made alive in the Spirit.' (3:18) And Paul,

in I Corinthians 15, says that 'if Christ be not risen, then is our preaching in vain'—for Christ is indeed risen. But he also says, in that same chapter, that there are both terrestrial bodies and celestial ones, that is, 'There is a natural body, and there is a spiritual body.' So Christ was raised in His celestial body, not His terrestrial one.

"His spirit returned to heaven even as the morning mist returns unto heaven. But now, the time draws near when the clouds of the Divine Spirit will once again condense and rain their bounty upon the parched earth of human understanding. And thus He will appear, just as He appeared before: First as a young child, with extraordinary knowledge—yea, innate knowledge—even as Jesus had."

Zach was so thrilled to read this that he wanted nothing more than to write immediately to Mr. Goodman. So as soon as the canal boat entered the lock at Fort Edward for the evening, he jumped off, ran to the general store, and bought some stationery. He began his reply that evening, hoping to dispatch it to London immediately upon his return to Perth Amboy.

He explained everything to Mr. Goodman—from his studies with his father to his father's death and the commissioning of his journey to his recent visit with Mr. Miller—how overjoyed he was to find someone who shared so many of the same insights and how he felt that they were truly kindred spirits. He also explained that he would be departing for England presently and how he would certainly call upon Mr. Goodman as soon as he arrived. And he described his plans to travel to the Holy Land in search of Christ's return.

He also explained that he hoped to find a traveling companion and inquired whether Elijah might either be able to join him in his travels or, perhaps, might know someone else with a similar view and interest who could accompany him. "All of the traveling expenses will be paid," Zach assured him.

*   *   *

REGAINING ONE OF THE schooners of the Thompson line in Albany, Zach was pleased that he and Jeremy were sailing with a full load of produce from the farms of the Erie Canal region. These goods, he knew, would fetch a good price in the hungry markets of New York or Perth Amboy. Some of the corn meal and other dried goods could be sold in Europe for an even better price. The profits from all of this trading was funding his travel plans and providing for the welfare of his family.

The washerwomen boarded, offering clothes-washing services to the travelers. This had to be completed soon, before the schooner reached the salt-water portion of the Hudson River, where there would be no fresh rinse water.

Also on board was a circuit rider—an itinerant preacher—who traveled from church to church each week, offering his services. Such preachers seemed to favor captive audiences.

Soon enough, he had a crowd of listeners on the deck of the boat. Zach listened, but from a bit of a distance.

It became apparent that Reverend Wilson had been listening to Mr. Miller or others who were preaching about the impending end of the world. Rev. Wilson's version was particularly lurid and terrifying, giving a vivid physical interpretation to many things that Zach had learned to take metaphorically. The reverend attracted the attention of most on board as his preaching reached a fevered pitch, with his arms flailing as he pointed in rapid succession to the crowd, then to his open Bible, and then to the Almighty in the sky.

When he finished, a hat was passed to take up a collection for his services. After the group dissipated, Zach wandered over to speak with him.

Rev. Wilson was excited to hear that Zach had just recently met with the famous William Miller. But he was taken aback at Zach's suggestion that there might be a different way to understand all of the prophecies about the colossal miracles that must occur when Jesus returned.

He pulled out his Bible and began fervently quoting various verses. Zach listened calmly and explained how he and his father had considered each of them and others and had discovered how each could be understood in a spiritual manner rather than adopting the physical interpretation that Rev. Wilson insisted upon. Zach provided him with various examples.

Finally, an exasperated Rev. Wilson asked, "And just how will the world be cleansed of its sin unless there is some catastrophe to chasten mankind?

Sin is everywhere! If Christ comes back as He came before, why, it would take several centuries before mankind learned its lessons, even as it took three centuries from the days of Jesus until the Roman emperor became one of His followers."

Zach had met many people who wanted a shortcut to the kingdom of heaven. Convinced of their inability to eradicate sin on a large scale, they seemed to think that Christ's coming and a miraculous cleansing of the world would resolve the question of evil.

Zach was not inclined to agree with this, so he simply said, "There are no shortcuts to God's Kingdom. We must teach people and provide an example for them. But *each one* must make his own effort to grow spiritually. *Making the effort* is the most essential part of spiritual growth. Shortcuts mean there will be no effort and, therefore, no spiritual growth. And *spiritual growth* is what the heavenly Kingdom is all about."

The reverend could scarcely imagine this. Wagging his finger, he admonished, "You just beware of the false prophets, whom Jesus warned us about."

"I certainly will," replied Zach. "But I am also mindful of that fact that Jesus did not ask us to reject *all* claims to prophethood. He explained that we could tell whether they were true or false by the fruits of their teachings. The very fact that Jesus said we must look into these fruits suggests to me that at least one would be true and that He would appear much as Jesus had appeared before—as a young teacher, probably with a new name, offering the fruits of spiritual knowledge and wisdom to those who are spiritually discerning."

Rev. Wilson looked baffled by these strange ideas. "But the Bible says clearly that Jesus went up into the sky and will return from the sky," he protested.

Zach replied calmly, "Eighteen hundred and forty-three years ago, Jesus came to us from heaven, but that does not mean that He came down from the sky. Moreover, the Jewish religious leaders understood their prophecies to mean that the Messiah would be a fierce king who would slay their Roman oppressors. Clearly, God did not feel compelled to follow human expectations back then nor is He compelled to do so today."

At length, Rev. Wilson relented. "We seem to have a difference in understanding. If you are right—if Christ returns as He came before and if He teaches the people in His immediate area as He did before—you will certainly have plenty of work to do for the next several centuries to eradicate sin and to spread the new message."

"Maybe," replied Zach. "Perhaps a period of spiritual growth that lasts for several centuries is part of God's plan."

Ultimately, they agreed to disagree on exactly what the future might hold.

The Star of the West—A clipper packet ship

Chapter 6

ACROSS THE WIDE OCEAN

THE SCHOONER ARRIVED BACK at Perth Amboy on June 10, and Zach thanked Jeremy for his assistance as he returned to his regular duties.

Zach posted his letter to Elijah Goodman immediately and then started his final preparations for the journey to London. He wanted to sail soon to avoid the height of the North Atlantic storm season, which would begin in early August. The warm weather of July would make the sailing easier along the normal eastbound route through the northern latitudes if storms could be avoided.

The next ship sailing on his father's line was the *Star of the West*, scheduled to depart on July 3, so he notified the captain of his plans to be on board. He remembered when his father had christened the ship with that name, thinking of the star that had guided the Magi westward and perhaps hoping it would serve as his own guide on a journey to the Holy Land. Now the duty of undertaking the journey had fallen to Zach.

When the day arrived, he bid a fond farewell to all of the members of his family. Sadness mixed with apprehension filled the hearts of many, but Zach asked only for their prayers. He assured them that he would either return shortly after the end of the next year or, if a change of plans was required due to a successful search, he would notify them.

Under a clear sky, with a warm wind out of the west, the captain gave orders to cast off the anchorage and unfurl the sails, driving the clipper ship eastward across Raritan Bay and then outward into the vast Atlantic.

Life on a sailing ship required some adjustments, as Zach well knew. Even the first-class cabins were small, and every inch of space was used carefully. Zach and the other sailors were, of course, well accustomed to the constant rising and falling motion of the ship on the ocean swells. But it made several of the less experienced passengers nauseated for the first day, and they spent much of that time on the deck near the railings. After the first night on board though, they usually acquired their "sea legs" and became accustomed to the constant motion.

Zach found the summer wind and the sea spray exhilarating, and he loved spending time on deck just watching the scenes of the sea and the sky or chatting with the captain or first mate as they piloted the craft. He still marveled at the ingenuity that went into the construction of these ocean-going "packet ships"—ships that carried a combination of mail, merchandise, and passengers of both classes. It seemed amazing that the invisible power of the fleeting wind could be harnessed to drive the ship across that vast expanse of the sea. Its billowing sails could be adjusted to meet every condition of wind and water, excepting, of course, for those days when the sea was becalmed and progress, if any, depended entirely on the ocean's current.

He marveled also at the tightly constructed hull, deck, and hatches that ensured that the sturdy vessel would remain afloat even if storm waves were crashing over her deck.

But he especially marveled at the ship's navigation instruments—the compass, the sextant, and the chronometer for direction, latitude, and longitude, respectively. Although the compass had been used for centuries, the sextant had been developed only about a hundred years earlier and the marine chronometer only about 60 years ago. They had become affordable for use on most ships earlier in Zach's lifetime.

These, together with the necessary astronomical tables and maps, enabled them to accurately determine their location anywhere on the face of the globe through careful observation of the sun and stars. With these tools, an experienced mariner could chart the most direct course to any port in the world.

Indeed, while most people simply saw a ship, Zach saw the embodiment of more than twenty-five centuries of experimentation, engineering, and innovation by countless people, all of whom desired to travel in relative safety across the vast, watery expanse.

*   *   *

THE PASSAGE TO LONDON would typically take a little more than three weeks depending on how well the winds blew, although it could take much longer if they were becalmed or if storms blew them seriously off course.

There were just a few first-class passengers on the ship as more people were moving westward toward America than eastward toward England. They passed the time in reading and, especially at mealtimes, in conversation.

Among the passengers, Zach found an Anglican priest, Rev. Woolworth, who was returning to England after completing a survey of the condition of the Episcopal Church in America. The Revolutionary War had disrupted the Anglican Church considerably. Many of its members had remained loyal to the British Crown and fled to Atlantic Canada for safety. Now the church had reorganized itself so that loyalty to the King or Queen was no longer essential for membership. The American branch had even replaced the Anglican name with "Episcopal" to distance itself from Britain.

Zach was interested to discover the Anglican Church did not have detailed expectations about the return of Christ. Yes, they acknowledged He would return in glory, but just how, or where, or when, the Reverend was unwilling to speculate.

Rev. Woolworth remained polite as Zach explained his own understanding of the Bible's prophecies and the purpose of his travels. He was amused by the notion that Christ might return much as He appeared the first time. He noted how unusual that perspective was, and then he asked why the prophet Joel referred to His coming as "*the great and terrible day of the LORD.*"

"If there are no outward miracles, how can the Holy Child's birth be the '*terrible day of the LORD*'?" the reverend asked.

Zach thought for a moment and then said, "It is not His birth—it is His revelation that can be terrifying. And what is terrifying about it is simply this: that the virtue of steadfastness, which you have always prized,

89

can quickly become the vice of attachment, *without any change on your part.* Unless you are spiritually awake and searching, you may become like the scribes and Pharisees of Jesus' age."

As the reverend paused to think about that, Zach continued, "Consider the Jewish priests prior to the appearance of Jesus. They were the most steadfast of all people in their adherence to the laws of Moses. And yet when the Messiah appeared, they utterly failed to recognize Him because the virtue of their steadfastness had become the vice of attachment and blind adherence.

"They had concluded that outwardly miraculous things would happen when the Messiah appeared, so there was no need to investigate and weigh the spiritual teachings of individual claims for themselves. There was no need to stay awake spiritually, because an alarm clock of outward miracles would quickly awaken them when He arrived. But these leaders were very badly mistaken."

Rev. Woolworth replied, "Are we supposed to listen to everyone who comes along claiming to be a prophet?"

Zach reflected on this and then said, "Did St. John ask us to reject every person who appeared, claiming to be a prophet? No indeed. In chapter 4 of his first letter, he instructed us to '*try the spirits*' to see '*whether they are of God.*' If we automatically reject them all, we are no longer spiritually alert or awake."

They discussed passages that seemed to suggest a specific time or condition and passages that indicated that "*no man knoweth the hour.*" Was the latter a reference only to those who were alive at the time of Jesus? Or was it intended to include all people in the future also? Did "the hour" mean also the year? The decade? The century? If no man could know any of those times, why did the Bible provide so many clues as to when Christ would return?

Zach pointed out that there were several Old Testament prophecies of the coming of Jesus that were in fact fulfilled. Rev. Woolworth replied that none of them helped the Jewish people find Jesus. Zach explained that while it was true that no Jews recognized Jesus through prophecy *before* He started teaching, Jesus' fulfillment of prophecies—even when done in unexpected ways—assisted many Jews *afterward* in setting them on their path toward becoming the earliest Christians.

"Perhaps it will be the same in this age," he concluded.

"Very well," replied Rev. Woolworth, "but let me offer one bit of advice: Do not listen to those preachers who have all kinds of ideas about the crazy things that are written in the Book of Revelation or the antichrist or other such nonsense." He was wagging his finger fairly vigorously by this point. "These things do have deep symbolic meanings. But there are far too many preachers out there who misuse these parts of the Bible. They are taking them out of context and mixing them with other quotes to assemble a concoction intended simply to scare people—to scare them into the pews and then to scare the money out of their pockets."

Zach assured the reverend he did not listen to such preachers.

"I find that the best defense against people like that is simply having good first-hand knowledge of the Bible," he said. "That kind of preacher is only successful if his followers don't read their Bibles thoroughly. Those people allow quotes to be taken out of context. They don't ask questions for themselves.

"For instance, I've heard some of them warning about the coming of that terrible figure called 'the antichrist.' But I know from my own Bible reading that an antichrist is not a single person. It is any person who denies that Jesus was the Anointed One sent by God. I know that the antichrist is mentioned only in two short letters of John and nowhere else in the Bible. I know that John explained that there were many such antichrists alive in the world even at the time of his writing—rather than a single figure who would appear only in the latter days. People who deny Jesus and who actively work against His followers have existed in every age. They are motivated by the antichrist spirit."

"Exactly so," replied the reverend. "I'm glad to see you know your Bible well. Some preachers will try to mix this antichrist spirit together with the beasts of the Book of Revelation, as well as the false prophet mentioned therein. But it makes no sense to those who have thoroughly studied the Bible. The message of Jesus was love, not fear. I am wary of anyone who is using fear to gather followers."

"My father," explained Zach, "was always searching for the spiritual meanings behind the words of the Bible. He knew many of the prophecies are given in parables or allegory—not always easily perceived. But he felt that the year of Christ's return could be reliably discerned based on Jesus' citation of Daniel's prophecies. He also felt that the manner of His return could be understood simply by looking at the manner in which all of God's prophets have appeared. All that remains is to find the place—and this is my task now. If I am successful, I will certainly ask Him about the correct understanding of the deeply allegorical references in the Bible. And I will try not to limit myself to my own particular interpretation nor to the interpretations of others, which may or may not be accurate."

The reverend wished him well. Although he did not think that Zach's search was likely to be successful, he was not one to discourage the effort. They had several helpful conversations during their trip.

Zach also got to know the other passengers over the dinners that the captain hosted for those in first class. The sailing was generally smooth, except for one storm midway through. Cloudy weather brought winds out of the west, which propelled the ship rapidly until they became so strong that the sails had to be furled to prevent damage. As the day turned into night, the waves grew in height, heaving the ship and its passengers up thirty to forty feet then dropping them down the same distance every ten seconds or so. The wind howled through the rigging. The crew had ensured all loose items were stowed away as the ship rolled from left to right and back. They battened down the hatches so that the waves occasionally crashing across the deck brought virtually no water into the tightly closed cabin spaces.

Zach understood how frightening this could be to passengers who had seldom traveled by ship. But he had been in such storms previously and was no longer bothered by them. He knew that the art of building seaworthy ships had developed greatly over the recent decades, and an undamaged ship with furled sails would float like a piece of cork.

"As long as we are far from the coasts during a storm," Zach explained to some of the frightened passengers, "we have nothing serious to fear." He assured them that they were in mid-ocean, with no rocky coasts within hundreds of miles.

On the deck on the evening after the storm, Ruth, the woman he had courted and hoped to marry, came to mind. Her fears of sailing were not totally unjustified, of course, for he himself was keenly aware that a storm could drive a ship onto a rocky coastline and destroy it. Poorly built ships could also founder during a bad storm in mid-ocean.

"It's a risk that all sailors must take," he thought to himself, "but I suppose some women feel that it is a risk that they don't want to take when choosing a husband."

The loss of Ruth's uncle, and the subsequent loss of her interest in marrying a seaman, had occurred more than ten years earlier. It still pained Zach to think about how deeply he had been wounded.

But as he sat on the deck that evening, he realized that had it not happened, he would likely have been married by now and would be a father to several children. Thus, he would have been in no position to undertake such a long search as this. He was glad to have the opportunity to take on this task. And as he sat pondering his past, he wondered whether it was all just a part of God's plan for his life. He wondered how often it happened that the seemingly tragic events in one's younger years might, in some unforeseen way, be the necessary foundation for something greater and far more important in one's later years. As the clouds cleared away and the stars twinkled brilliantly in the dark, moonless sky, he felt that perhaps, in some way, they were smiling down on him.

He spent much of the rest of his trip reviewing some of the notes from his father, as well as various biblical passages. He entered his thoughts in his diary. Between all of this, he tried to imagine what life in the Holy Land would be like. And he hoped Elijah Goodman in London would be willing to join him in this journey.

Chapter 7

CONVINCING JAMES IN LONDON

UPON ARRIVAL IN LONDON in late July, Zach wasted no time finding one of the hansom cabs and provided the cabbie with Elijah Goodman's address. He had been looking forward to meeting him face to face and was hoping to find a willing traveling partner.

When he arrived at the modest home, he was pleased to find Mr. Goodman there but somewhat chagrinned to discover he was an older gentleman, about as old as his own father had been, and not a likely candidate for travel.

Elijah expressed his delight in meeting Zach and warmly welcomed him as he offered him tea and lunch. They discussed the views they shared on the likely manner of Christ's return. Zach was encouraged by his friendliness. Elijah reminded him much of his own father. He realized now that the forthright tone that he had heard in Elijah's letter to Mr. Miller was the tone of an older man writing to a preacher who was somewhat his junior.

After an hour of getting to know more about each other, Elijah brought up the topic from Zach's letter regarding accompanying him to the Holy Land. "As you can see, I am much too old for such a journey," he noted.

"Yes, the thought did cross my mind," admitted Zach in a disappointed tone.

"But do not be dismayed. I have been casting about in my mind for someone who might accompany you. My attention was drawn to one of our congregants, a young professor by the name of James Lawrence. He is a lecturer of geography at the University College of London. He shares our religious perspectives. *And* he's an Orientalist—he spent several years in Egypt prior to his appointment at the college."

"That sounds ideal," said Zach enthusiastically, "but is he willing to travel?"

"I've shared your letter with him, but you'll need to meet with him to discuss it. He didn't seem to feel that it was out of the question. He told me he'd like to meet you in any case, once you'd arrived. He said he's most readily available on Saturdays, and that would be tomorrow."

After they concluded their discussions, Elijah handed Zach the address for Professor Lawrence. Zach expressed his gratitude for the reference and the hospitality. Then he headed off to find lodging near the University College while anticipating his meeting with the professor.

James Lawrence had taken a position as a lecturer in the recently established Department of Geography at the University College of London. Born in 1805, he was three years older than Zach. When James was eighteen, his father arranged an appointment for him to work under *Henry Salt*, the British Consul-General in Cairo. James spent five years there, assisting with the cataloging of the hieroglyphs being translated with the help of the *Rosetta Stone* and collecting archeological artifacts for the British Museum.

While there, he picked up a good knowledge of Arabic as well as a basic knowledge of Arabian customs and the Muslim religion. He had hoped to visit Jerusalem, but the press of work made it impossible. Upon his return to England in 1828, he studied the Middle East, with a focus on religions—Jewish, Christian, and Muslim. He received appointment from *Capt. Maconochie* as a lecturer in geography with a focus on Oriental studies in 1836.

"The following year, I married Caroline, a lively and intelligent young woman I had met here at the college," James explained. "And shortly thereafter, we were expecting our first child."

A panic flashed though Zach's mind—a worry that James' family obligations would preclude his ability to travel.

But James continued with a grave expression, "Alas, problems arose on the day of her delivery, and both she and young Joseph died in the childbirth attempt."

"I am so terribly sorry to hear of your loss," replied Zach sympathetically. "It must have been heartbreaking."

"Indeed it was," James affirmed, "so much so that I have had no thought of marrying ever again. I dedicate a part of my income—the part that would have been spent on our dear Joseph—to the local orphanage to help those poor children who have no parents."

Zach shared with James the reason that he was unmarried. "But the depth of your loss certainly dwarfs mine," he added.

As Zach heard more about the professor's knowledge of life in the Holy Land, he was thrilled to realize his near perfect credentials for this journey.

"Yes, Mr. Goodman gave me your letter," said the professor. "We share the same understanding of the significance of the coming year. We also agree that Christ's appearance this time will be similar to His previous appearance—not a huge miracle of coming down from the sky but rather being born and growing up similar to most men, except perhaps for having the same sort of innate knowledge that Jesus had as a child."

As the professor prepared some tea, Zach noted his features. He was slightly taller than Zach, with deep-set eyes and an alert gaze that quickly picked up details. He was somewhat lean and less muscular than Zach, never having had any significant manual chores. Broad sideburns descended from a head of bushy brown hair.

"But finding Him would be another matter. For although the Holy Land looks small on the map, nevertheless, when we get there, it will seem like a huge task. We might have to wander from city to city—every city with a church or monastery at least—asking if there has been any child born with extraordinary knowledge and intelligence during the last 30 years or so. This could be a formidable task indeed."

Zach replied, "Yes, it is possible that it will go that way. But it is also possible that such a person would have received some renown by the year that His teaching begins. The news would almost certainly have spread locally.

"Besides, did you ever think of the Magi—how they traveled all the way over land from Persia? They didn't know where to look exactly—they only knew, by the star, when to start their search. They must have known from the prophecies of their own religion that a star would be the sign to herald the coming of the Promised One of the Jews. The fulfillment of that prophecy must have been a great confirmation for them."

"I wish I knew the exact prophecy," said James. "I've heard that it is lost to history due to the destruction that various invaders have wrought in that land."

"In any case," Zach continued, "we know that although they started with just the prophecy and the star, they received some guidance along the way, first from the chief priests of the King—however corrupt his motives—which led them to Bethlehem. When they got to Bethlehem, Matthew suggests that the star was directly above them."

"But how could they have determined so precisely which house or inn to look in?" James wondered.

"Perhaps they simply spoke to the townsfolk," suggested Zach, "many of whom had probably heard the story from the shepherds, who, only a few days earlier, had witnessed the miraculous events that Luke described."

"It's possible," acknowledged James.

"So my point is that like the Magi, we do not need to know *exactly* where to look. We already know the time. We know the approximate place. We must make the effort and trust in God that the guidance will come as we seek Him."

James sat for a moment, thinking it over.

"Well, in any case," said Zach, "*I* am going. I made a promise to my father on his deathbed that I would go. And I have a sense that he is watching and guiding me.

"Besides," he continued, "even if we should fail, it will be good for your career. As a junior professor of the history of the Middle East, you will be much better off for having visited the Holy Land and seen it firsthand.

"And personally, I *need* you. I need to have someone who knows the language and the ways of life—someone who has been to the Arab world. I cannot do this alone."

James paused a while, thinking, then said, "You can afford to take me along? I don't have adequate savings for such a major trip."

"Money is not an obstacle," Zach assured him, knowing that his father had given him almost a carte blanche to use his family's fortune. He explained how he had brought funds to cover the costs of two or even three travelers.

But James was reluctant to make such a big commitment. He thought of the students who were planning to hear him teach. He thought of the research work he hoped to accomplish during the coming year and of his friends, who expected him to be around to help them. He thought of his home and repairs that needed to be tended to. His mind started to fill with the practical implications of such an absence.

Finally he said, "I don't know, Zach. There is so much going on in my life. I really can't afford to take a year off to pursue this—as exciting as it is."

Zach was crestfallen. He felt that James was missing the big picture. He paused a moment as a thought came to mind. He then asked, "James, how long ago did your family convert to Christianity?"

James thought it was a rather odd question, but he answered, "Well, I don't have a documented family history that stretches back that far, but I like to think that some of them were among the converts when the early missionaries first reached these shores in or around the year 600 AD. Why?"

"So at least some branches of your family have been practicing Christians for more than 1,200 years, I suppose," said Zach.

"Yes, very likely. But why do you ask?"

Doing some quick calculations, Zach continued, "That is to say, perhaps about 40 generations for parts of your family."

"Possibly 50 generations—the generations were often shorter in those ages," replied James.

"And how many of them heard the stories of Christ's promise to return?"

"I suppose almost everyone. It has always been a significant part of the Christian message."

"How many, then, thought about how *wonderful* it would be to live in the age when Christ would return? How many *longed* to live in the age in which we now find ourselves? How many would have given anything to live in this age?" Zach continued.

"I suppose most of them," sighed James, beginning to realize where Zach's line of reasoning was going.

"Precisely!" said Zach. "I have a sense that it is not just my father who is watching over me, guiding me on this journey. I have a sense that all of my ancestors—at least everyone who ever longed to see this day—is *watching*. To me, giving up a year or two to pursue this may seem like a big thing. But they are all exclaiming, 'Throw such cares away! The promised day is come! Now is the day to act! Fail not to seize so priceless an opportunity!' When we hear their calls, how can we sit back and do nothing? And how shall we answer them when we join them in the greater Kingdom?"

Zach paused briefly then continued, "When you were a child, did you ever wish that you might have the chance to witness Christ's return? Did you ever pray and ask God that you might see it?"

James looked startled, saying, "How did you know that?"

"Don't be so surprised," continued Zach. "Most of us have done the same. When I ask those questions of the Millerite followers in America, most tell me yes, they have carried that wish or that prayer in their hearts from their childhood.

"So if you have asked God to open the door and now the door stands wide open before you, will you fail to go through it? Will you say, 'Thank you, dear Lord, for answering my prayers, but now I will ignore Your answer'?"

James thought for a while. He thought back to his childhood and remembered hearing the lessons about Christ's return. How much simpler life seemed back then; how much easier it would have been to let go of everything! And the words of Jesus came to him: "*Whosoever shall not receive the kingdom of God as a little child, he shall not enter therein.*"

Tears started to well in his eyes.

As he thought of all the cares that he carried, like large bags weighing him down, the words of the gospel came to him again, saying, "*It is easier for a camel to go through the eye of a needle, than for a rich man to enter into the kingdom of God.*" Perhaps he needed to let go of some of these things to enter God's kingdom.

And then the scene from Matthew came to his mind, in which one of Jesus' disciples asked to be excused so that he could go to bury his father who had died. Jesus replied, *"Follow me and let the dead bury their dead."*

Jesus seemed to be saying that those who were spiritually alive should not let themselves be distracted by the cares of the material world, especially when the call of the Messiah was at hand.

Zach, thinking of James' wife and child, as well as his own loss of Ruth, added, "We have both suffered losses in recent years. But let it not be said that we suffered those losses in vain. Let it rather be said that they have opened the door of opportunity to pursue the greatest search of a lifetime, which can also be a balm to a wounded heart."

James was pleased with the thought that the loss of his wife and son could possibly result in some good, and he thought that they, too, might be watching over such an effort.

With these thoughts in mind, James realized that the only reasonable response was to go. Zach's arguments and the lessons from the gospel were overwhelming.

So he smiled slightly and simply said, "When shall we leave?"

Jumping up out of his seat, Zach clapped his hands and said, "Praise be God!" and then, "We can go as soon as you are ready."

James replied, "I have an assistant whom I've been training over the past several semesters. I suppose he'd welcome the opportunity to take my place for the year. I'll need to make arrangements with the head of the department, but he has always encouraged us to pursue research and outside studies. I don't think it will be a problem. Perhaps I could ask my neighbor to look after the house and maybe let it out to a visiting professor."

"Great!" said Zach. "How soon, then, can we set sail?"

"Give me fifteen days," said James. "I think I can wrap things up by then."

"Wonderful! I'll check down at the Jerusalem Coffee House to find out who is sailing," replied Zach, referring to the place where all the ship captains would gather and post their sailing plans.

"Good," said James, "but come back to my home every evening, and bring plenty of paper and a pen set."

101

CONVINCING JAMES IN LONDON

"For what?"

"You'll need this time, and most of our travel time, to learn Arabic."

"Oh...yes. That's a very good point." He hadn't given it much thought until now.

And with that, Zach was up and out the door.

Chapter 8

CATHOLIC LESSONS ON THE SHIP TO ROME

ON A HOT DAY in mid-August, their ship sailed outward through the mouth of the Thames and into the English Channel. The captain unfurled its full sails to the clear blue skies, carrying them southward. Zach felt pleased to be on board once again, and this time he was not alone. James was elated with the feeling that his life had been endued with a new sense of adventure and purpose. The latter, in particular, had been lacking since the loss of his wife and son five years earlier. He felt as if he were beginning to see that tragedy in a new light.

The captain was interested to hear of Zach's seafaring experience and was pleased to share some of his own knowledge of the nautical world. He mentioned that he had just recently read of the July 19 launch of the *SS Great Britain* in Bristol—the largest ship in the world and supposedly the inauguration of a whole new era in ship design.

"What is different about it?" inquired Zach.

"You may know," the captain said proudly, "we Britons have been working for some time to adapt the dependability of steam power to our ocean-going ships. Various paddlewheel designs have been tried, but they've proven unreliable on the high seas when tall waves may toss a ship left and right.

"Well, the *SS Great Britain* has no paddlewheels. Rather, it is driven forward by a rotating screw that extends out the bottom of the ship's stern, where it remains constantly below the waterline. And to hold all of the machinery together tightly, we've made the entire ship from iron instead of wood."

"That's fascinating," Zach replied. "In America, I've heard that our navy is building a similar ship—the *USS Princeton*. It's a military ship, but I can see how the design could be adapted for cargo and passenger service. As I recall, it is due to be launched next month."

They both paused for a moment, contemplating how different the future might be.

"Aye," said the captain wistfully, "if these succeed, we're going to have to learn a whole new trade. Feeding a boiler with coal day and night and keeping pipes and valves working is a different world from the setting and trimming of sails in the wind."

"True indeed," Zach said. "My brother, who runs our family's shipping business, would love the predictable schedules of these steamships. But for my part, I will always love the friendly tug of the wind and the quiet elegance of the sail."

*   *   *

ZACH'S LESSONS ON THE fundamentals of Arabic, both in script and in spoken form, continued on the ship. He was an attentive student. And he had a great incentive to learn—knowing they would soon be traveling in a land where this was the only language used by most of the people.

The ship carried few passengers on this trip, and of them, fewer still seemed to have much interest in religion. Some seemed amused at the idea of making a "pilgrimage" to the Holy Land—it was not a common practice at the time. Most warned of the dangers in traveling through such foreign places.

Zach took this in stride, not giving great credence to the opinions of people who had not themselves visited the lands they felt free to opine about. He was, however, deeply grateful to have found James. Foreign countries were not nearly as foreign when you were traveling with someone who knew the land, the language, and the people.

One passenger who had a definite interest in religion was a Catholic priest heading to Rome from his parish in Ireland. While passing the Straits of Gibraltar one day after lunch, Zach struck up a conversation with him.

Father Timothy was interested to hear of James and Zach's plans to visit the Holy Land, and he inquired as to what had led them to undertake such a journey. Zach explained the story of his father's interest in the teachings of Mr. Miller.

"Ah, then you are Millerites," said Father Tim. But James explained how they shared his belief in the expectation that Christ would return during the next year but had different ideas regarding the manner of His coming, and thus they were traveling to search in the Holy Land.

"But enough of our story," said Zach. "I have also been taking every opportunity to inquire from others concerning their own understandings of the Bible's teachings on this topic, but I must confess that I have not had the opportunity to hear directly from a Catholic clergyman. So tell us about the Church's understanding of these things."

Father Tim paused to collect his thoughts and then said, "The Church is very much looking forward to the second coming of Christ. Yea, wondrous things will happen in that day. But we generally do not say *exactly* what will occur or how it will occur or when. There are too many individual interpretations that can be, and have been, offered, for the Church to say which is correct and which is not. So we will just await the appearance of some of the many miraculous things that will occur, and then we will know for certain that the time has come."

Zach was somewhat disappointed by the vagueness of this response. It reminded him of Rev. Woolworth's Anglican-Episcopal perspective during their discussion on his Atlantic crossing. He was inclined to inquire as to why Jesus had repeatedly warned his followers to remain spiritually awake and on the lookout for His return. After all, if outward miracles were going to make it so obvious, why would Jesus have emphasized the need to remain spiritually awake?

Zach thought again of how many await outward miracles as an alarm clock to wake them up. However, out of respect for the priest and a true desire to hear all of his views, Zach did not mention his objections.

Instead, he inquired, "What about the indications of the year of Christ's return? You have no doubt read of how Mr. Miller and thousands of others have studied the prophecies of Daniel and how they point to the year 1844."

"Yes," responded the Father, "I have read of them. In the Church, however, we are disinclined to pay any attention to the sort of numbers that you find in the books of Daniel and Revelation."

"But why is that?" inquired Zach. "Surely God revealed them to Daniel and John for some purpose."

"Perhaps so, but we Catholics have a long history, stretching back further than any of the Protestant churches can claim." He looked away, as if unsure whether he wanted to go into any details. Then he added with a certain sadness, "Yes indeed, and we have learned a thing or two from that history."

"What do you mean?" Zach pressed.

"Well, putting a date on the return of Christ can have bad consequences," he replied. "Suppose you are wrong? You will be the laughingstock of the entire community. And once you have set a date, you can be sure that the community will be watching—and they'll not let you forget it."

"Did something like that happen?" asked Zach.

"Well..." Father Tim paused again, as if trying to decide how to proceed with a delicate topic. "Well, yes, there was a monk, who lived in the twelfth century, by the name of *Joachim of Fiore*. He studied the Book of Revelation intently for a long time. He came forth from this study with many new ideas and became one of the most outspoken thinkers on the subject. But one of the conclusions he reached, along with some of the Franciscan monks who followed him, was that the apocalyptic cataclysms would occur, and a new age would begin, in the year 1260 AD because of the references to 1,260 in Matthew, Revelation, and Daniel."

"I know about the 1,260 references in Daniel and Revelation," noted Zach, "but are they found in Matthew as well?"

"Yes, although indirectly. The first chapter of Matthew cites 42 generations from Abraham to Jesus, and since a generation is typically 30 years, Joachim expected that Christ would return after another 42 generations. That would be in the year 1260 AD."

"I have puzzled over similar references myself," replied Zach. "It is clear to us that the references in Daniel to 490 years were fulfilled exactly with the crucifixion Jesus. It seems equally clear to me that Daniel's 2,300-year prophecy will be fulfilled next year. But I don't have a clear understanding of his references to 1,260, 1,290, and 1,335 found in the last chapter of Daniel's book. I might have been inclined to ignore them, except that the 1,260 figure is repeated several times again in Revelation, and now, as you've mentioned, it seems to be in Matthew as well.

"But tell me, did Joachim find anything special that happened in 1260?"

"Fortunately for him," replied the priest, "he was born too early to reach that date. He died in 1202. But his teachings became very popular, and the Franciscans remembered them; it created much excitement and controversy as the date approached. But when nothing of significance happened in 1260, it was, of course, a major embarrassment for their followers and for the Church in general. In 1263, the Church condemned those teachings as heretical. And since that time, the Church has been wary of traveling down such a path of date-setting ever again."

"I see," replied Zach, reflecting on what he had heard.

The priest added, "I do fear that your William Miller may suffer the same fate sometime next year."

A twinge of panic went through Zach's mind as he considered this possibility.

James, who had been listening, noted Zach's expression. "Well, we thank you for your insights," he said to the priest. He nodded to Zach that he would be on the upper deck. Zach excused himself and followed James.

Looking out at the wide expanse of the Mediterranean Sea, Zach commented to James, "That was an interesting story and a bit worrisome, I will confess. Do you think there's a chance that we'll suffer the same fate?"

James said, "I think our evidence is much stronger than what Joachim of Fiore had. In addition to the clear lines of reasoning from Daniel, we also have available to us the confirming prophecy of Revelation 9:15."

"And what is that?" asked Zach.

"You aren't familiar with it? I thought all of Miller's followers had heard of it."

"I'm afraid I must have missed that one. What does John say?"

"It is the point where he refers to the slaying of a '*third part of men*.'"

"Ah, yes, I recall the passage, but how is it connected to 1844?" Zach inquired.

"Well," responded James, "several students of the Bible, including Mr. Miller, noted that the '*third part of men*' could refer to a third of the Christian world.[6] For much of its history, Christianity was regarded as being divided into three major areas—the Western or Latin portion, headquartered in Rome; the Eastern or Greek-speaking portion known as *Byzantium*, with its center in Constantinople; and the North African one, including Egypt. Although the forces of Islam were able to take over all of North Africa shortly after the death of Muhammad, they were unable to conquer the Byzantine Empire at first.

"The *Ottoman* Muslims from central Asia eventually took over Asia Minor and parts of Southeast Europe. But try as they might, the massive walls of Constantinople—built by *Theodosius II* in the mid-400s withstood every attack for 1,000 years. All onslaughts—at first by pagan tribes and later by several Muslim leaders—were incapable of breaking through those massive walls.

"It was not until these Muslim Turks learned how to build and use large cannons that they were able to conquer Constantinople in 1453 with '*the fire and smoke and brimstone*' coming out of what John perceived to be the 'mouth' of a specialized 'horse'—all as mentioned in the latter half of Revelation Chapter 9. Thus, many scholars regard 1453 as the date of the loss of one of the three sections of the former Christian world, that is, metaphorically, the *'slaying of a third part of men.'*"

"Interesting," replied Zach, "but what does it have to do with 1844?"

"There is a time reference in that verse. It seems to indicate that this is taking place *'an hour, a day, a month and a year'* before the coming of the next main event. So how much does that add up to, using our understanding that 'a day in God's sight is as a year to men'?"

Zach thought for a moment then said, "Since a biblical 'day' is regarded as a year in human terms, then a 'month' would be thirty years, and a 'year' would be 360 years. So I suppose that would add up to 391 years."

"Correct!" declared James. "And what year would it be then—391 years after the fall of Constantinople in 1453?" asked James.

Zach did a quick calculation. Then he smiled broadly and said, "That adds up to exactly 1844!"

"Quite right," said James. "You see, it is not only Daniel who points to this year. It is also found, however indirectly, in the Book of Revelation."

"That is *amazing*!" exclaimed Zach. "I had always just assumed that when John wrote of the *'hour, the day, the month and the year,'* he was just poetically referring to our various measurements of time."

"I thought the same thing when I first read it," replied James. "But I noticed, when I reread it, that he had left out any reference to a week, which should have been included if he was poetically listing human references to time. So I always wondered if it didn't have some deeper meaning, until one day when one of the members of our congregation explained to me this interpretation."

Zach thought about it for a moment and then observed, "Then there is one additional—and very important—aspect to that prophecy: Since the start date for this prophecy is in the AD years, not the BC years, there is no confusion here about whether there was a 'year 0' in the Roman calendar, as was the case with the 2,300-year prophecy of Daniel. In this prophecy, simple addition takes us from 1453 to 1844. So this also confirms my father's explanation of the 2,300-year prophecy from Daniel—that the absence of the zero in the Roman numbering system means that the 2,300 years would be fulfilled in 1844, not in 1843."

"An excellent point," said James enthusiastically. "Here is another interesting observation about this prophecy: The fulfillment date could not even be calculated at the time it was revealed since the starting time was based on an event in the future, whose date was unknown.

"So if one was inclined to doubt that John's revelation was a true revelation and therefore thought that he had somehow 'designed' his 391-year prophecy to end at the same time as Daniel's 2,300-year prophecy, it would have been impossible for him to do such a thing because the fulfillment date of the 391-year prophecy was dependent on the occurrence of a future event—the fall of Constantinople in 1453 AD. And John obviously had no way of knowing that date when he was writing this around 100 AD."

Zach and James pondered awhile as they stood on the deck, watching the waves of the blue Mediterranean pass by. The sails were billowed by a warm breeze from the west, which drove them eastward almost as quickly as the white clouds moved in the sky above them.

Then Zach said, "There is yet one more thing that is special about that prophecy."

"What is that?" replied James.

"Something that might help us in our search: In addition to showing us that the 'day' refers to the year 1844, the prophecy also mentions 'the hour.'

"If we follow the same reasoning—that a 'day' in the Lord's sight is a year in man's normal reckoning—then an hour, that is, a twenty-fourth part of a day, would be a twenty-fourth part of a year, or a half of a month. So to carry the formula to its logical conclusion, this prophecy refers to a period of 391 years *and* a half-month. So perhaps we could have some idea of more exactly when, within 1844, the Promised One will appear."

"Yes," said James, "the same thought occurred to me. And I did some research at one point to determine more exactly the date that Constantinople fell to the Turks. But the battle itself raged for almost two months, so I couldn't tell if one should take the starting date, one of the turning points, or the final date of the battle. But the best I could figure was that the battle raged from April 11 to May 29. Of course, that was the Julian calendar, so in today's Gregorian calendar, we would say it went from April 20 to June 7. So adding the 391 years plus a half-month would lead me to guess that it will occur sometime between May 5 and June 22, 1844.

"But then another thought struck me. In Matthew 24 and 25, and again in Mark 13 and Luke 12, Jesus says that 'no man knoweth the hour' that the Lord will return. So perhaps we cannot get that specific."

"Perhaps that is true," agreed Zach, "but perhaps Jesus was referring to no man alive at the time He was speaking to them. Indeed, since the future start date of this prophecy was unknown, no one could have understood John's reference to the hour until at least 1453 AD.

"Moreover, in those same passages, Jesus says that 'no man knoweth the day.' In biblical terminology, that could be taken to mean that no person would know the year that He will come. But for us, in this age, the year seems to be understandable. So I think the purpose of His statement was that people should remain spiritually awake. Although the time-related prophecies are helpful, we cannot rely on them alone. We must also look for the spiritual qualities of the Promised One."

"That is certainly true," acknowledged James. "I am certain that the year is 1844, but I'm going to keep my mind open for a fulfillment anytime within the year."

"Fair enough," agreed Zach.

As the ship surged forward, Zach was pleased to be learning not just from the new people he had met but also from James as well.

*   *   *

UPON REACHING THE PORT of Ostia at the end of the Tiber River, they booked passage on the next ship scheduled to depart for the Holy Land, in about a week. They had decided to follow the normal pilgrimage route to the port of Jaffa, and from thence travel inland to Jerusalem and Bethlehem.

If nothing could be found there, they would head northward along the Jordan River to the Sea of Galilee, where Jesus had taught, and from there, westward to His boyhood home in Nazareth if necessary.

The ship's captain was British. He said emphatically that they would depart on Monday, September 18, at 3 p.m. "Don't be late," he said sternly.

Zach and James decided to use their waiting time to travel up the Tiber and to visit some of the sites in Rome, the "Eternal City."

Zach had felt that his visit to London was a step backward in time, but he felt it even more so here. While London had roots stretching back eighteen centuries, Rome was founded another eight centuries before that, with earlier settlements being established before the dawn of history. Though they were both Protestants and thus disinclined to pay much attention to the current pope, they could not help but feel a sense of the immense history of the West associated with this city and with all of the great monuments they saw.

They went to St. Peter's Basilica first—the spot beneath which St. Peter was reportedly buried after his crucifixion in Rome in 64 AD. They took time to pray that they would be guided, hoping that when the time came, they might be as detached as Peter had been in his willingness to walk away from his previous life. They hoped to be able to recognize the new Christ through His teachings and His actions, just as Peter had done on that day so long ago on the shore of the Sea of Galilee.

Although the architecture and the sculpture that had developed over the last 1,500 years were marvelous, Zach and James both felt that the most marvelous thing of all was the example of Peter's life—how an untrained fisherman could become one of the most significant people in all of Western history by having the courage to follow the Christ instead of listening to the religious orthodoxy of his day.

They similarly prayed at the Basilica of St. Paul, who had been beheaded there at about the same time as Peter was crucified. They asked God that they, too, might have the kind of detachment that enabled Paul to follow Christ when He appeared to him and to turn away from the old Jewish practices, recognizing that the promises of the prophets of old had indeed been fulfilled in the teachings of Jesus, even if the fulfillment had been contrary to the particular expectations of the religious leaders who had been his companions.

112

They learned about Pope Gregory XVI, who had been serving as the pope and ruler of the Papal States of central Italy since 1831. Zach was pleased to learn that although the pope was conservative in many ways, both he and Queen Victoria had condemned slavery.

"I wonder how long it will be before my country will be able to follow their example," he thought.

From **West** to **East**

Black Sea

Constantinople

Patmos

Cyprus

Aegean Sea

Ionian Sea

Mediterranean Sea

Rome

Beirut

Damascus

Akka

Jaffa

Jerusalem

Red Sea

Nile R.

Mecca

Chapter 9

TOWARD THE HOLY LAND—AND A SOLUTION TO THE 1260 RIDDLE?

THEIR DAYS IN ROME soon came to a close, and they arose early on the appointed morning to have plenty of time to return to Port Ostia for their departure. The riverboat they boarded was ready to leave, except for the captain, whose arrival was delayed without explanation.

Zach was frustrated by this delay, but James observed, "I have noticed during my years in these areas that the peoples in the lands without winter have a much more relaxed attitude toward time than we do. Perhaps winters force a certain sense of timeliness upon us."

Zach was less philosophical about it. "Unfortunately, the captain of the ship to Jaffa is British, and he will not tolerate any such delays."

The riverboat captain eventually arrived. A jovial fellow, he made no apologies for his tardiness. They cast off, but the river was low and moved sluggishly as it was now near the end of the dry season. The windless day made matters worse, leaving the sail hanging limp much of the time. Zach felt agitated and began to wonder if walking would be faster.

Eventually they reached the port—just in time to see their ship leaving the harbor. Their dismay was worsened when they discovered from the shipping agent that it would be at least another week before the next ship would leave for Jaffa. Zach grumbled, "When we prayed for guidance, this is not exactly what I had in mind."

Noting their frustration, the agent mentioned that a Turkish ship was scheduled to leave for the northern port of Akka the following day. James considered the option.

"You know," he said, "Akka is near Nazareth. We could reverse our plans...visit Nazareth first then follow the Jordan River southward from there to reach Jerusalem and Bethlehem."

Zach had no objection to this as a way to recover their lost time. So they booked their passage and set off the following day.

James continued to teach Zach more Arabic. And on this ship, there were many Arabic-speaking travelers with whom he could practice.

*   *   *

WITH CLEAR SKIES IN mid-September, their ship pushed courageously southward through the Strait of Messina then followed a southeastern course across the Ionian Sea and into the blue Aegean. While passing near the island of Patmos, southwest of the Turkish mainland, Zach started thinking of the revelation that had come to St. John while he was imprisoned on that island some 1,750 years earlier. Many were the mysterious allusions contained in that book, and fascinating were the similarities, as well as the differences, between the things St. John had seen and the things Daniel had witnessed in his visions some six centuries earlier—as if they had each seen almost the same place in heaven.

He thought particularly of St. John's frequent reference to the 1,260 "days" as 42 months or as 3-1/2 years, or more poetically as *"a time, times and the dividing of time"* in chapters 11 and 12 of Revelation. Daniel had used the same phrase in chapter 7 and again in the last chapter of his book. Zach still felt unsatisfied with the explanation that Mr. Miller had offered. He had asked James for any insights that he might have, but James was equally mystified by its significance.

So a couple of days later, he decided to mention it to his fellow travelers on the ship—those who spoke English at least. Not that he expected that they might have an explanation, but as a seeker, one never knew what might turn up. And there was no harm in asking. He had previously shared the purpose of their pilgrimage with many of his fellow passengers.

116

At dinner, he explained, "Although Daniel's prophecy of the 2,300 years seems to clearly point to the year 1844, I'm still not so clear about the meaning of his prophecy concerning the 1,260 years. If we go 1,260 years forward from the date of Daniel's prophecy in 457 BC, we come to 804 AD. Nothing particularly significant happened in that year. If we take 1,260 years after the birth of Jesus, we get to the year 1260 AD, and again, nothing especially significant happened at that time. Nor did anything happen 1,260 years after Jesus' crucifixion. So, what, really, is the meaning of the 1,260 years?"

The ship's cook, who had entered to serve the dinner, was of Turkish descent. Most Turks of this position knew little English, but he appeared to have picked some up in his travels and had been listening to at least some of what Zach had been saying because he interjected in broken English, "Habibi (my friend), this year...it is not 1260. This year is 1259."

Zach replied, "What do you mean?"

"What I mean, sir...the year now, here, in Ottoman lands...it is 1259."

Zach turned to James with a quizzical look. "What is he talking about?"

James blurted out, "By God, I think he's right! I never thought of it until now! Although I was in Egypt, that was more than a decade ago, so I never made the connection—but this year in the Muslim calendar is 1259 AH...and that means that the Muslim year 1260 will start sometime in the Christian year 1844 AD."

Zach sat upright and squinted while thinking. Slowly he said, almost to himself, "That is a very strange coincidence. What are the chances of that?"

"Well, I suppose it is one chance out of 1,260, or 1,844, or 2,300, depending on how you look at it," said James matter-of-factly, "but either way, it is most remarkable."

He turned to the captain and asked how many months and days it would be until the beginning of the year 1260 AH. After a little calculation, they understood that 1260 AH would start on January 22, 1844 AD. And since the Islamic lunar year had fewer days than the Christian solar year, he and James determined that 1260 AH would end on January 9, 1845.

Turning to James, Zach said, "This is extraordinary! It's nearly a perfect overlap—almost all of the year 1844 AD falls in the year 1260 AH. Could this be just a coincidence?

117

"But why on earth would Daniel and John have heard a number that would come from a pagan calendar?"

One of the Turkish passengers at the table said, "Perhaps the religion of Islam is less pagan than you think."

James shot a glance at Zach as if to warn him to be more mindful of the people with whom he was sailing. Zach assured the gentleman that he meant no disrespect. But his mind was so preoccupied with these thoughts that he left his meal unfinished and rose to have some private words with James on the deck above.

"Is that possible?" Zach asked excitedly. "Is it really possible that the 1,260 of Daniel and the Book of Revelation could be the same as the 1260 of the Muslim calendar? Could it *really be* that the prophecy of the 2,300 years and the prophecy of the 1,260 years are both pointing to the same year—1844 AD on our current Christian calendar and 1260 on the Islamic calendar? Or is this just some sort of strange coincidence? But how would God allow such a thing to happen? It makes no sense!"

He felt dizzy with all of these thoughts as he paced back and forth on the deck.

"This is surely the most bizarre twist in our search—more bizarre than anything I could have imagined. And you know as well as I do what makes it so completely bizarre. The first question that our brethren will ask us when we return is the one that even now is reverberating in my head: Why on earth would the angel who spoke to both Daniel and to St. John have made reference to a pagan calendar—the calendar used by a people who have fought the religion of Jesus for centuries?"

James paused for a moment and then said, "Perhaps my previous years living in this part of the world have affected me, but I don't see as wide a gulf between the Islamic religion and our Christian one as you do."

Zach returned a look of surprise, but James continued, "Consider this, Zach: Although we may be inclined to call the Mohammedan a pagan, in reality, he is a believer in God, right?"

"Well, so they may claim," said Zach.

"He is a monotheist—Muslims are adamant about the fact that there is no God but God, right?"

118

"But they seem to believe in someone called 'Allah,' not God!" Zach protested.

"Allah," James explained, "is just the Arabic word for Elah, and Elah was the Aramaic word for God. And Aramaic is the language that Jesus spoke. So actually, the Arabic word for God is much closer to the term Jesus used than the English word. But in any case, they all mean the same thing."

This surprised Zach. But he remembered that he was speaking with a professor, who knew this part of the world far better than himself, so he held his peace. Inwardly, though, he struggled with the idea that "Allah" and the God of the Bible could be the same. As a Quaker, he had been taught that the "inner light" could be experienced by all people. But could Muhammad have experienced the revelation that he claimed? This seemed too strange.

James continued, "Muhammad taught that Abraham, Moses, and Jesus were all Prophets. He claimed that the angel Gabriel dictated the words that became the Quran. He did not deny that Jesus' message came from God. He only claimed to have a similar message."

"Perhaps so, but he certainly did not teach that Jesus was God, as we believe."

"True enough," said James. "When we get down to the details of doctrines, I know there are differences. But from a broader perspective, is it really any different from what you explained to me about how the accuracy of the Zoroastrian prophecy that guided the Wise Men testified to the divine source of that prophecy? It, too, was monotheistic, like its contemporary, the Jewish religion, was it not?

"Surely many of the details of the Zoroastrian religion are contrary to our own, but does that mean that it was wrong from the start? Or does it only mean that some truth has been lost over the centuries, during which it was managed by men who were not always so wise?"

Zach was perplexed. But James continued, "So if the Zoroastrian religion, which is outside of the Judeo-Christian tradition, could have come from a true prophet, perhaps it might be that Islam also came from a true prophet."

"But Zoroaster accurately predicted the coming of Jesus," Zach protested, "and Muhammad did not."

"Of course not." James reminded Zach, "Islam came *after* Jesus, so obviously it could not predict His coming...but..." he paused, thinking it through, "it *could* predict His return."

"All right," Zach responded in a bit of a challenging tone, "if the religion of Islam was in accord with the teachings of Daniel and the teachings of the Book of Revelation, then it should teach that the Promised One would be returning next year, in 1260 AH. So do you know of any such predictions in all of Islam?"

"They sometimes speak of the end of the world, but I've never studied the details. My knowledge of Islam is still growing," answered James. "At least I can say that we are now headed in the right direction."

Zach inclined his head and furrowed his brow, wondering whether their discussion had taken them in the right direction at all.

But James interjected, "I mean, my good fellow, that we are on a ship headed east toward the Holy Land, where there will be plenty of people to inquire of about all manner of understandings of these things."

By this point, Zach's mind was exhausted, and he wanted some time to think quietly. He excused himself to go to his cabin.

But that night he could hardly sleep. He felt stunned, as if a lightning bolt had struck the shell of his limited world and cracked open a hole, through which some of the teachings of one of the world's largest religions might seep.

He pondered the implications of the possibility that some of the teachings of Muhammad might be true revelation, which, according to Muhammad, had been delivered by Gabriel—the same angel who had given Daniel the prophecies that had brought them here. Could some of these teachings be as true as, perhaps, those of other Old Testament prophets? Or perhaps, even if Muhammad had only been an occasionally inspired man, had God, in His mercy, allowed the Muslim people access to some measure of prophecy so that they, too, might see the truth and become Christians when Christ returned?

If so, the fighting and killing between Christians and Muslims in the name of the same God for the better part of the past twelve centuries must surely be the greatest tragedy in human history. How, he wondered, could Christianity—which was the true religion of God—have spent so many lives and so vast a fortune fighting Islam if Islam also had some element of the divine within it?

After pondering this for a while, it occurred to him that Christians believed both Judaism and Christianity had been initiated by a revelation from God, and yet in spite of that, Christians had fought with and persecuted Jews for centuries.

"Oh, the miserable condition of men!" thought Zach. "God gives us free will, and what do we do with it? We develop all kinds of excuses for killing each other. How very few seem interested in finding some common ground in understanding the true spirit of God's teachings!"

As he lay in bed, Jesus' words from John 14:2 came to his mind: *"In my Father's house are many mansions: if it were not so, I would have told you. I go to prepare a place for you."*

He wondered, "Could our heavenly Father have provided a mansion for Muslims in addition to the one that Jesus prepared for His followers? Are the true Christians and the true Muslims, who recognized the common spirituality of both religions, living side by side in neighboring mansions in heaven while a vast number of others, who had grown to hate and kill each other, live in a hell of their own making?"

And again, as he thought about it further, the words from John 10:16 came to his mind: *"And other sheep I have, which are not of this fold: them also I must bring, and they shall hear my voice; and there shall be one fold, and one shepherd."* Jesus had spoken these words long before Christianity started to divide into various groups, so He wasn't referring to the gathering of various Christian groups.

Surely the true Zoroastrians—those Wise Men who were so attuned to the teachings of their faith that they were able to find the infant Jesus—must have been from one of the other folds. This being so, was it too impossible to believe that at least some of the people of Islam might be one of the other folds who would be gathered in at the time of Christ's return? Zach realized that he knew so little about Islam, having always regarded it as pagan and not worthy of any attention. Now he realized he needed to learn more about it.

He wondered why it might seem all right from a Christian perspective to accept that the Zoroastrian Magi were correct, and by implication that Zoroaster's prophecy and revelation must have been true, and yet it was impossible for the Christian world to acknowledge that any truth could come from Muhammad. Perhaps it was because Islam was such a large religion and had been butting heads with Christianity for so many centuries that the Christian world felt threatened. But then he remembered what James had mentioned. The real problem lay in its chronology.

With respect to other religions, including Judaism and Zoroastrianism, Christians could afford to acknowledge that God may have revealed some truths to them but that Christ's teachings, being more recent, were the most complete. If there was anything in the theology of either Judaism or Zoroastrianism that didn't agree with Christian teachings, the obvious choice was the Christian teachings since they were God's most recent revelation and thus spoke to humanity's more recent conditions.

However, Christianity could not say the same thing about the revelation of Muhammad, which was about 600 years younger. If a Christian were to acknowledge Islam as being divinely inspired, the obvious next question would be "Then why don't you follow it?" There was no option of saying that Jesus' teachings were more recent. But Zach could not imagine following a religion that he still regarded as outside of Jesus' teachings.

Even so, he was greatly agitated by all the implications of this change in perspective. It felt like a great tribulation had crashed upon his head, even as a mighty wave crashing upon a rocky reef. But as soon as the word "tribulation" crossed his mind, the words from Matthew 24 began to echo in his head: *"For then shall be great tribulation, such as was not since the beginning of the world to this time, no, nor ever shall be."*

What tribulation could be greater than this—that the world's largest religion might need to accept at least some of the truths that were taught by a prophet whom they had rejected for more than 1,200 years? And yet, if and when they could overcome such a tribulation, they could rest assured that no greater tribulation would ever occur since Islam was the only religion more recent than Christianity.

As he lay on his bed, his thoughts returned to the question that his first traveling companion, Jeremy, had posed after sailing up the Hudson back in May: *"What about you, Zach? Have you thought about the fact that you, too, might have some misunderstandings and might have to change something about your own expectations?"* He had told Jeremy that he had prayed to have the necessary humility to recognize that some of his previous understandings might not be correct. But he had never contemplated coming upon a change in understanding of this type or magnitude. Finally, he sat up and repeated his prayers, asking God to protect him from error and to guide him at every turn.

At last, Zach was able to drift off to sleep.

*   *   *

WHEN ZACH AWOKE THE next morning, he had only one thought in mind: He must ask about whether Muslims expected any major event to occur during the upcoming year, 1260.

So he went to the Turkish-speaking cook and tried to ask in simple English, "Do the Muslims expect a prophet to appear next year, or the end of the world, or any such thing?"

But the cook only rolled his eyes and shook his head back and forth. Then he made a signal with his fingers pointing to his head in a circular motion, as if to suggest insanity. And the only word he would utter was "She-yah."

The captain, even more adamantly, refused to discuss the topic. Zach asked James what this meant.

He said, "Well, since we are heading into the Muslim world, it is time that you learn at least a little about the religion of Islam. Whether it has any bearing on our search or not, we will be living among the Muslims for the coming year, so you ought to know a bit about their background. You should bear in mind that just as Christianity is divided into three main branches—Catholic, Protestant, and Eastern Orthodox—Islam is divided into two main divisions. One is called *Sunni* and the other *Shia*.

"But unlike Christianity, Islam divided immediately after the passing of Muhammad. One group of believers was inclined to adhere to the Arabic custom in which the community would appoint its next leader from among the senior leaders of the group. This led to the selection of *Abu Bakr*.

"But others said that Muhammad had verbally appointed his own son-in-law, *Ali,* to lead the community. From that time onward, there were two groups. One recognized Abu Bakr and his successors as the legitimate heads of Islam. They were called the '*Sunnis*' with Abu Bakr as the first '*Caliph*,' or successor. The other recognized Ali as the legitimate leader and source of authority. He was known as the first '*Imam*,' or 'religious leader,' appointed as successor by Muhammad. He was the first in a line of twelve descendants of Muhammad. The followers of this line of authority became known as the '*Shiites*,' that is, 'followers' of Ali.

"As the years went by, the Sunni Caliphs persecuted the Shiite Imams, killing them one by one and scattering their followers. Although both sides based their beliefs on the Quran, they had different understandings of the details and applications of its teachings. And so they tended to fight each other. The Sunnis generally prevailed, while the Shiites became a minority scattered in various places across the Islamic world."

"So," said Zach, "I gather that our captain and the cook are Sunni and don't want to talk about anything that is Shiite."

"That would certainly make sense," offered James. "But beyond that, I'm wondering if the year 1260 might have some significance to the Shiites. Otherwise, the cook and the captain would not have so rigidly refused to discuss the subject."

"We'll need to be careful when exploring this question when we reach Akka," said Zach.

At this point, their port—the ancient city of Akka in the northern part of the Holy Land—lay just two days ahead.

Chapter 10

AKKA: THE DOOR OF HOPE

Sailing south of Cyprus with a favorable wind, on the second day, they saw the hills of Lebanon on the eastern horizon. Drawing closer, they swung south, passing first the rocky shoreline of the ancient city of Beirut, home during its 5,000-year history to the Phoenicians, Greeks, Romans, Byzantines, Arabs, Crusaders, and, now, Ottomans.

Like much of the Holy Land, history here was found in layers, with new rulers building upon the remains of the cities they had conquered. As a trading port on the eastern Mediterranean, it was a rival to Akka and had revived somewhat after *Ibrahim Pasha*, the ruler of Egypt, came north to capture Akka from the Ottomans in 1832.

Farther south, they passed Sidon and then Tyre, both mentioned in the Old and New Testaments, which provided a sense of excitement that they were now entering into biblical lands. But as they were watching from the side of the ship, a thought occurred to Zach that had not come to mind until that point.

"James," he said, "whenever I think of the Holy Land, I tend to think of it in biblical terms, as if it were still occupied by Christians and Jews. But of course, they are now just small minorities among the general Muslim population."

"Yes," replied James, "and in the case of the Jews, a *very* small minority."

"So I'm now thinking," continued Zach, "that *if* some aspects of Islam could possibly be true and *if* the Muslims are expecting a Promised One,

125

they are probably expecting that He will be a Muslim. But we, ourselves, and any other Christians who are looking for a non-miraculous return, naturally expect Him to come from a Christian background. And the Jews, of course, are expecting a Messiah who will be a descendant of King David, or at least a descendant of his father, Jesse, as prophesied in Isaiah 11, and therefore they must be expecting someone who will be Jewish."

"Yes, of course," James replied.

"So would God send three Messengers...one for each religion?"

"Of course not," said James. "The latter-day Messiah of the Old Testament *is* the return of Christ from the New Testament. It is true that people have many different understandings as to how the prophecies will be fulfilled. When He appears, we will realize that some of those understandings were correct while others were not. The Jews will find that they have to adjust many of their previous expectations. And Islam—if any of its prophecies are accurate—will have to adjust many more of its own interpretations."

"And what of us?" Zach asked, echoing Jeremy's earlier question. "Do you suppose we will have to change any of our own understandings?"

"There are many different Christian understandings, so I'm sure that almost everyone will have to change in some respect. They cannot all be right," James explained.

"Yes," Zach continued, "I suppose that if anyone was right all the time, we would have no need for a Promised One. After all, Jesus said that when the *'Spirit of truth is come,'* He will guide us *'to all truth.'* That certainly implies that none of us have all of the truth yet; otherwise, we wouldn't need His guidance.

"But still, I'm wondering whether He will appear in the Christian community or whether He might possibly be born to a Jewish family, as Jesus was. Or possibly He might come from a Muslim village," Zach continued, seeking to probe James' limits. "In any case, at least two of the three groups are going to be very disappointed."

"Well," said James, "it had better *not* be us who are among the disappointed. I cannot imagine going back to England to explain that the returned Christ was found and that He was a Muslim, a Jew, or from some pagan religion."

THE WISE MEN OF THE WEST

They both chuckled at the thought. But the logic of it bothered Zach. If God were to send the Promised One to the people of the most recent religion, as had occurred with the coming of both Jesus and Moses, the most recent religion would now be Islam.

If He were to send the Promised One to a pagan people—a people who worshipped many idols, as He had done in the time of Abraham and, more recently, with the coming of Muhammad—that again would *not* be to a Christian people.

Either way, it would be very difficult to explain to people back home how the return of Christ had *not* come particularly to Christians alone. He pushed the question to the back of his mind, trusting that this would not be the case. "Surely even these people of the 'other folds' would recognize Him as the returned Christ, regardless of their background," he thought.

Before long, they could see the walled city of Akka, brilliantly illuminated now by the sun setting in the west. As they drew closer, however, Zach noticed that the walls were pocked with holes.

"Yes," James explained, "our naval ships, together with Austria's, pummeled Akka and some of the other cities on the coast here a few years ago as we assisted the Ottomans in regaining Syria and Palestine from the Egyptians. But not all of that damage is ours—some of it was caused by the Egyptian leader, Ibrahim Pasha, when he captured the city eleven years ago on behalf of his father, *Muhammad Ali Pasha*, the Viceroy of Egypt. And some of it was *Napoleon's* when he attempted to lay siege to the city in 1799. It looks like repairs have been going very slowly, if any have happened at all."

Akka was indeed a well-fortified city. Built on a peninsula, it was surrounded on three sides by seawalls. And on the land side, there was a double wall with a moat between them. It had a single land gate as well as a sea gate. Unwanted visitors were easily repelled.

"It has survived for millennia," James continued. "It was mentioned in the Bible by the prophets Isaiah and Hosea. In the second chapter of his book, Hosea referred to the valley of Akka as a *'door of hope'* on the day when its people return to faithfulness."

Zach gazed across the valley—to the right, where the Carmel range rose, and then to the left, where the hills of Galilee stood. "Well, he said, "it certainly is a door of hope for us—our entryway into the Promised Land."

Zach thought about how impossibly distant life at William Miller's farm in Low Hampton now seemed. It was not simply far away geographically but far away in ways of thought. Back there, thoughts of life in the Islamic world were rarely considered, so foreign and far-off they seemed!

Yet now, the realities of life in this part of the world were beginning to settle in on him, even as their ship approached this city of stone. As they drew into the shelter of the bay, he heard for the first time the chant of the muezzin, "Allah-u-Akbar!" calling the faithful Muslims to prayer from atop one of the minarets of a nearby mosque.

"God is the most great," explained James. "You will hear it proclaimed constantly while here."

"There is so much to learn in this strange world," Zach thought to himself, "so full of both mystery and history and, yes, hope. I hope and pray that God will open some doors for us here too."

The ship swung around the southern tip of the walled city, and as they slowly approached the sheltered side, he could see a small opening in the wall—the sea gate—adjacent to a cannon tower that defended it. The sailors cast the ship's anchor at a nearby spot in the bay as small wooden tenders approached to unload both passengers and cargo. Even the tenders had too much draft for the shallow rock over the final few yards on which the walls were built, so porters came wading across to carry them over the wet rocks and then up into the city through the sea gate.

The air of the city was putrid. They later heard that this was due to a dearth of fresh water. They were arriving near the end of the dry season— it had not rained since late May—and the main aqueduct bringing spring water to the city had been ruined when the city was controlled by the Egyptians.

The Ottoman takeover in 1840 had not yet led to any significant repairs. The city had open channels for sewers, which awaited the coming rainy season for their contents to be flushed out to sea.

The captain of the ship advised that they would find accommodations most to their liking in the Christian Quarter on the west side of the city and to inquire at churches there about possible places to stay. They soon found the Greek Orthodox Church of St. George, and there James explained to the black-robed priest that they were on a pilgrimage and seeking accommodations.

The priest directed them to inquire at the nearby home of Father Alexi Kallistos, one of their older priests, whose English was passable and who frequently housed such travelers. There they were welcomed by him with warm hospitality and encouraged to stay. Both James and Zach were grateful not only for the hospitality but also for its location on the seaward side of the city, where the sea breeze greatly improved the air's quality.

The priest's wife provided an excellent dinner, during which Father Alexi requested that they explain more about the purpose of their pilgrimage. Zach and James took turns explaining the reasoning that led them to search for the return of Jesus in the Holy Land that year.

The priest was interested to hear how Zach's father's quest began with a discussion with a Greek priest about the "end of the world." He reaffirmed that the original Greek references in the Bible spoke of Christ's return at the "end of the age" rather than at the "end of the world."

But Father Alexi was rather surprised to hear their belief that Christ would return as a child rather than from the sky. He assured Zach and James that he had not heard of any child in all of the Holy Land who was reported to have the kind of innate knowledge Jesus had.

The priest explained that many amazing things would happen when Christ returned, but he acknowledged some might be metaphorically described. Then he added, "I do not try to decipher their meanings, nor do I make calculations regarding the time. I look for one sign, which our Lord described in His parable of the vineyard. Do you remember it?"

"Yes, of course," replied James, "from Mark 12, as I recall."

"Correct. It is also found in Matthew and Luke as well. It describes the world—a vineyard—as having been given over by its owner to certain caretakers, how they failed to keep their part of the agreement, how they beat up any messengers the owner sent, and how he finally sent his own son. But the caretakers killed the son. So, Jesus asked, when the lord of the vineyard himself returns, how will he treat those caretakers? He will utterly destroy them!

"Gentlemen, those caretakers are the rulers of mankind—the kings that have ruled by divine right. God has given them a right to rule, but He requires that they rule with justice and they be the living embodiments of righteousness and morality—the best possible example for their people to follow. Instead, these kings have almost always ruled solely for their own benefit, to increase their power and wealth, while paying lip service to the true teachings of Christ.

"Truly I say unto you, when you see that the kings and their monarchies have fallen, and when their power has been given out to other rulers who are *not* kings, then you will know that Christ has indeed returned, whether He be visible or not."

"Well," offered Zach, "in my country, we have established the first large republic in modern times. We have no kings."

"Your country," James commented, "began with no king or queen. It is an entirely different thing to try to remove an existing monarch. And removing *the institution* of monarchy as a whole is nearly impossible. Just look at the French. For more than fifty years, they have been trying to end their monarchy, yet *King Louis Philippe* rules today.""

"Yes," added the priest, "the large majority of the Christian world still finds itself ruled by monarchs—monarchs who must necessarily be deposed when the Lord of the Vineyard returns."

James and Zach had to admit, it would be an astounding revolution if such a thing were to occur. Kings or emperors had ruled since ancient Roman times. Could a world without them be imagined?

They continued to discuss their understandings of the signs of Christ's coming until well into the evening.

*   *   *

** The French monarchy ended 4-1/2 years later when King Louis Philippe abdicated. Napoleon III was elected as president in 1848 but then proclaimed himself Emperor in 1852. His empire met its demise 18 years later at the Battle of Sedan and, with it, all echoes of the age of monarchy in France.

130

THEY AWOKE EARLY THE next morning upon hearing the muezzin's call to prayer and decided to use some of the early morning time for their own prayers for guidance.

After breakfast and some discussion of travel routes and methods, there came a knock at the front door. "There is a shaykh here who wants to see you," the house servant told James and Zach.

"What's a shake?" Zach asked James.

"A sha-yeek," explained James while attempting a more exact pronunciation, "is an educated and respected elder in the Muslim community."

They both went to the door of the house, where they met the older Arab gentleman. He had a long white beard, which swayed in the sea breeze with his long white robe. He walked with a cane.

"You are the ones searching for the return of the Christ?" he inquired earnestly in Arabic.

"Perhaps so," explained James cautiously, not wanting to lie but not ready to give too much information away. "But who are you, and what brings you here?"

"I am Shaykh Hakim,†† a neighbor of Father Alexi. We have much to discuss. Can you join me for a short walk now?"

James glanced toward the priest, who nodded to indicate that he recognized the shaykh and that there was no cause for alarm.

So James and Zach agreed, and they headed out toward the nearby seawall.

"How do you know about us and our search?" inquired James politely.

"News of strangers from distant lands travels quickly in a small town such as ours," replied the shaykh. "I am often at the mosque, and while there yesterday, I met your captain, who had come to give his thanks to God for having arrived safely after his travels.

"In listening to him talk after his prayers, he told of his passengers, including two young men from the West, who had come in search of the Promised One of the Christians."

†† Historical note: While Shaykh Hakim (doctor) is a fictional character, it is reasonable to suppose that there were Shiite elders living among the population of Akka at this time since there was a substantial Shiite population living in the villages of the nearby hills northeast of the city.

"Surely," said James, "we are not the first Christian pilgrims you have met who have come to the Holy Land seeking enlightenment about the past and the possible future appearance of our Lord."

"Indeed," replied the shaykh, "many Christian pilgrims have passed this way. I pay no attention to most of them. But the captain commented that you had asked him about the year 1260. You are the first I have ever met who have mentioned that year."

"It is an important number," said James, "that appears in biblical prophecies. And I now understand that the Muslim year 1260 will commence within a few months. We wanted to know if this year has any particular significance to the Muslim community. We asked the captain, but he refused to say a word about it."

"The year has no significance to him—he is Sunni. But I am a Shiite, and..." The shaykh paused to glance around, as if to make sure no one else was within earshot. Then, looking James straight in the eye, he said slowly, "We are certain that the Hidden Imam—the promised *Qaim* (kah-eem) of Islam—will return next year. We Shiites have waited to see this date for a thousand years."

James was so struck by the intensity of the shaykh's clear statement, its implications, and its parallels to Christian expectations that he gasped and then turned his gaze toward the sea, leaning on the seawall.

"What is it?!" exclaimed Zach, who was not certain that he had heard the Arabic words correctly.

"It is exactly as we thought it might be, Zach...indeed, as I *feared* it might be...." James paused to gather a breath then added, "It is no coincidence that the Muslim year 1260 is the same as the Christian year 1844. The Muslims—at least the Shiite Muslims—are expecting their Promised One to appear next year too!"

On the ship a few days earlier, they had considered this as a possibility. But it was only theoretical then. Now it was real. Zach joined James in staring out at the sea while contemplating the immense significance of this as well as the immense problems it implied.

"I am sorry," offered the shaykh, "if I have said something that has offended you. I know that people hold their beliefs very close to their hearts, and it was never my intention to offend."

"No, not at all," replied James. "We have come here on a mission of discovery—a search for the truth. And you have now given us so much to think about. It is just...overwhelming."

"Well," said the shaykh, "I have many more things I could tell you. But perhaps we should leave them for another day, when you will be better able to hear them. When you are feeling ready, come by to visit me, and I will share with you what I know. And I hope you will tell me what you know."

Using his cane, he pointed northward along the road by the seawall. "I am living over there. Ask for Shaykh Hakim. I will tell my family and neighbors to expect you."

Zach and James remained at the seawall as the shaykh went home. At first, they were too confounded by what they had just learned to speak. Finally Zach asked, "How can this be? How can it be that these Muslims are expecting the return of their Promised One in the same year as we are? The shaykh seemed to say that this was the fulfillment of a thousand-year-old Muslim prophecy, so it is *not* something borrowed from the Bible.

"Yet why would God guide *them*? They may talk of Jesus as one of God's prophets, but they don't recognize Him as the only begotten Son of God."

James replied, "I've been pondering this question since our discussion on the ship, and it's led me to wonder how the Bible and the Quran could both be true. It occurred to me that the only way this could be is if we peel away centuries' worth of human interpretations. For instance, regarding our understanding of the nature of Jesus, how much of those teachings are clearly from the words of Christ, and how much comes from men?"

"Well, I don't know," Zach replied. "I know there is some confusion on how to reconcile verses like the statement in John 10, '*I and my Father are one*,' with other statements like in Mark 10, where He asks, '*Why callest thou me good? There is none good but one, that is, God*,' which certainly suggests that Jesus is not God."

"Yes," agreed James, "I have read enough about the struggles of the early Christian church to know that there was *immense* confusion about the true nature of Jesus—whether He was simply a great teacher, a Prophet, or actually part of God. And there are quotes in the Gospels that point toward all three possibilities. So naturally, there was a lot of room for argumentation on this matter. The religious leaders argued about it for centuries before most agreed on the three-Gods-in-one doctrine, while the rest were chased out of the church."

"So your point is...?"

"My point is that perchance they got their theology wrong *back then*. It was, after all, a man-made doctrine. Perhaps we have misunderstood the true nature of Christ."

The mere implication of this left Zach feeling thunderstruck.

"Ooohhhh..." he groaned. "I can see us taking that idea back to England and America. They would likely load us into cannons and blast us both into the sea—or some worse fate!"

"Seriously, Zach," James continued, "I've been rethinking some of what I learned from my time in Egypt. Muhammad recognized the legitimacy of Jesus as a Prophet, like Himself, and recognized the truth of all the biblical prophets.

"What Muhammad's revelation had done to Jesus' teachings was essentially the same thing that Jesus' teachings had done to the Old Testament: They both affirmed the underlying spiritual truths of the past Prophets, updated some of the laws and practices to suit the needs of that age, and washed away those accumulated manmade teachings that tended to obscure spiritual truths."

Zach wrestled with this notion. His mind remained resistant to the notion that Muhammad could be similar to Jesus in a way that would make them peers.

James continued, "The former scriptures still provided valuable guidance, context, and history, but they would need to be understood in light of the newer revelation. Thus, the sanctuary of human religion was cleansed."

"Why didn't the Christian world follow Muhammad then?"

"Well, many of them did—many of the Christians of North Africa, Syria, and much of the Middle East became Muslims gradually. But in places where there were enthroned Christian political and religious leaders who were unwilling to give up their positions of power, they would have none of it. So they blocked the spread of Islam into Europe, much as the

Jewish religious and political leaders had conspired against Jesus and the Christians in the first century.

"Now, mind you, I don't mean to suggest that the things that Muhammad's followers have done were always rightly guided. Indeed, even many Muslims speak of their first four leaders as 'the rightly guided caliphs' who led the religion for the first thirty years. This suggests that the caliphs after that were *not* always rightly guided. Indeed, I've heard how some were terribly corrupt. The religion inspired sacrifice and communal cooperation, which soon led to wealth and power. But these, if not carefully controlled, tend to corrode those very positive values upon which the power and wealth were built.

"The history of Islamic leadership, after those first four caliphs, includes many examples of those who failed to take Muhammad's teachings seriously. But there were also others who successfully resisted the negative tendencies."

James paused as he thought about it and then added, "I suppose one could find some examples of similar vacillation within Christian history as well."

They gazed for a long while out to sea, trying to fathom the implications of this prophetic linkage.

As they walked slowly back to Father Alexi's house, they agreed that if two independent prophecies, coming from two completely independent sources and ages, were both pointing to the same year, there could be no doubt that the prophecies, and the prophets from which they came, must both be drawing from a single All-Knowing Source. In spite of any subsequent misunderstandings of their religious leaders or misdeeds of their followers, the accuracies of the prophecies pointed to a common divine Source, which could not be ignored.

But oh! The very thought of trying to teach their fellow Christians to recognize that there might be some truth in the teachings of Muhammad after having fought against his followers for over 1,200 years!

That seemed like an impossible task—like climbing a mountain of impossible heights.

The parting words of the shaykh had a familiar ring to them. Then it dawned on Zach that they sounded so much like Jesus' words from John 16:12–13: "*I have yet many things to say unto you, but ye cannot bear them now. Howbeit, when He, the Spirit of Truth is come, He will guide you into all truth.*"

Perhaps the very idea that there were other true revelations that taught the oneness of God would have been too much for the early Christians to bear.

"But now, since we are indeed living at the 'close of the age,' that is, in the 'latter days,' when the hidden meanings of the scriptures would be 'unsealed,' shouldn't we be ready to bear these new truths?" Zach wondered. But how could his fellow Christians, even now, bear such news?

That evening, sharing dinner again with Father Alexi, they were reluctant to explain their quandary. When he inquired about why the shaykh had stopped by, they briefly explained that he wanted to discuss some things about his religion, and they let the topic pass.

That night, though, Zach dreamed of climbing a tall mountain and seeing a wide valley below and, beyond that, another tall mountain. On that other mountain, he could see the shaykh. And while at first glance they appeared to be normal mountains, upon looking more closely, they each seemed to be standing on a mountain of books.

Then he heard a deep, booming voice, seeming to shake the whole world, saying, "*The Day hath come!*"

And with that, the mountains of books seemed to quiver and then turn into dust so that both of the mountains slumped down to nothing while their dust filled up the valley below. Then he and the shaykh could easily walk toward each other on this new plain.

When he awoke, he could not stop thinking about his dream. It reminded him of a verse from Isaiah. So he checked his Bible until he found it in chapter 40, verses 4 and 5, which read: "*Every valley shall be exalted, and every mountain and hill shall be made low: and the crooked shall be made straight, and the rough places plain. And the glory of the LORD shall be revealed, and all flesh shall see it together: for the mouth of the LORD hath spoken it.*"

Zach understood this passage now in a new light. He realized these were not physical mountains but rather they were the mountains of peoples' opinions—their interpretations and commentaries, their doctrines and theology. These, seen in his dream as books, had built up over the centuries into large mountains of religious dogma.

The followers of the various religions all stood on their respective mountains of man-made ideologies, which left a great gulf standing between them. But when the Promised One appears, the authority of all those positions, opinions, and interpretations will be swept away in one clean stroke, just as Jesus swept away the mountains of legalistic reasoning and disputations of the Jewish leaders of His day.

Anyone standing on such a mountain of old theological pride would see his exalted position disappear and his feet slipping out from underneath him, while those who lived in the valley of humility—those like the disciples of Jesus, who could sense intuitively the truth of the Promised One without relying on the dogma of men—would be exalted and raised up by His coming.

All people would have an equal chance to respond with their own spiritual ability to recognize the truths taught by the Promised One. The religious leaders who had been at the top of the mountain of dogma as well as those who had been in the valley—all people of all religious backgrounds, indeed, "all flesh," would have an equal opportunity to see it together.

"Yes," he thought, "how could all humanity see the coming of the Promised One together if those mountains of dogma that separate the religions are not first removed?"

He thought of the vast differences between the legalistic dogma of the Jewish leaders of Jesus' time and the changing polytheistic teachings of the Greco-Roman world and how both of these mountains were both demolished by the teachings of Jesus.

"Yes," he acknowledged, "the process of rebuilding necessarily begins with the tearing down of the mountains of old debris in order to reach a common, solid foundation."

With that, his fear of the mountain of troubles that would await him upon his return to America seemed to abate. In the morning, he discussed his dream and his understanding of it with James.

"It seems we can learn a lot from our dreams, as you have undoubtedly learned from this one," James said. "I do not treat them as scripture, since they are sometimes colored by our own thoughts and desires. Nevertheless, if it seems to accord with the Scriptures and sheds new light on our understanding, I would hold to it."

Zach agreed.

Chapter 11

THE NEW ELIJAH AND THE GREAT CROSSING

WITH HEARTS THUS PREPARED to bear some new possibilities, Zach and James set out that morning to visit Shaykh Hakim at his home.

There they were welcomed and treated with the utmost hospitality, as was the common practice among Muslims receiving a guest. Food and tea were brought to them as they sat down for their discussions. Yet none was given to the shaykh or any of the members of his household.

"It is Ramadan," he explained, "our month of daytime fasting."

"Yes," said James, "we heard on the ship that it had started. But the sailors said they were exempt."

"This is true. All travelers are exempt. Christians are exempt too," he said with a nod and a smile.

"We are reluctant to eat in front of one who is fasting," replied James.

"No, please go ahead. We all had a full meal before dawn. It is not a problem," the shaykh assured them.

James explained how their study of prophecies had forced them to conclude the revelations of Jesus, Abraham, Moses, and the Old Testament prophets, as well as Zoroaster, had all come from one common divine Source. He explained in particular their understanding of their Christian prophecies—how Jesus' statement in Matthew 24 pointed to the prophecies of Daniel 8 concerning the '2,300 days' and how this led William Miller and hundreds of thousands of others in America and England to the conclusion that Christ would return in 1844.

139

He explained their confusion over the meaning of the 1,260 years mentioned in both Daniel and the Book of Revelation and now their amazement to find that this very same number was the year on the Islamic calendar that was equivalent to the year 1844 on the Christian calendar.

This was forcing them to consider the possibility that some aspect of the revelation of Muhammad might be a part of this overall prophecy.

"We were astonished," James concluded, "not only because these two numbers point to exactly the same year on two different calendars but, more significantly, that Islam—at least the Shia portion—is expecting the return of their Promised One in the very same year that we in the West are expecting the return of Christ. And so we are interested to know the reasoning that leads you to this conclusion."

Shaykh Hakim paused, considering where to begin. Then he said, "Tell me, do you expect to see only the return of Jesus next year? Some of my Christian acquaintances tell me that the return of Elijah, or someone like John the Baptist, must come first."

Zach explained that his father had asked the same question and how different interpretations could point toward either position.

James added that the recent focus on the return of Jesus had, to some degree, pushed aside considerations of the return of Elijah, as described at the end of Malachi. But in any case, finding the one would certainly lead to finding the other.

"What does the prophecy of Daniel say will happen after 2,300 days?" the Shaykh inquired.

"'*Then shall the sanctuary be cleansed*,'" James quoted by heart.

"And what will actually be cleansed? Will someone arrive with a bucket and brush to clean the sanctuary of the old temple in Jerusalem? Will someone bring a whip to drive out the money changers and the sellers again, as Jesus had done, according to the Gospel of John?"

James perceived that the shaykh was not favorably disposed toward literal interpretations. This was good since neither he nor Zach were inclined toward that approach either.

Zach was surprised at the shaykh's willingness to discuss the Bible. But then he recalled how James had explained that many Muslims generally regarded the Bible in some ways similar to the way that Christians regarded the Old Testament—as a source of God's Word, though not as accurate as the more recent one—the Quran—which Muhammad had reviewed and confirmed during His lifetime.

"No," James replied. "We feel that the cleaning of the temple is an allegorical reference. For Jesus also explains in the verses that followed in that same chapter of John how the temple could be destroyed and He would rebuild it in three days. I understand that the real temple is the faith of the body of believers in God. The physical temple is just an outward manifestation of this faith.

"The faith of the disciples was destroyed on the Thursday evening when Jesus was arrested. The disciples were scattered. Peter denied Him three times the following morning. But by late Sunday—three days later—they became aware that the true Jesus continued to live, in spite of the crucifixion of His body. Their faith—the true temple—was rebuilt. It is upon such faith that all physical temples are built.

"So I believe the cleansing of the sanctuary of the temple means the cleansing of the core of our faith in God, which has acquired too much misunderstanding, dogma and human interpretation over the centuries. All of us may need to let go of many old ideas, which have become a sort of clutter in our hearts and minds, in order to prepare for His coming. The cleansing, which John the Baptist also did symbolically by baptizing his followers, will need to be done once more."

"Well said!" replied the shaykh enthusiastically. "Well said indeed! But to return to my question: Will this be done by Jesus, or will there be a forerunner?"

"It certainly seems possible that a forerunner would be necessary," replied James.

Zach thought for a moment and then spoke to the question. "The prophet Zechariah wrote in chapter 4 of his book about the two anointed Ones who '*stand by the Lord of the whole earth.*' Inasmuch as 'Messiah' and 'Christ' are simply the Hebrew and Greek words for 'Anointed One,' I think Zechariah may be telling us that there will be two who will appear nearly together, just as in Jesus' day. Zechariah speaks of them as being the two olive trees, feeding their oil to the lamps of faith. I have often wondered about the meaning in the two anointed ones. It seems very possible to me that there will be a forerunner, like John the Baptist, before Jesus Himself returns."

"Yes!" exclaimed the shaykh. "Then your understanding of this is very similar to ours. We believe there will be two trumpet blasts. We, in the Shia branch of Islam, believe that the first to appear will be the Qaim, which simply means 'He who shall arise.' He will be followed by the return of the *Imam Husayn*—that blessed grandson of the Prophet who willingly accepted martyrdom on the plain of Karbila. Many of us believe the Qaim will arise next year—in the year 1260—as the first of two Messengers.

"We Shiites follow Muhammad's teaching regarding the leadership of Islam. He taught that after His days had ended, God would guide His descendants. By words and deeds, He indicated that His son-in-law, *Ali*, was to be its first leader, or Imam. However, He did not write it down. At the very end of His life, Muhammad asked for paper to write down something to prevent His followers from being led into error. But *Umar*, one of the community's leaders attending Him, felt He was in fever and did not comply. So the true instructions were never dictated explicitly by Muhammad Himself nor recorded for all to see. Therefore, from the time of His passing, there have been the followers of Ali and the followers of Abu Bakr and Umar. These developed into the Shia and the Sunni branches of Islam respectively. Neither one recognizes the legitimacy of the other.

"Ali led his followers for twenty-nine years, until he was killed due to the intrigues that resulted from the lust for power that had affected some of Muhammad's original followers. But before he died, he appointed his son, *Hasan*, to be the second Imam. Although Hasan was forced to relinquish his position, he was still poisoned and died at a young age. His brother, Husayn, became the third Imam.

"Husayn struggled to keep Islam pure. He had been invited by a large band of Shiites in Kufa, south of Baghdad, to move from Mecca in western Arabia and to rule from Kufa. However, when this band was threatened by the Sunnis, they lost their nerve. As a result, Imam Husayn, grandson of the Prophet, was killed in the most tragic of circumstances on the plains of Karbila, not far from Kufa. Ever since, the sacred centers of Shia Islam have been there, along the Euphrates River, at the edge of the Arabic and Persian worlds. Ever since, we have mourned Husayn's tragic martyrdom and awaited his return, much as the Christians mourn the tragic crucifixion of Jesus and await His return.

"The pattern continued—each Imam appointing the best of his sons as the next Imam while living under fear of persecution by the Caliph, the leader of the Sunni branch. Some Imams were able to live and guide the community for 30 years before being killed. For others, their time was much briefer.

"Finally, in 260 AH, the eleventh Imam was killed. He had appointed his son, *Muhammad al-Mahdi*, as the twelfth, but the boy was only five years of age. So one of the faithful took the child into hiding in a cave beneath the earth. His seclusion was careful and complete. The only communication he had with the rest of the Shiite followers was via this intermediary, who was vigilant in making sure he was never followed as he carried messages back and forth.

"For many years, God provided guidance through this 'hidden Imam' and his intermediary. This was called the 'Lesser Occultation' because, although he was hidden, we could still ask for his guidance, and he would provide it. But after about 70 years, the intermediary announced that al-Mahdi (the Guided One) had gone into the 'Greater Occultation' and no further communications would come from him until the end of time, when he would arise from out of his hiding place in the earth to overcome those who have persecuted the rightful branch of Islam and establish justice throughout the earth shortly before the return of the Imam Husayn Himself."

"When and where will this be?" inquired James.

"The first Imam, Ali, hinted at it by saying, 'In Ghars (planting) the Tree of Divine guidance shall be planted.'"

"And just where is Ghars?" Zach was puzzled.

"No one could understand to what, or where, he was referring," the shaykh replied, "until someone suggested that he was alluding to 'when' instead of 'where.' For if we consider the numerical value of the Arabic letters, Ghars adds to 1260. 'Gha' has the value of 1,000, for 'r' it is 200, and 's' is 60. Some of the later Imams and others have also alluded to the same year. And in 260 AH, it became clear that the year would be exactly 1,000 years after the death of the eleventh Imam and the disappearance of the twelfth."

"Another sealed prophecy," marveled Zach, "that became understandable only long after the prophecy was given."

"Thus," the shaykh continued, "some say that the year 260 marked the start of our separation from direct divine guidance that had been given by the Prophet and the Imams. This was the beginning of the 'day of separation,' as mentioned in the seventy-eighth chapter of the Holy Quran. The return of divine guidance shall come at the end of this day of separation, *'the day whose length shall be a thousand years of those which ye compute,'* according to chapter 32 of the Quran.

"We have long awaited the return of this guidance—a thousand years after its disappearance—that is to say, in the year 1260 AH. And that blessed year begins just a few months from now."

"Astounding..." Zach was speechless at first. Then he added, "It is the exact same number as in Daniel and Revelation, but it's derived in an *entirely* different manner and from a different source. And as to the 1,000 years, it sounds identical to Peter's comment in chapter 3 of his second letter: *'one day is with the Lord as a thousand years.'* But then, I suppose that Muhammad must have read these things first in the Bible."

"Muhammad was unable to read," noted the shaykh, "and in any case, Bibles were uncommon in the Hejaz, where Christians were few and their books were even fewer. But I have no doubt that Peter and Muhammad drew their verses from one common Source of inspiration, although it was not of this world."

Here was yet another discovery to astound Zach. How could an illiterate Arab have derived such an insight—save by divine inspiration?

Then the shaykh continued, "So you can see why many of the Shiites today believe the Hidden Imam will arise next year, in 1260 AH. Even many of the Sunnis expect the Promised One to appear around the middle of this century, according to some of their traditions, but they do not know the exact year. And most of both groups believe in all manner of amazing things that will happen at that time, such as the sun being darkened and the mountains being scattered into dust."

Zach looked at James. This sounded so much like many of the things he had heard from his Christian friends regarding their beliefs about the amazing things that would happen when Christ returned.

But James had a question: "You said *most* believe this. But not all?"

"There are, of course, some branches within Shia Islam that have other interpretations. These are taught by various religious sages, who offer a different understanding. Some of us have, in recent years, been following the lessons of a great teacher from Bahrain and Iraq, whose name was *Shaykh Ahmad*.

"He affirmed that the Qaim—the Mahdi—would arise at the promised time, but he taught that it was al-Mahdi's *spirit*, which had lived through all these centuries, not his physical body, and that his *spirit* would arise and appear in a new human body.

"Of course, this teaching was very controversial and—for many of the religious leaders of Islam—even blasphemous. Many of them had based their *entire* theology on their belief that all kinds of amazing, miraculous things would happen at the time of al-Mahdi's coming.

"They understood 'the Last Day' to mean the end of this physical world. To suggest that the promises could be fulfilled in a manner similar to the coming of Muhammad or Jesus—as a simple teacher with a revelation from God, a teacher who would have an enormously powerful spiritual effect but only a gradual material affect—would completely undercut the whole theology of these clerics as well as their power and the sway that they held over their congregations."

James and Zach were stunned by this explanation. It seemed to be an exact parallel of their own situation with respect to many of their Christian acquaintances. So many had come to believe the return of Christ would be associated with huge outward miracles. They had forgotten that the real miracle was the spiritual revelation He would bring and the transformation this new understanding of the Word of God could cause in the hearts of people.

Zach wondered how many of the clergy intentionally misused the metaphorical language of prophecy in a purely literal way—often as a means of dazzling and frightening their congregations. He knew, from things he had witnessed at home, how effective this could be in drawing together large crowds and how it could frighten people into becoming followers.

He also knew that if those people had taken the time to do a careful study of the Scriptures and had reflected on its deeper meanings, they would be immune from the influence of such preachers. But alas, there were very few people willing to devote their time to this kind of study and reflection.

Therefore large congregations were left with a fanciful imagination of world-ending physical disasters associated with the coming of the Promised One. Zach knew these allegories were never intended to be understood in such a material manner.

"So," Zach thought to himself, "not only are both the Christian world and the Islamic world expecting their Promised One in the same year but they are also largely in the same spiritual condition, in terms of their general unwillingness to recognize the coming of a new Messenger unless He is accompanied by huge outward miracles."

Although he remained skeptical about the nature of Muhammad's revelation, he could see these additional parallels.

James wanted to return to the Islamic prophecy. "So the 1,260 years of the Muslim prophecy comes from the ending of direct guidance under the Imams in the year 260 AH plus the thousand-year period of separation."

"Indeed," replied the shaykh.

"And these two numbers," said Zach to James, "the 1,260 from Islam and the 2,300 from Daniel—these are from two completely difference sources, and yet they converge exactly on the same year. And both are associated with the coming of the Promised One, although from two different religions."

"Actually, from three different religions," interjected James, "the Quran and its traditions from Islam, Daniel from Judaism, and the Book of Revelation from Christianity—in addition to Matthew's reference to Daniel."

He sighed then continued. "There is no denying that all three religions foretell the coming of the Promised One in 1844 AD or 1260 AH, which is next year in both cases. It is impossible for me to understand how this specific prophecy from Islam, which agrees so perfectly with our own, could be a part of a false religion." Zach shared the sense of conflict that James expressed.

"Of course," said the shaykh calmly, "the answer is that Muhammad's revelation was a true one sent by the God of Jesus, the God of Moses, and the God of Abraham. So why do you sigh?"

"You have *no idea*," ventured James, "how difficult it will be for us to explain this to our countrymen and how, being steeped in almost two thousand years of their own traditions and the trappings of Christianity, they will almost certainly reject it without any hesitation or thought, even when the evidence is perfectly clear."

"Alas," acknowledged the shaykh, "we have many people like that within our own religion, who also cling to the form, having forgotten the inner spiritual essence. It will no doubt be a long time before they are ready to change.

"I know you have a difficult struggle ahead of you. But..." The shaykh paused, as if composing a thought, and then said slowly and deliberately,

"O Seeker of Truth!
 Know thou of a certainty
       that truth has consequences.
 But fear not these consequences,
       if thou wouldst remain
       a Seeker of Truth.

 For if ye choose to flee
       from truth's consequences
       and if ye would hide from truth's light,
 Where shall ye stop?
  How shall ye account for your life,
       when your final day arrives?"

These words penetrated deeply into the minds and hearts of both Zach and James.

Zach thought back on the many times he had prayed for God's guidance. He had arrived in the Holy Land seeking the truth about the coming of the Promised One.

He turned to James and said, in English and with great earnestness, "We have prayed repeatedly that God would open doors for us. When we see that a door has opened, can we refuse to go through it? Just because the truth comes with difficult consequences, can it be ignored? And if we choose to ignore new truths, after having asked God to send them, will God ever listen to our prayers again?"

147

Finally, James sighed once more and said, "Maybe we will just have to deal with those consequences somehow when we return."

But then he added, on a more hopeful note, "Or maybe, if we continue our search in the Holy Land, we will find someone else whose background will be more like what we were expecting."

But first, Zach wanted to find out more from the shaykh. "And where do you expect the Messiah to appear? Will He return to Jerusalem?"

"If we are speaking now of He who embodies the spirit of the Imam Husayn—that is, the spirit of Jesus—we have good reason to believe that He will arrive here. I do not simply mean here in the Holy Land. I mean here in Akka," explained Shaykh Hakim.

"Right here? Right in this city?" inquired James urgently. "Why do you think He will appear here?"

"Several of the most reliable of our traditions—the records of the things Muhammad said—speak of the great significance of Akka," he replied, "and since it has not been a very significant city in the past, we think it will be so in the future. One of the most important traditions speaks of how the supporters of al-Mahdi will be Persians and how the last remaining one will arrive on the plain of Akka.[7]

"Another quotes a statement from Muhammad: '*By the shore of the sea is a city, suspended beneath the Throne, and named Akka. He that dwelleth therein, firm and expecting a reward from God—exalted be He—God will write down for him, until the Day of Resurrection, the recompense of such as have been patient, and have stood up, and knelt down, and prostrated them-selves, before Him.*'[8] And so we will wait here."

Zach thought about the verse from Hosea 2 that James had quoted while on the ship, regarding how the valley of Akka would be a '*door of hope*' in the latter days.

"So you believe that this last remaining supporter of the Mahdi will be the Messiah—the second of the two Messengers—and will come from Persia. And you hope to meet Him here when He arrives?"

"Yes, He will come here. But alas, I do not imagine I will still be here when He arrives. For it may be another thirty years or so before this comes to pass."

Shaykh Hakim appeared to be at least sixty years old, so the likelihood of his passing to the next world during the coming thirty years was entirely understandable.

"But," Shaykh Hakim continued with hopefulness, "we will surely train our children to watch for Him." He nodded toward some of the young children playing outside.

Zach thought about how much could happen in thirty years. Thirty years —1873— seemed far into the future. He himself would be sixty-five by then and possibly too old to travel. Then he made the transition to the Muslim calendar and did the simple addition.

"Thirty years from next year will be 1290 AH. Do you expect something extraordinary to happen in that year too?"

"No doubt there will be many eventful things that occur while the Messiah is here," replied the shaykh. "Why do you ask?"

Zach looked at James, who looked back. "Are you thinking what I am thinking?" he asked.

James said, "The number from Daniel 12:11?"

"Absolutely! Here, then, may be the answer to two of the three mysterious numbers from the last chapter of Daniel's amazing book of prophecies. This would explain both the 1,260 and the 1,290. Only the 1,335 number would remain."

"That's certainly a fascinating thought," said James. "But we may have a problem. We are living in 1843, and we are here to find the Promised One. Whether that be the Messiah or Elijah, we are here to witness the great One whose coming was foretold for next year, that is, 1844."

So he asked the shaykh, "If the Messiah is to come here in 30 years, from whence will His forerunner—the Qaim or Mahdi—come? And in which town should we start our search when the year 1260 begins? We have come a long way, and we are hoping to witness that blessed event next year."

As they spoke, Zach could not help but think of the original Wise Men, who had come to the Holy Land seeking the birth of the Christ child, and how they needed to ask the religious authorities under King Herod regarding the details of where it was prophesied to occur. Today there was no King Herod, so there was no official high priest or other single religious authority to ask. They would need to ask several people to see if they could get a consensus or find someone who had some compelling knowledge.

The shaykh replied, "We do not know the exact town, but we believe that He will arise in the East—from the land of ancient Elam, known today as Persia."

"From Persia?!" exclaimed Zach, his eyes popping out. "We were planning to look throughout the Holy Land, not throughout the whole of the Orient!"

Shaykh Hakim shrugged. "You can search here if you wish. But you may need to search for thirty years. If instead, you seek the fulfillment of the promise of 1260 during the coming year, you do not need to look throughout the whole of the Orient. But you will need to make the Great Crossing."

"The Great Crossing?" asked Zach. "What is that?"

The room seemed to hush as the shaykh paused and then explained in a slow and deliberate voice.

"It is...the crossing between the two great centers of the world's religious civilizations—the ancient Mesopotamian-Persian Holy Land of the East and the eastern Mediterranean-Red Sea Holy Land of the West.

"It is the crossing that Abraham made when He was exiled from His home in Ur and came here, to the western Holy Land. It is the crossing that the Jewish people made, including Daniel as a child, when they were taken eastward as captives by the Babylonians, before the Persians took over Babylon. When the king of Persia released them and told them to return and rebuild Jerusalem, they made the Great Crossing once again, heading westward this time.

"It is the same crossing the Magi took from Persia in order to find the infant Jesus. It is the crossing that Ali, son of the Prophet, made in his journey to Kufa and that Husayn, the son of Ali, made on his way to martyrdom in Karbila, on the shores of the lower Euphrates. And it is the same crossing that new Husayn, or Jesus, or the Messiah, whichever name you wish to use, will take upon His return when He comes from the East and arrives here in the West, in the city of Akka."

The thought of such a journey was still reverberating in Zach's mind. But the mention of East and West pricked his memory, and he recited in a tone of wonderment, the verse from Matthew 24: "*For as the lightning cometh out of the east, and shineth even unto the west; so shall also the coming of the Son of man be.*"

The shaykh continued, "Yes...indeed...if you wish to succeed in your quest for the Promised One, who will arise in the East next year," the shaykh paused and then looked Zach straight in the eye, "then you, too, must make this Great Crossing.

"Although Shaykh Ahmad passed to the next world almost twenty years ago, you will find his leading disciple, *Siyyid Kazim*, teaching all about Shaykh Ahmad's views in the city of Karbila, on the banks of the Euphrates. He will be able to tell you much, much more about the coming of the Qaim than I can offer. I know of others from our land here who have made the journey to learn from him. They were not disappointed. Today the door is open; ever since Palestine and Syria have been returned to Ottoman control, the entire distance is within the Ottoman domain.

"So if you wish to find the Qaim—the Promised One who will appear next year—you must travel to Karbila. And then perhaps from there into the land of Persia—the land of Daniel's vision and prophecy, which will no doubt be fulfilled."

There was a long pause. Zach and James had not previously considered such a distant search. But it was certainly true that Daniel's vision of a prophecy regarding the 2,300 days occurred in Persia. Did that mean that it would also be fulfilled in Persia? They acknowledged this was something to consider.

It would be an ironic twist, thought Zach, that they would be retracing the steps of the original Wise Men, but in the opposite direction, in order to find the Promised One, who might, in this age, appear in that same country from which those original Wise Men had come.

"However," explained James after a pause, "we have much searching to do here in the Holy Land first, in any case. We have been discussing the places we wish to visit while we are here. We are on our way to Jerusalem. We were planning to travel from here through the Jezreel Valley in the Galilee to Nazareth then down to the River Jordan, following it south to Jericho and from there up to Jerusalem and Bethlehem.

"We must go to those places and learn from others about their understanding of the coming of the Messiah—where they think He will appear and why. From thence, we shall decide which course to follow."

151

"And how do you plan to reach these places?" asked Shaykh Hakim.

"We plan to buy a horse and donkeys to carry our belongings and will ride upon or walk beside them," replied Zach.

"My friends," said the shaykh kindly, "do you realize how perilous this would be, traveling in this country as a foreigner without protector or guide? There are many thieves out there who may attempt to steal everything even from a protected traveler. How much more from foreigners who are alone and without protectors!

"In this land, the government will not protect you. You are protected by your family. People refrain from attacking others for fear of retribution from their family. Then what of people who travel through these parts with no family members in sight?"

Until now, Zach had not given much thought to this aspect of the journey. In America, he had heard of feuds and rivalries between families that could become violent. But these were the exceptions, and clearly the violence was outside of the law. Such a state of affairs was more common in the unsettled territories of the American West, where the system of law had not yet been well established.

He hadn't considered how to travel safely under such conditions in the Holy Land. Certainly carrying a gun and threatening force would not work. They were foreigners and would be quickly outnumbered. "What do you suggest?" he inquired.

"I have a friend, Siyyid Youssef. He told me that he was planning to travel this route to meet with his uncle, who is currently in Jerusalem. I will speak with him, but I have no doubt that he would be pleased to travel with you. He will make sure that you travel with caravans so that you are not alone. His large family is strong and well known. None would dare harm him. Neither would they dare harm his traveling companions.

"And," the shaykh added, "he is very well read and knowledgeable."

"This is very kind of you," replied James, who was more familiar with such arrangements due to his earlier experience in Egypt. "When traveling in foreign lands, nothing is more valuable than a trustworthy guide who knows the land and the ways of the people."

"We must show hospitality to all travelers," replied the shaykh. "I will check with Youssef and let you know soon as to when he is planning to leave. And tomorrow I shall send you my servant to take you to the market to obtain some local clothing. While you travel, there is no benefit in showing everyone that you are a foreigner. In addition, if I may suggest," he said with a smile, "you should give your razors a rest."

James and Zach smiled too. The broad moustache common among American men of the time and the large sideburns of the British would betray their origins at a glance. They agreed that growing full beards would be a good idea.

Their lighter complexions and brown hair were not entirely different from segments of the Arab population as a result of centuries of interactions with Europeans. Wrapped in local clothes and headdress, wearing full beards, and carefully limiting their use of Arabic, they might be able to pass as locals, at least part of the time.

As they rose to leave, the shaykh pulled Zach aside and said, "And one special piece of advice for you, my friend: If you should get into any trouble along the way, you might do well to tell people that you are British. The American government is a long distance away and exercises no influence in these parts. The British Empire, however, is an entirely different story."

Zach thought about the damage that British ships had inflicted on the walls of Akka a few years before, and he understood the shaykh's point. All of the lands from the eastern Mediterranean to India and beyond felt the effects of Britain's presence.

"We are greatly indebted to you for all of your advice and assistance. How can we repay you?" James inquired.

"No charges," insisted the shaykh generously. "Just provide me, upon your return, with any news of whatever you have found during your search. This will be my greatest reward."

James and Zach thanked the shaykh profusely for his hospitality and his kind assistance as they all arose and walked toward the door.

"You have given us much to think about," said James as they departed.

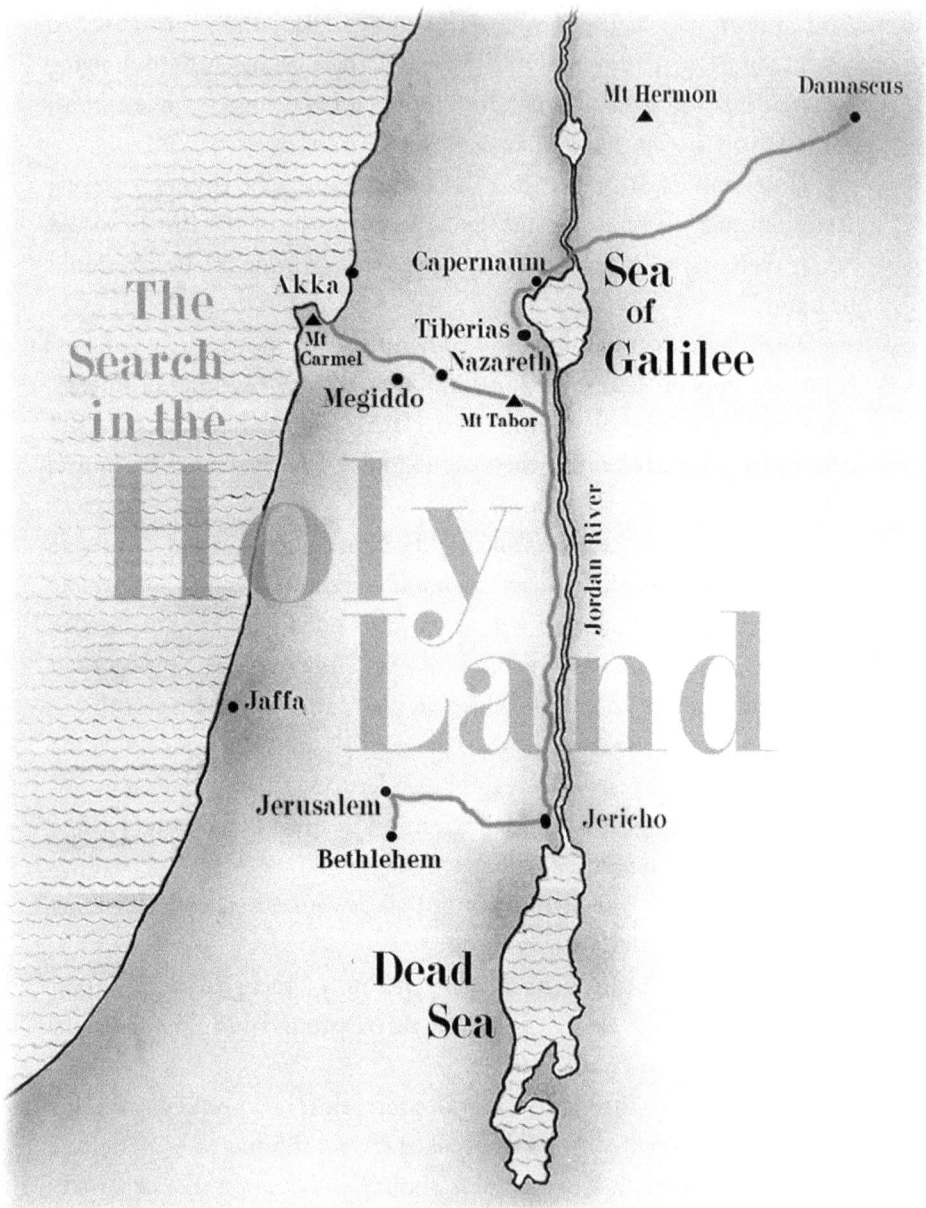

The Search in the Holy Land

Damascus

Mt Hermon

Capernaum

Sea of Galilee

Akka

Tiberias

Mt Carmel

Nazareth

Megiddo

Mt Tabor

Jordan River

Jaffa

Jerusalem

Jericho

Bethlehem

Dead Sea

Chapter 12

JEWISH EXPECTATIONS AT THE CAVE OF ELIJAH

James explained to Zach that "Siyyid" was a title of respect that indicated a man who was a direct descendant of Muhammad. A siyyid typically wore a green turban to signify this status.

James also noted many Arabic first names were simply the Arabic version of a biblical name. For instance, since the English "J" was the Arabic "Y," "Youssef" was the Arabic version of "Joseph."

"Don't worry," he said. "After a while, you'll develop an ear for it."

Siyyid Youssef was a good deal younger than Shaykh Hakim; he appeared only slightly older than James. He was muscular and stood erect with a princely bearing. His green turban stood out in brilliant contrast to his bright white robe. With trips like this, he assisted his larger family with its trading business.

Having purchased two donkeys, a horse, and various supplies for their travels, they thanked their Greek hosts and set off for Jerusalem on the path that Zach had described, except that Siyyid Youssef needed first to stop at the hamlet of Haifa. It was a small village of a few hundred people that sat at the foot of Mt. Carmel, marking the south end of the long bay, while Akka marked its north end.

As they rode along the beach, Zach was still feeling rather dazed and disoriented by all he had learned. James had warned him of the difficulties of experiencing too many new things all at once, as often happens during an initial visit to a foreign culture. The normal adjustments to a new language, climate, foods, sounds, scenery, smells, and behaviors were enough to tax the mind heavily. He found himself often looking up at the clouds in the sky because they were the only thing that seemed familiar to him here.

But adding to his discomfort, they had not yet found anyone who had heard anything about a child with innate knowledge recently born in the Holy Land. Nor had they found any Christians with additional clues to aid them in their search. To his surprise, they had found that at least a portion of the Muslim population was expecting the return of their own Promised One in the same year as the Christians were.

Curiously, the number of this year on the Muslim calendar, 1260, matched exactly the number that had been mentioned in the two most prophetic books of the Bible: Daniel and the Book of Revelation. While he acknowledged that this could not be a coincidence, its implications were huge. How could Muhammad have been a true prophet? He recalled the broadminded lesson from his Quaker upbringing and a quote from its founder, George Fox: *"God, who made all, pours out of His spirit upon all men and women in the world, in the days of His new covenant, yea, upon whites and blacks, Moors, and Turks, and Indians, Christians, Jews, and Gentiles, that all with the spirit of God, might know God and the things of God...."* While it was easy to accept this teaching at a distance, he had never considered the possibility that one of the people upon whom God might have poured out His spirit, at least with respect to the 1260 prophecy, could have been the founder of the religion of Islam. It seemed impossible to reconcile with the more commonly held views of his non-Quaker friends.

Secondly, should they be searching for the return of someone who would come first, before the return of Jesus, as John the Baptist had—someone who would come with *'the spirit and power of Elijah,'* as Gabriel had explained in the first chapter of Luke?

Finally, and most difficult of all, should they even be looking in the Holy Land? Or should they be looking to the East, as Jesus had suggested in Matthew 24:27? Traveling all the way to ancient Babylon and Persia—the areas associated with the prophet Daniel, as well as the Wise Men of the East—was difficult to conceive. Zach's head began to throb from thinking of it all. And Jeremy's question still haunted him: *"Have you thought about the fact that you, too, might have some misunderstandings and might have to change something about your own expectations?"* This was all proving to be much more difficult than he had imagined.

It was easier for James. He had lived in Egypt; the language and culture here were not new to him. Even the notion that the revelation of Muhammad might have had some positive benefits was not so strange to him. He started to share with Zach some thoughts that he had been mulling over.

"You know," he said, "the idea that some of Muhammad's teachings may have come from God would solve some of the questions that I, as an historian, have long held."

"Such as what?"

"Well, we know that Christian civilization started to flourish after the conversion of *Emperor Constantine* in 313 AD. In the West, it started a decline in the fifth century as pagan tribes attacked, mostly from northern Europe, and as the church itself became divided over several doctrinal issues. The Christian empire based in Rome collapsed around 480 AD, and for about twenty years, there was not a single Christian king in all of Western Europe.

"Meanwhile, the Eastern Church, and the whole Byzantine civilization along with it, was weakened by doctrinal divisions and supposed heresies and then by a long series of wars with the Persian-Zoroastrian civilization further east. As a result of all these tribulations, Christian civilization entered the 'Dark Ages,' which continued from roughly 500 AD to 1500 AD.

"And just as Christianity was declining, the Islamic civilization appeared and started to grow rapidly. So I've often wondered why God allowed Christian civilization to decline so much while also allowing a pagan civilization such as Islam to expand, flourish, and become the world's leading civilization of its time. I never considered that perhaps it was not really as pagan a civilization as I had been taught."

"Was Islamic civilization once the leading civilization of the world?" asked Zach incredulously.

"Yes indeed," replied James. "It expanded rapidly, and then they began to collect knowledge from all over the known world under the *Abbasid* Caliphs. Their kingdom lasted about five centuries—from 750 until about 1250 AD. Known as the *Islamic Golden Age*, it illuminated the world of knowledge while Europe was in the heart of its Dark Ages.

"If we entertain the possibility that Muhammad was indeed a true messenger of God, then it might be easier to understand why Christian civilization faltered during this period while Islamic civilization flourished. Under the Abbasids, people of all religious backgrounds were encouraged to share their knowledge. Much of our knowledge of the ancient Greek civilization was not preserved in Western Europe and might have been lost had not some Christians brought it to Baghdad, the center of the Abbasid civilization, where it was preserved until, centuries later, it was retranslated into languages of the people of the West.

"In Bagdad they established the *House of Wisdom*, which became a focal point for scholars of all backgrounds. They sought to bring together learned men from every land. It was responsible for great advances in the fields of medicine, mathematics, geography, astronomy, and others.

"And not just there; a similar *House of Knowledge* was established in Cairo in the middle of this period. Some say that these were actually the forerunners and models for the modern Western universities—places devoted to the pursuit of knowledge of all types."

Zach replied, "That is amazing. I can see that there is much that I missed in my history lessons."

"Indeed, our studies in the West focus on our own history, and they leave out much of the rest of the world. But I managed to learn more about the history of these parts during my time in Egypt almost twenty years ago."

Zach was once again deeply grateful for having found such a knowledgeable traveling companion.

James continued, "I have often wondered how different the world would have been if the leaders of Christianity in the seventh century had accepted Islam instead of fighting against it. If these two great civilizing forces—the teachings of Jesus and the teachings of Muhammad—had built upon each other instead of working against each other, what would have happened?

"I concluded we can get some idea of an answer by looking at the result of even the limited contacts between Islam and Christianity during *the Crusades.*

"You see, some historians have recognized that one of the side effects of the Crusades, which occurred near the end of the Islamic Golden Age, was to open the eyes of many Westerners to the benefits of Islamic advances in knowledge. However much they may have deplored the Islamic theology, they brought back to Europe not only some of the knowledge that they had learned but, perhaps more importantly, a recognition of the benefits of knowledge and a resulting desire to learn and improve.

"As I mentioned, the Caliph of Cairo established the House of Knowledge there in about 1000 AD. Some Europeans apparently saw the benefit of it because eighty-eight years later, they established the first university in Europe, in Bologna, Italy.

"After the Crusades, the early Renaissance started in northern Italy because it had been in direct contact with the Holy Land and was an important route for the Crusaders. Thus, in some respects, we can understand that the Renaissance, and all of the discoveries since then, were the result of a mixing of Christian and Islamic civilizations and the re-ignition of the quest for knowledge in the West. What benefits would have accrued if the mixing had been complete from the beginning and without the constant fighting? One can only imagine how much more rapidly civilization might have advanced," said James wistfully.

But Zach was more cautious. "Certainly Christianity would be *very* different from what it is today."

*   *   *

MOUNT CARMEL LOOMED EVER larger as the little band moved gradually southward along the sandy track near the edge of the bay. Zach remembered the story of Elijah, from the Second Book of the Kings in the Old

159

Testament, and his reckoning with the prophets of Baal on Mt. Carmel. He was pleased to be approaching this first place in the Holy Land that seemed to have a direct connection with their search.

Here was the mountain of Elijah, from the times of the Israelites, whose return was promised at the very end of the Old Testament—a promise that, as Jesus had explained in Matthew 17, was fulfilled with the coming of His forerunner, John the Baptist. And James and Zach were here today, hoping to find perhaps his next return—the new Promised One, who would also go forth *"in the spirit and power of Elijah,"* as the angel Gabriel had described to John's father, Zacharias, in the year before John's birth.

The mountain itself looked dry and was barren of trees or cultivation. Thorny shrubs grew between the rocks, where the occasional rain might collect. But no rain had fallen since their arrival during this latter part of the dry season, and the dryness was unfamiliar to Zach.

They occasionally passed ancient wine presses, cisterns, and other relics abandoned long ago but providing silent testimony that the land had once been cultivated with vineyards and other crops. Indeed, the name "Carmel" had come from the Hebrew for the orchard, or vineyard, of God.

Reaching the village of Haifa at sundown, they found a small inn. That evening, when speaking with the townspeople, James and Zach learned of the Cave of Elijah, near the point where the end of the mountain jutted into the sea. Since Youssef would spend the following day at the market trading some of his goods, James and Zach decided to spend their free time visiting this ancient holy site.

*   *   *

THEY ARRIVED IN THE late morning and entered through a small stone building leading to an opening of a "cave," which appeared to have been hewn from a layer of the relatively soft limestone rock of this part of the mountain. It was not a large space, but one could easily imagine it would have been enough to provide Elijah with the limited shelter a religious ascetic might need.

160

Cave of Elijah overlooking the Mediterranean Sea

The stone walls reflected little light. The candles on a Star-of-David-shaped chandelier helped somewhat but had covered the ceiling with enough soot to suggest that the place had hardly changed since the days of Elijah.

There were a few people milling around, none of whom appeared to be pilgrims. They found a place on the floor where they could sit and pray for guidance. For although they were intrigued by what Shaykh Hakim had taught them in Akka, they were not yet ready to abandon their search in the Holy Land.

After much prayer and meditation, they arose, stretched their legs, and stepped outside. An old man with a long beard and an unusual turban had been watching. He now approached them.

"You are, perhaps, Christian pilgrims?" he inquired gently. "The Christian monastery is at the top of the mountain," he said, pointing uphill.

"We are pilgrims, of a sort," offered James kindly, "but not in search of a monastery. And who might you be?"

"I am Moshe," he replied while taking a slight bow, "the keeper of these premises."

James recognized the name as the Hebrew form of 'Moses' and realized this site was maintained by a small group of Jews. He introduced Zach and himself and explained they were scholars seeking to learn more about Elijah. Moshe was happy to oblige. He started a long explanation of the details of Elijah's life in this region.

At length, Zach thanked him for the explanation and then added, "We are also interested to learn about his return as it is mentioned in the Book of Malachi."

"Oooohhh," replied Moshe. "You wish to know about the *great and terrible day of the Lord*' that will come upon us when Elijah returns?"

James and Zach both nodded.

"But first, answer me this," continued Moshe, his voice becoming quiet as his eyes gazed intently first at Zach and then at James. "Do you believe that we now live in the time that Moses called the *'end of days*'?'"

"Yes indeed," affirmed Zach, "for Jesus clearly told His followers that when His gospel was preached to the entire world, the end would come.

And we know now that within the past few years, the Christian gospel has been taken to the last countries where it had never been preached before. So we believe that we are now living in what we call 'the latter days'—the end of the age."

"Well, I know little of what Yeshua taught," said Moshe, referring to Jesus by the Hebrew version of his name. "But consider what Moses revealed in the fourth chapter of His final book, the Devarim (Deuteronomy). He taught us, the Jewish people, about the end of days, saying:

"And the LORD shall scatter you among the nations, and ye shall be left few in number among the heathen, whither the LORD shall lead you.

"And there ye shall serve gods, the work of men's hands, wood and stone, which neither see, nor hear, nor eat, nor smell.

"But if from thence thou shalt seek the LORD thy God, thou shalt find him, if thou seek him with all thy heart and with all thy soul.

*"When thou art in tribulation, and all these things are come upon thee, **even in the latter days**, if thou turn to the LORD thy God, and shalt be obedient unto his voice;*

*"(For the LORD thy God is a merciful God;) **He will not forsake thee, neither destroy thee, nor forget the covenant of thy fathers which he sware unto them.***"

"And hear again, in Chapter 30 of that same book, wherein He says:

*"And it shall come to pass, when all these things are come upon thee, the blessing and the curse, which I have set before thee, and **thou shalt call them to mind among all the nations**, whither the LORD thy God hath driven thee,*

"And shalt return unto the LORD thy God, and shalt obey His voice according to all that I command thee this day, thou and thy children, with all thine heart, and with all thy soul;

*"That then the LORD thy God will turn thy captivity, and have compassion upon thee, and **will return and gather thee from all***

the nations, whither the LORD thy God hath scattered thee.

"If any of thine be driven out unto the outmost parts of heaven, from thence will the LORD thy God gather thee, and from thence will he fetch thee:

"And the LORD thy God will bring thee into the land which thy fathers possessed, and thou shalt possess it; and he will do thee good, and multiply thee above thy fathers."

"If we live at the end of days," Moshe explained, now gazing out across the sea, "then surely the Jewish people will return to this land. And surely we will possess it and build here a great nation."

Zach was surprised at the power of Moshe's presentation. "I've read Deuteronomy, but I must admit that I haven't studied it deeply enough to put those two passages together. It seems clear that the latter days and the ingathering of the Jewish people to the Holy Land are connected as a part of God's promise to Moses."

James, however, was a bit skeptical. "How do you propose to possess the Holy Land, which has been held for centuries by the Ottomans and by other Muslim rulers before that? The Jewish people live in small communities—often in impoverished ghettos—scattered in many nations across the whole face of the world. None of them has any political power to speak of and certainly no military strength. Few have any wealth. Most are persecuted. How could they possibly succeed in taking possession of the Holy Land from the might of the Ottoman Empire?"

Moshe acknowledged, "Yea, indeed, we are cut off into parts, our bones are scattered and dried up, and our hope seems lost. And I, too, would lose all hope were it not for the vision that the prophet Yechezkel wrote down concerning our dry bones."

"Ezekiel," interjected James for Zach's benefit, "chapter 37, as I recall."

"Surely, you will recall this," continued Moshe:

"The hand of the LORD was upon me, and the LORD carried me out in a spirit, and set me down in the midst of the valley, and it was full of bones; and He caused me to pass by them round

about, and, behold, there were very many in the open valley; and, lo, they were very dry.

"And He said unto me: 'Son of man, can these bones live?' And I answered: 'O Lord GOD, Thou knowest.'

"Then He said unto me: 'Prophesy over these bones, and say unto them: O ye dry bones, hear the word of the LORD: Thus saith the Lord GOD unto these bones: Behold, I will cause breath to enter into you, and ye shall live.

"'And I will lay sinews upon you, and will bring up flesh upon you, and cover you with skin, and put breath in you, and ye shall live; and ye shall know that I am the LORD.'

"So I prophesied as I was commanded; and as I prophesied, there was a noise, and behold a commotion, and the bones came together, bone to its bone.

"And I beheld, and, lo, there were sinews upon them, and flesh came up, and skin covered them above; but there was no breath in them.

"Then said He unto me: 'Prophesy unto the breath, prophesy, son of man, and say to the breath: Thus saith the Lord GOD: Come from the four winds, O breath, and breathe upon these slain, that they may live.'

"So I prophesied as He commanded me, and the breath came into them, and they lived, and stood up upon their feet, an exceeding great host."

"That is an interesting prophecy," said Zach, "but how do you know that it is an allegory about the return of the Jewish people to the Holy Land?"

"Very simple," replied Moshe. "Many of the allegories of prophecy are not explained, so the reader must try to reason them out. But in this case, the Lord explained it directly to Ezekiel. He said:

*"Son of man, **these bones are the whole house of Israel;** behold, they say: Our bones are dried up, and our hope is lost; we are clean cut off.*

"Therefore prophesy, and say unto them: Thus saith the Lord GOD: Behold, I will open your graves, and cause you to come up out of your graves, O My people; and **I will bring you into the land of Israel.**

"And ye shall know that I am the LORD, *when I have opened your graves, and caused you to come up out of your graves, O My people.*

"And I will put My spirit in you, and ye shall live, **and I will place you in your own land;** *and ye shall know that I the* LORD *have spoken, and performed it, saith the* LORD.

"Yea, the spirit of the many Jews who were persecuted and killed over long centuries will awaken a spirit among the living, which shall cause them to return here, to the land of our forefathers, Israel."

Zach and James had read this prophecy before, but in the context of the earlier ones from Deuteronomy, it seemed to have a new clarity.

Moshe added, "There are several other places in the Tanach—what you call the 'Old Testament'—that speak of the 'end of days' or, as some of the Christians call them, the 'latter days' or the 'last days.' Most of them are associated with the return of the Jewish people to the land of Israel. The prophet Isaiah spoke of it, as did Jeremiah, Hosea, and Zechariah."

"Yes," replied Zach, "it is even so within the teachings of Jesus. He predicted, in Luke 21 as I recall, that Jerusalem would be *'trodden down of the Gentiles'* but not forever. It would only be so *'until the times of the Gentiles be fulfilled,'* that is to say, until the Jewish people return. And He clearly associated this with the time of His return—or the coming of the Messiah," Zach quickly added, remembering that a reference to the return of Jesus might not sit well with members of the Jewish community.

"So what year do you expect Elijah and the Messiah to return, and where do you expect them to appear?" inquired James.

"As to the exact year, I do not know, but I think it will be sometime in my lifetime. Have you read the teachings of the Rabbi *Judah Alkalai* or the *Ga'on of Vilna?* Through their studies of our scripture and the mystical teachings of the *Kabbalah,* they concluded that Elijah and the Messiah will appear during this coming century. Rabbi Alkalai said this is the time, and we Jews must prepare for it by returning to the land of Israel and by buying property here wherever we can until the whole land is ours. Because of their teachings, small groups of Jews from all over the world have started to move here to the Holy Land during the last 35 years.

"As to the place of Elijah's return, I should think that he will return to this very mountain—for this is the place where he stayed and where his most important miracle occurred. And this is exactly why I and this small community of Jews," he nodded toward those around him, "remain here."

Regarding the timing, Zach thought of asking about the prophecies of Daniel and of presenting the reasoning of his father and William Miller, which pointed to the upcoming year of 1844.

But then he remembered that in order to understand this prophecy, one had to understand the other prophecy from chapter 9 of Daniel, concerning how the Messiah would be 'cut off' or crucified at the end of 490 years. And he knew that the Jewish community would certainly not be ready to recognize the crucifixion of Jesus as being the fulfillment of that prophecy.

So instead he asked, "And how will you recognize Elijah when he returns?"

Moshe took a step back in surprise.

"There will be many amazing things to witness. The sun will be darkened, and the moon shall turn to blood, and the stars shall cease to shine."

"But those are prophecies from the New Testament!" protested Zach, thinking of Matthew 24.

Moshe replied, "If Yeshua taught them, then he was just repeating what was already spoken by Joel and by Ezekiel, Isaiah, and Micah."

James nodded, for he knew it was true.

By now, both Zach and James could see the same pattern they already knew from their own Christian communities and from what they had learned from Shaykh Hakim as well: Prophecies that were intended to convey spiritual meanings were, instead, being understood in a material manner. So James simply nodded to Zach to indicate that it was perhaps time to leave.

"You have given us much to think about," said Zach respectfully, "and we thank you greatly." But as they started to walk down the path together, Zach had one more question.

167

"I thought that the Jewish people were banished from the Holy Land. How is it that you and your community are still here?"

"My forefathers were banished," Moshe explained. "They wandered for many centuries before settling on the Iberian Peninsula, the land you now call Spain. They migrated there in about 750 AD, shortly after Islam had defeated the Christian *Visigoths* there.

"The Muslims were generally tolerant of religious minorities and did not persecute either the Jews or the Christians much. My ancestors lived in the town now called Madrid until the Christians conquered the area around 1250. All of the Jews and the Muslims were forced to convert to Christianity or to flee. My ancestors fled south to the province of Granada, which remained in Muslim hands. There, in Cordoba, was a most wonderful age, where Muslims, Christians, and Jews worked, learned, and lived together in harmony.

"But in 1492 the Spanish Christians once again pushed south. Although they promised tolerance toward people of other faiths, they quickly forgot their promises and again forced Jews and Muslims to convert or flee. Some converted but secretly remained Jewish or Muslim. So the Spanish created their 'Inquisition' to hunt down and kill anyone suspected of being insincere.

"My family, along with tens of thousands of other Jewish families, fled to north Africa, where they were welcomed by the Ottoman Empire. My ancestors gradually migrated eastward until they settled in Cairo.

"As a young man in 1800, I decided to join one of the early groups of Jews to make Aliyah, the 'coming up' into the Holy Land. We settled in Jaffa. But after long study of the Torah and our other sacred books, I became convinced that Elijah would return soon, and so I set out for this place, here at Mount Carmel.

"For many centuries, Jews were not supposed to be here. The Ottoman rulers here provided no protection for us from assault or murder. Yet some Jews, like myself, came because we felt impelled to be here. As long as we remain quiet and poor and stay out of other people's way, the Ottomans generally seem content to leave us alone. And being supported here entirely by the contributions from our home community in Egypt," he shrugged, "we are not likely to become rich.

"But now the prophecies of the *Talmud* and the *Zohar* seem to be coming true."

"What's the Zohar?" asked Zach.

"The Zohar is the main mystical book of our faith, and it predicted that our plight would start to improve in the year 5600 of our calendar.

"It says: '*In the 600th year of the sixth thousand, the gates of wisdom on high and the wellsprings of lower wisdom will be opened. This will prepare the world to enter the seventh thousand, just as man prepares himself toward sunset on Friday for the Sabbath.*'[10] Many took this to mean that the Messiah would appear in 5600, and this is why so many Jews have started to migrate to the Holy Land during the past forty years."

"When will the year 5600 occur?" Zach inquired.

"It already occurred—four years ago, in the Christian years 1839 and 1840. Although it is true that the Messiah did not arrive in that year, several important changes happened.

"Our former ruler, *Muhammad Ali of Egypt*, had refused our request in July 1839 to be permitted to buy or even to lease farmland so that we could better support ourselves. But in that same month, the old sultan of the Ottoman Empire to our north passed away, and his son came to power. The young *Sultan Abdulmejid* brought new ideas of ways to modernize the empire. A few months later, in 5600, he issued the *Edict of Gulhane*, which gave rights to everyone in the Ottoman realms, regardless of their religion. It included the right to own property. He started his reorganization plan, called the '*Tanzimat.*'

"This would have had no effect on our community here. But later in 1840, the Ottomans, with help from the British and Austrians, ended Muhammad Ali's rulership over the Holy Land. And thus the Jewish community—here now as citizens of the Ottoman Empire—are allowed to buy land and can start farms to support themselves. I believe the Sultan will continue on this Tanzimat path and more Jews will be able to return, because once land is purchased, they will no longer need to depend on contributions from their home communities. And thus I feel that the first 'wellspring of lower wisdom' has already opened for us, and the congregation of Israel shall arise from the dust of exile during the coming century, exactly as the Rabbi Judah Alkalai has taught."[11]

"That's certainly fascinating," noted James. "We hope, for your sake, additional wellsprings of lower wisdom will be opened."

"And we will continue in our search," added Zach, "looking for the 'gates of wisdom on high.'"

They shook hands and thanked Moshe and then parted.

On the path back toward the village of Haifa, Zach was pondering over the things Moshe had said.

"It is fascinating to realize that groups of Jews, Muslims, and Christians are all expecting the Messiah to appear. All three are focused on these current few years, and all three have arrived at their conclusions through independent references to their holy books. I don't see how this could be a coincidence."

James agreed. "We came here searching for the return of Jesus, and we've already discovered that there is a lot more to this than we had imagined."

"Do you think it is possible that the Jewish people could return to the Holy Land and actually rule it once again? It seems hard to believe."

"There are some in the West who think it could be done," James replied. "Some see it as a solution to the problem of Jewish ghettos in Europe and the anti-Jewish persecutions that have happened in many parts of Europe and Russia.

"Others, who are religious, see it as a necessary part of the return of the Lord. Why, just the year before last, one of the Latter-day Saints, *Orson Hyde* as I recall, was sent to Jerusalem by Joseph Smith to prepare for the ingathering of the Jewish people there.

"But I must say, I cannot imagine how they could rule over this land. The Ottoman Empire would never stand for it. It would take a miracle," James said confidently and then added, "No...it would take *many, many* miracles."

"Yes, I suppose that is true...but then again," Zach paused and then simply added, "God has done many, many miracles here before."

Chapter 13

LESSONS IN THE GALILEE

THEY REJOINED YOUSSEF AT the inn. While speaking with people there, they asked whether anyone had heard any stories of a child with rare knowledge—someone who seemed to know things without ever having been taught. It was one of the first recognizable signs of the Holy Spirit in the young Jesus. They felt certain that it would be an early sign in the coming of the Promised One as well. But the people they asked only shook their heads to say no. A few would squint and pause, as if they might imagine the reason for the question, but they too said no.

So they set out the following morning with a small caravan heading east into the Galilee area, toward Nazareth, the boyhood home of Jesus. Zach wondered whether Jesus might have walked this very same path as His parents brought Him to Nazareth after spending His earliest years in Egypt.

But he was also pondering the story of a more recent immigrant from Egypt: Moshe, the Jewish keeper of the Cave of Elijah. Zach had always seen European-Christian history from the inside, looking out. But Moshe viewed it from the outside, with all of its consequences for his family. It was not the picture of the wonderful, progressive, and civilizing influence Zach had taken for granted.

At length he said to James, "It was an interesting story that Moshe told of his family's background and how they were forced to leave Spain. I had always heard that Islam was forced on the people—'spread by the sword,' as they say. Yet in this case at least, it seems that Christianity was the religion that was being forced on people, not Islam."

"Yes," replied James, "the Christian *Reconquista* of the Iberian Peninsula and the Spanish Inquisition that followed were certainly *not* among our religion's finest hours. As to the notion that Islam was 'spread by the sword'…I have read some history that has led me to wonder about this. But let us ask our friend Youssef here for his views also."

So they switched to speaking in Arabic and inquired.

Youssef replied, "I've heard this comment from Christians before. But first let me ask you, which of God's Messenger's said, '*Think not that I am come to send peace on earth: I came not to send peace, but a sword*'?"

Zach paused and then said, "Well, yes, I know—that was Jesus, in Matthew 10 as I recall. But I think you are taking it out of context. I mean, if you read the whole passage, you would see that He was not promoting war. Rather, He was saying that love of God must be stronger than love of family. He taught that His followers must be willing to cut themselves off from their families if the family would not believe in Him. Therefore the 'sword' is a symbol of detachment from the love of the things of this world in order to follow Him."

"Yes," replied Youssef, "and that is *exactly* my point. If you do not stop to read the whole chapter, you may easily misunderstand its context. For instance, when the Quran mentions 'holy war,' it does not usually mean war between soldiers."

"That is true," agreed James, to Zach's surprise. "I remember looking this one up when I was in Egypt. '*Jihad*' can more accurately be translated into English as 'spiritual struggle' rather than 'holy war.'

"This encompasses the struggle that each person has each day to pay more attention to his spiritual development and to avoid undue attachment to material things. Saying one's daily prayers, fasting, giving alms to the poor—all require a daily 'spiritual struggle' against our more material tendencies."

"Exactly so," Youssef replied. "Although it is true that jihad can imply sufficient detachment from material things so that one is ready to go into battle for the protection of the faith, the real meaning of jihad is much wider than that.

172

"The actual references in the Quran to fighting are narrowly defined to defending Muslim realms against armed attackers, or they pertain to particular circumstances of those times, which are not found today. But if you take them out of context, you can easily lead people astray—lead them into thinking that the Quran encourages the use of force to convert people to its beliefs. And when people, whether Muslim or Christian, have not read the Scriptures for themselves, they can be easily misled by their so-called 'religious' leaders, who are more inclined to serve their own patron, their sultan or king, than they are inclined to truly serve God.

"Let them all read the second chapter of the Holy Quran, wherein Muhammad says, *'There is no compulsion in religion.'*[12] Truly it is impossible to force anyone to believe something. We Muslims will recite the words of God to them. And if, by God's grace, they accept it, we give thanks to God. But if not, we will leave them to themselves and pray God to guide them.

"As you know, Jesus brought His message to the Jewish people—a people who already shared a belief in the oneness of God, and it spread in the West. Also, Zoroaster had brought teachings of the oneness of God to the Persian people, which helped unite them.

"But Muhammad's revelation came, instead, to the place in between, where monotheism was not yet widespread. It came to our people when we lived in *Jahiliyyah* (the 'age of ignorance'), when we worshiped many idols. We were a people whose loyalties extended no further than our own families. Our many tribes were constantly fighting each other. But with the Prophet's teachings, in the crucible of our wars, God melted away our age-old allegiance to family. And from this there emerged a new allegiance—an allegiance to the one true God. This allegiance knew no geographic bounds, so it could spread widely and ultimately transform much of mankind.

"The Quran brought a higher purpose to the lives of the people. They were called to come together to worship the one God and to abandon their previous animosities. Because of the fighting that existed all around them, these people were also capable of fighting. But as their new religious community expanded to new areas, the fighting that had once existed throughout Arabia was now transmuted into the worship of the one God. As the 'house of Islam' continued its outward spread beyond Arabia, larger areas were brought into this realm of peace, and the fighting, if any, was limited to the frontier areas.

"Muhammad made a provision for the existing monotheists, the 'people of the Book,'" Youssef explained. "Those who believed in one God could continue in their old beliefs if they did not want to accept Islam. They were to pay a reasonable tax for the protection that Islam had brought. In return, they were not called upon to serve in the Islamic army. Perhaps one day they or their children would read the Quran and recognize that this was indeed a message from God. But there was to be *no compulsion*.

"Muhammad set a great example in His capture of Mecca, which had far-reaching implications, for He did not slaughter the people who had opposed Him nor pillage their city. He destroyed only the idols that the polytheists had been worshipping at the sacred *Kabaa* there. He did not force them to become Muslims.

"This pattern was followed on many future occasions. After a city was surrounded, Islamic generals would offer terms similar to what Muhammad had offered so that the city could be taken without force or destruction. This way, it was much easier for the city leaders to accept new rulership, knowing they would not be harmed nor forced to follow the new religion.

"The Muslim armies lost fewer men and maintained relatively good relations with the local population, so it was unnecessary to leave a large garrison force behind. This meant that more men could move on to the next city. Thus did Islam spread over the course of just a few decades; it went westward across North Africa and throughout Spain and eastward across Arabia, Mesopotamia, Persia, and into central Asia."

James added, "It was also Islam's good fortune to arrive on the scene just at the time when both the Roman-Byzantine Empire and the Persian-Zoroastrian Empire had exhausted their strength through decades of nearly constant war with each other."[13]

Youssef smiled. "Was it simply good fortune? Or did the All-Knowing Creator look upon the sorry state of His two leading religions and realize that mankind was in need of a fresh measure of His divine guidance?"

Zach, while not yet thinking of these religions as equals, was neverthe-less amused to see how the same set of circumstances could appear entirely different from these two different perspectives.

"Did you know," Youssef continued, "that Muhammad had sent messages to the rulers of both empires, *Heraclius* of Byzantine Rome and *Khusro II* of Persia, inviting them to recognize God's new message? But the leaders of both empires turned their backs on Him, and so God swept most of their dominions away."[14]

"Frankly," offered James, "I don't think either empire had any idea of what was happening in Arabia. For centuries, the Byzantines and the Persians suffered occasional attacks by small Arabian tribes that never amounted to any significant threat. And as long as those tribes were disunited and squab-bling amongst themselves, they would never have been a serious threat.

"But Muhammad's teachings transformed their disunity into a far greater unity, which transcended tribal and family loyalties. Neither the Byzantines nor the Persians noticed what had happened in western Arabia until it was too late.

"Furthermore, the Christian cause was not helped by its own disunity. There were so many different branches of Christian belief that had been disowned or marked as heresies by the church fathers in Constantinople and Rome. Whether it was the *Monophysites* from Armenia to Ethiopia, the *Nestorians* in Persia, the *Coptics* in Egypt, the *Arians* in the West, the *Syriac Christians*, or even the Christian *Ghassanid* tribes in northern Arabia, all had been badly treated by orthodox Christianity.

"So when Heraclius needed help from his Christian brothers in many realms, very few had any sense of loyalty or devotion to him or to his church, which had rejected them. Furthermore, his negative attitude toward the Jewish community did not help. It encouraged the Jews to help the Persians as they temporarily took over Jerusalem in the year 614, and again, a couple of decades later, it encouraged them to assist the Muslims in some of their early battles against Byzantine cities."

"Yes," interjected Youssef, "the Jews usually found themselves more welcome in Islamic countries than in Christian ones."

Zach reflected on how that seemed to be consistent with what he had recently heard from Moshe regarding his family's history in Spain.

"And from what I've read," James continued, "Persian unity was also shattered but in a different way. After Khusro II was killed in a coup in 628 AD, various Persian factions, including the contending clergy and the military factions, tried to set up their favorite new leader. A succession of twelve short-lived leaders attempted to rule over the next four years. By the time *Yazdegerd III* finally consolidated power in 632, the forces of the expanding Muslim nation were nearly at his doorstep.

"By 637 his western defenses were shattered, and he was forced to abandon his capital. For the next seven years he retreated across Persia, after which he was forced to flee his country altogether. His death, another seven years later, marked the final end of the Sasanian dynasty and its empire."

"Yes indeed," Youssef replied. "The Islamic armies were able to push forward rapidly. No doubt God helped them. Circumstances may have helped. Muhammad's example of how to treat conquered cities certainly helped. But the bravery of Islam's army was also helped by the vision that the Prophet provided for His followers of a paradise that was so certain and so wonderful that risking one's life in battle would have a positive outcome, regardless of whether one lived or died on the battlefield.

"Still, in the midst of all their success, there was always the Quranic restraint against compulsion in religion. Thus, it was only gradually, over the course of centuries, that the wisdom of the Quran convinced large parts of the population to recognize Muhammad as God's most recent Prophet.

"Even today, there are often small communities of Christians and Jews in Muslim lands whom we will not harm nor force to convert. If you were to travel to northern India, you would find some realms there that have been controlled by Muslim rulers for over eight centuries. And yet the majority of the inhabitants of those lands still remain Hindu because *there is no compulsion in religion.*"

Zach replied, "Surely there must have been some instances of forced conversion or intolerance. I recall reading that the Crusades started because of Muslim intolerance of Christian pilgrims."

"Of course there were some instances over the long course and wide expanse of Islamic history," Youssef said. "Islam had taken over the city of

Jerusalem peacefully and without destruction of its holy places or its inhabitants. And for over 350 years, Christian visitors made their pilgrimages to Jerusalem without any Muslim impediment.

"But a hundred years before the Crusades began, *Al-Hakim bi-Amr Allah* inherited the role of Caliph in Egypt at age 15. He was erratic, and for a period of about eight years, he was fanatically disposed against Christians. His destruction of the Church of the Holy Sepulcher in Jerusalem in 1009 and his forced conversion of some of the Christians in his realm was an aberration in our history.

"But within a few years, he changed his ways. After he died, his son also made amends, allowing any forced conversions to be annulled and allowing the Byzantine emperor to rebuild the church. The state of peace between the religions returned for almost fifty years, but it was again shaken as control of Jerusalem switched back and forth between the Egyptians and the Turks.

"Although Christians were not directly involved in those conflicts, this instability—together with memories of the earlier caliph's intolerance and the expansion by the Turks into Byzantine territory in Anatolia—provided some reasons for the Europeans to start their Crusades."

"Yes," James added, "expansion by the Turks forced the Byzantine emperor to call for knights from the West, but they were not motivated to fight the Turks in Anatolia. To them, Jerusalem and the Holy Land were the only prizes worth fighting for.

"I also recall that the pope of that time, *Urban II,* had many other reasons to start the Crusades that had nothing to do with Jerusalem and everything to do with extending his authority over a wider range and acquiring more popular support.

"Zach, you may recall from your studies of Christian history that this pope and the previous pope had been forced out of Rome by another man, Clement III, who claimed to be the proper pope. So an internal power struggle provided a lot of motivation for the Crusades as well. Some say it was a greater motivation than the concern for the treatment of Christian pilgrims, although the pilgrimage issue certainly provided a rationale."

Zach had heard this story from some of his Protestant friends in America, many of whom held the pope in low esteem.

Youssef continued, "In any case, the whole episode demonstrated yet again the truth of Muhammad's teaching that '*there is no compulsion in religion.*' The Caliph's persecution of the Christians during those eight years was foolish. There have been a few other overzealous Muslim leaders in history that made the same mistake. When these leaders have ignored this teaching of the Quran, they have suffered serious consequences. In this case, Islam lost control of the Holy Land for two centuries.

"But the Crusader mistreatment and wholesale slaughter of the Muslims in the Holy Land and in the Holy City was also unwise. And thus, it seems that God eventually enabled Islam to push the Crusaders out."

Turning now to Zach, he added, "I am told that your new country of America takes pride in offering religious freedom to everyone."

"Yes," replied Zach proudly, "this was something guaranteed to all our citizens when my grandfather's generation wrote the American Constitution."

"It is a good thing," replied Youssef. "But why was it considered so special, so extraordinary, or so necessary?"

"Many of the people of my country came from Europe to avoid the religious persecution there, my own ancestors included."

"Was there much religious persecution in Europe?" Youssef inquired.

"Yes, of course there was. Why, ever since the Protestants broke away from the Catholic Church more than three hundred years ago, there have been many wars over religion in Europe. Much of the population of Germany was killed during the *Thirty Years' War* there."

"So it would seem," offered Youssef, "that many of the people of Europe believe that religion is something that can be compelled—first through the forced suppression of heresies, later by Crusader wars, then by wars between Protestants and Catholics. Is it possible that this European tendency to think of religion as something that can be forced on others is one of the reasons that Europeans are inclined to think that Islam is trying to do the same thing? Is this perhaps more of an expression of European thinking than of reality?"

Zach could see Youssef's point. James, too, having been raised in a country that had suffered enormously in the Catholic–Protestant wars, had to admit the Christian record of compulsion in religion was, at best, no better than the Muslim one and quite possibly worse.

Youssef added, "I am pleased to hear that the founders of the American republic have learned that there is no compulsion in religion. Have you ever wondered how different the history of Europe might have been had they accepted this one simple principle from the time that Muhammad taught it?"

Youssef had given much for James and Zach to think about, and they continued on their way for some time, just reflecting on the histories of the two religions and the mirror-image perspectives they sometimes had of each other.

Zach and James were pleasantly surprised to discover their traveling companion was so well educated. "Some of this I learned in school," explained Youssef, "but most comes from my habit of reading a little every morning and every evening. Over the years, one's knowledge grows."

After a thoughtful pause, James returned to the theme, saying, "I've always suspected that there may have been an additional reason why the Christian clerics wanted to promote the idea that Islam was spread by the sword."

"And what is that?" inquired Zach.

"Ever since the conversion of Constantine at the *Battle of Milvian Bridge*, Christian clerics had taken this victory, and subsequent Christian military victories, as a sign that God was on their side."

"Yes...and what is wrong with that?"

"Well, it creates somewhat of a theological crisis when your side *loses* a military campaign, as happened when Islam spread so rapidly. The natural implication is that God is *not* on your side. Or at least that He didn't help enough. How do you explain that to your followers?"

"Yes, I can see how that would be a problem."

"And thus, I believe, they came up with the story that the religion of Islam was 'spread by the sword.' They claimed that people only became Muslims under threat of death rather than out of free choice."

The trail was starting to rise gently through the foothills of the Galilee. The grass and brush on either side was parched by the dry season's sun.

As they continued on their way toward Nazareth, Zach thought about why the people back home never seemed to even consider the religion of Islam or other religions.

"One of the things that I was always taught," remarked Zach, "was that we must 'beware of false prophets.' So I, like most Christians, did not ever consider looking at anything outside of Christianity, until my father convinced me to consider the religion of the Magi."

"Yes," replied James, "I've often heard that quote cited. Unfortunately, they seldom finish the quote. You may recall that the disciples immediately asked Jesus how to distinguish the true prophets from the false ones. Jesus did *not* say that there would be no more prophets after Him. Instead, He provided us with a means for determining which were true and which were false. Do you remember?"

"Yes," said Zach, reciting the verses from Matthew 7 clearly:

> *"Beware of false prophets, which come to you in sheep's clothing, but inwardly they are ravening wolves.*
>
> *Ye shall know them by their fruits. Do men gather grapes of thorns, or figs of thistles?*
>
> *Even so every good tree bringeth forth good fruit; but a corrupt tree bringeth forth evil fruit.*
>
> *A good tree cannot bring forth evil fruit, neither can a corrupt tree bring forth good fruit.*
>
> *Every tree that bringeth not forth good fruit is hewn down, and cast into the fire.*
>
> *Wherefore by their fruits ye shall know them."*

"Exactly," replied James. "And one of the first fruits is whether he testifies to the truth of Jesus, as Jesus testified to the truth of Moses and Abraham."

"Certainly," Youssef added, "the Holy Quran testifies to the truth of Jesus as well as Moses and Abraham and all of the prophets. Much of it is the recitation of the stories of the Bible to Muhammad's followers. Of course, He did not recite the dogma that Christians added after Jesus' time.

The angel Gabriel provided Him with new ways of understanding some of the old stories.

"But these teachings were directed, first and foremost, toward the savage tribes of Arabia, during the time when our people were deeply devoted to idol worship and when fighting between the many tribes was the norm. Although many Christians and Zoroastrians became Muslims, Muhammad's teachings had an appeal beyond them. They could reach tribes that the Christians and the Zoroastrians had been unable to reach.

"It spread among the nomadic peoples across the Sahara; it spread down almost the entire eastern side of Africa. And to the north and east, it spread not only across the Zoroastrian lands of Persia but also widely among the nomadic people of Central Asia—people who had not responded in large numbers to the Christian message.

"Eventually, Muhammad's teaching spread into western China and parts of Mongolia, across northern Hindustan, through parts of southeast Asia, southward through the Malay peninsula, and across the islands of the eastern ocean. And in all of these places, the people learned of the truth of Jesus because of what God had taught Muhammad in the Holy Quran."

Zach was taken aback. "I had never thought of it that way before," he replied.

"Indeed," continued Youssef, "until about three centuries ago, when Europe started spreading the Christian message by sailing the oceans, it was surely the case that more people around the world knew about Jesus as one of God's Messengers by learning it from the Quran rather than from the combined efforts of all the Christian countries."

After reflecting on this, James added, "I have to admit that Youssef may be right. Up until the late 1400s, Christianity was mostly confined to Europe, apart from Coptic Christians in Egypt and Ethiopia and a scattering of smaller Christian communities in various places in Asia."

"So spreading the teachings about Jesus and Moses and all of the past prophets to distant lands was one of the good fruits of the Prophet Muhammad. But there are many more; shared values across these wide areas, in which people were willing to submit their will to the will of God, led to the flourishing of civilization while Europe remained in its Dark Ages."

As the trail crossed over some of the low hills in the valley, Youssef pointed across the flat plain to larger hills about ten miles distant. "Nazareth," he said, "lies just beyond those hills."

They were about halfway there and the day was half spent, so they retired to the shade of a tree near a small spring for a midday meal while their animals drank their fill of the fresh water. The sun was strong, and the air was dry, so all enjoyed this break from their travels.

Youssef's account of the success of Islam raised questions in Zach's mind.

"If Islam was the pinnacle of civilization in the 1200s, as James indicated, then why are its people in such a condition as we find them today?"

Youssef winced slightly at this question. It was a topic he preferred to avoid.

"There were probably many reasons," he started. "One of the greatest was the destruction we suffered at the hands of the Mongolians with the rise of *Genghis Khan* and his descendants, with armies that swept across central Asia, into Eastern Europe, and down into Persia, Baghdad, and Damascus. They were finally stopped militarily by the Egyptian Mamluks just a short distance from here, at Ain Jalut." He nodded to the southeast.

"They caused untold destruction to the vast stores of knowledge housed in our leading cities. But they failed to convert the Muslims to a Mongolian belief system. On the contrary, in the generations that followed, most of the descendants of Genghis Khan, who ruled over vast areas across central Asia, adopted Islam instead.

"Alas, we never fully recovered from the Mongolian invasion. The Ottoman Empire arose from its ashes. It expanded until it dominated most of the Muslim world. It expanded even into Christian lands in southeast Europe. But our love of knowledge and discovery seemed to have been replaced by a love of power and wealth." Youssef sighed.

"Meanwhile," added James, "the love for knowledge and discovery was rekindled in Europe, sparked perhaps by the knowledge that some of the Crusaders discovered while in this Muslim area.

"And when the expansion of the Ottoman Empire blocked our overland trade routes to the East, we developed sailing ships, which opened our access not only to the East but to the whole world. That Ottoman blockade became a blessing in disguise for us."

"In more recent times," replied Youssef, "your missionaries have traveled around the world to teach the message of Jesus. They have reached some areas that Islam never reached.

"But when they reached Muslim communities, they had little success, because as Muslims, we already believe in Jesus. We would simply recite unto them the verse from the Holy Quran:

> '*We believe in God, and that which hath been sent down unto us and that which hath been sent down unto Abraham, and Ishmael, and Isaac, and Jacob, and the tribes, and that which was delivered unto Moses, and Jesus, and that which was delivered unto the prophets from their Lord: We make no distinction between any one of them, and to God are we resigned.*'[15]

"Since we already believe in Jesus, these missionaries had nothing to offer but their own interpretations and man-made doctrines, which were often confused—and which had already been the cause of much fighting even within the Christian communities. Who would rightly exchange the clear explanations of the Holy Quran for the argumentations and disputations of the various Christian churches?"

"That's an interesting perspective," acknowledged Zach. He found himself starting to understand more of the Islamic perspective than he originally thought he would.

Youssef continued, "The fruits of the Islamic civilization are clear for every unbiased mind to see: At a time when Christianity had carried the belief in one God little beyond the bounds of Europe, Islam arose to spread monotheism from the west coast of Africa to the islands of the Far East and from Africa's southeastern coast to the steppes of central Asia and western China.

"Muhammad's revelation has provided the foundations for a vast civilization, in which large parts of the world were at peace and the pursuit of knowledge and of sciences and the arts, as well as systems of law and justice, flourished. During the ages in which Christian Europe was sunk in darkness, Islamic civilization led the world in its discoveries, its architecture, and its devotion to learning.

"And the foundation for all of this was a high sense of morality and the obligation to do good based on the firm belief in one God and in a clear vision of the next world, wherein the good would be rewarded and the evil punished. All of this was brought to us through Muhammad's revelation of the Holy Quran.

"So please tell me, if these fruits are not good, what is? And since these are clearly good fruits, then, by Jesus' own standard, Muhammad is a good tree that has brought forth these good fruits. Therefore, He must be what He claimed to be—a true Prophet of God."

James and Zach sat quietly for a couple of moments, pondering in their minds what Youssef had said.

Finally, James simply nodded and said, "That is a very good argument. I might be able to cite a few bad leaders over the course of Islamic history but no more frequently than I could cite some bad leaders over the course of Christian history."

Back on the trail again, they rode on for a couple of miles as Zach reflected on this broader understanding of history. As they were climbing the hill leading toward Nazareth, Youssef paused, looked to the right, and pointed to a hill at the base of the Carmel range a few miles away. "The Hill of Megiddo," he said. "You may know of it by its Hebrew name, 'Armageddon.'"

"From the Book of Revelation?" Zach asked. "So this is where the final battle is to take place?"

"Only if you take the book literally," cautioned James. "This valley of Zebulon here was, in John's day, a vital strategic crossroads of ancient trade routes. So many groups fought to control it that 'Megiddo' became synonymous with 'major battle.' It doesn't mean that it will necessarily happen right here."

Entering Nazareth, Zach was surprised to find it was mostly an Arab town, although with several Christian holy places. Given its significance in Christian history, he had imagined it would be mostly Christian. He soon learned, however, the town was, in fact, mostly Christian. But these Christians spoke Arabic and wore Arabic clothes. He was finding here that is was necessary to let go of his old stereotypes, including the one that said all Arabs were Muslims and all Christians necessarily looked like Europeans.

"Do not make the same mistake as the Crusaders," James cautioned. "They inadvertently slaughtered many Christians during their campaigns, simply because these people spoke Arabic and wore the robes of the East."

They spent a couple of days there, visiting Christian holy places but also speaking with people in shops and inns and wherever they could, inquiring about whether they had heard reports of any children who seemed to have knowledge of things without having been taught. But the answer was always negative.

Zach was interested to learn that different Christian denominations could have different holy places that commemorated the same event. They visited the Roman Catholic Church of the Annunciation, which had been built a hundred years earlier over the sites of previous churches, which in turn were originally built over a grotto or small cave. This was believed to have been the childhood home of Mary, where she was living, presumably, when the angel Gabriel announced to her what would soon take place.

Then Zach and James found the nearby Greek Orthodox Church of the Annunciation, built over a spring from which, according to their tradition, Mary was drawing water when Gabriel appeared to her.

They were also surprised to discover both of these churches had been built under the encouragement of the local Muslim ruler, *Zahir al-Umar*, who had controlled this region during much of the 1700s. His example of religious tolerance had encouraged more Christian settlement in Nazareth and Akka as well as Jewish settlement in nearby Tiberias. Learning of him seemed to confirm much of what Youssef had taught them about tolerance between religions.

Chapter 14

VISIONS: MT. TABOR AND THE JORDAN VALLEY

THE FIRST RAIN OF the season fell during the night before they left Nazareth, cooling and clearing the air. Thus it was on a sparkling clear morning in mid-October that they departed from Nazareth with a south-bound caravan.

But at Zach's request, the trio broke off from the caravan to take a side trip to the top of nearby Mount Tabor. He had always wanted to see the place where Jesus' transfiguration had occurred, and he felt that it could be an important place in their search.

With the hot, hazy air of the summer gone, the day's journey would be short but steep. For although Mt. Tabor lay only a few miles east of Nazareth, reaching its summit required an ascent of almost 1,500 feet.

Matthew had simply described it as a "high mountain apart" in chapter 17 of his gospel, for unlike most of the hills of the Galilee, which were linked to adjoining hills, this one was surrounded on all sides by broad plains. The climb up the winding path leading to the top was exhausting, but the views from its heights were spectacular, especially on such a clear day.

Zach saw the great Jezreel Valley through which they had come spread out before him to the southwest. It was the major east–west connection, coming from the Bay of Akka-Haifa and its Mediterranean coastal trade routes at the west end, leading past Megiddo, and extending to the Jordan Valley at the east. That valley had its own north–south trade routes from the Hejaz along the shores of western Arabia up to Damascus and beyond.

The Jezreel Valley was the only place along these two north–south routes where the land rose smoothly and gradually from sea level before descending, again gradually, more than 1,000 feet to the Jordan River below. Thus, it had been for millennia a vital link between major trade routes in this part of the world. To control it was to control a large part of the region's wealth.

Gazing to the west beyond Nazareth, they could see a bit of the Mediterranean on the far horizon, while the northern horizon was dotted with the rolling hills of the Galilee. To the northeast, Mount Hermon— the tallest height in the Holy Land—was clearly visible and would soon be snow-capped.

Farther down and slightly farther toward the east, they caught glimpses of the Sea of Galilee, an area forever remembered as the site of so many of Jesus' teachings. To the east, across the Jordan Valley, lay the adjacent high land of the Syrian province. And to the southeast, the Jordan Valley itself was clearly visible, with the Jordan River at its center—the site not only of John's baptisms and his preparations for the coming of Jesus but also the river whose crossing had become synonymous with entry to the Holy Land itself, as the followers of Moses had done after their escape from enslavement in Egypt and their forty years of wandering in the wilderness of the Sinai and Jordan. Thus, from this spot, they could see not only the entire width of the Holy Land but, in some respects, much of the panorama of Western religious history.

"Being here, it is easy to understand why this spot was the scene of Jesus' transfiguration," thought Zach. "There is something about high places with panoramic vistas that inspires larger thought and loftier reflections. Whether it is simply that one has removed himself from the day-to-day life of the fields, farms, and markets or whether the clear skies and vast scenes inspires one to ask larger questions and think larger thoughts, I do not know. But this is certainly an inspiring place!"

Alas, the very benefits of the view had, over the centuries, led to a problematic history. Sitting high above strategic trade routes had a military significance in addition to the religious one.

Although three Byzantine churches and a monastery had been built here in the early Christian centuries, the Islamic conquest, later Crusaders' attacks, and finally the *Mamluk Sultan* of Egypt had succeeded in destroying most of what had been built.

Within the few remaining rooms of the ruined fortifications, there lived a couple of Franciscan monks—the only ones who were there to greet the travelers when they arrived at the summit. They spoke little of any of the languages that Zach, James, or Youssef knew and seemed to come forth from their dark rooms more out of curiosity rather than to offer any hospitality.

But the travelers had no cause for complaint, as they had not been certain whether anyone would be up there, and they were fully provisioned. The top of the mountain had a flat area that afforded plenty of room to pitch their tents without disturbing the monks.[16]

After sharing an evening meal, as the sun was setting over the Mediterranean Sea in the distance, James set out to find the ruins of one of the ancient churches, built there over a thousand years before. Finding it, he discovered a large stone slab upon which to sit and started his evening prayers and meditations.

He thought particularly of that time long ago when Jesus, Peter, James, and John had been on this mountaintop—perhaps in this very spot—and how the disciples had witnessed a vision of Jesus transfigured, with His face shining *"brighter than the sun"* and His robes shining with light. And even more miraculously, how they heard the voice of God coming from a cloud and had seen Jesus talking with Moses and Elijah.

He thought about how this indicated that those two ancient beacons of God's guidance were still alive in the world of the spirit.

His disciples were no doubt heartened when Jesus explained to them, as they descended down the mountain, that John the Baptist was Elijah. Although John had recently been beheaded by Herod, it was clear that he was still very much alive in the spiritual world—a world in which Jesus seemed to be able to dwell even while He was also living on Earth.

In this spot, James prayed long and arduously that Jesus would guide them in their search and that their efforts might not be in vain. He also remembered Caroline and Joseph, his deceased wife and son, and prayed fervently that they might hear his call for guidance and somehow help in showing him the right way. The sun had vanished, and a clear, moonless night had descended, with thousands of glittering stars, by the time James finished and found his way back to their encampment.

His companions were already sleeping. The journey of the day had tired him, and soon he, too, was fast asleep.

At some point during the night, as he was dreaming, he found himself back at the spot overlooking the surrounding vistas. It was earliest morning, and the sky was just getting light in the east. But as he looked, he saw a peculiar sight: The light was growing brightest at two points on the horizon— one to the northeast and one to the southeast.

As he watched toward the northeast, he saw a large arch of illumination appear over the horizon above the area where the sun was rising, in the direction toward Damascus. Upon the arch were emblazoned the letters M-A-G-I.

And as he looked farther, he saw men on camels coming through the arch, silhouetted by the rising sun and carefully carrying their Holy Book, the Zoroastrian *Avesta*, with them as they proceeded toward the Holy Land from their homeland in northern Persia.

Then he turned to the southeast, and looking down the length of the Jordan Valley, he saw more men on camels. They, too, were coming through a brilliant arch, silhouetted by a rising sun. On this arch were emblazoned the numerals 1-2-6-0. They, too, were carrying a Holy Book—the Quran. He realized these men represented the Islamic nation coming northwest along the Hejaz from Mecca and from thence into the Holy Land via the Jordan Valley.

Prophetic linkages connecting to the Holy Land

He realized, as he saw this, that in the same way that the story of the Magi was a gateway to recognizing that the Magi followed a true revelation, so also the fulfillment of the prophecies in both Daniel and the Book of Revelation regarding the year 1260 was a gateway leading to a recognition that the revelation of the Quran must also be true.

The fact that 1260 in the Islamic calendar was the very same year as 1844 in the Christian calendar, and that both dates were exactly 2,300 years after the Zoroastrian king's order to rebuild Jerusalem, just as Daniel had foretold, seemed to tie all of these religions together. How could it be otherwise?

As he was thinking this over, he noticed a light glowing from behind him. He turned and was startled to see three brilliantly luminous figures. He wondered if these might be the same as the three who had been described in Matthew. They were pleased to see that James had reached this new understanding. They smiled to see both the coming of the Magi and the coming of the Muslims.

They then shifted their gaze, looking due east across the Jordan Valley. And as they looked, the lights of the Magi and of the Muslims faded while a brilliant new star appeared above the distant eastern horizon. It appeared the same as the star that James had always imagined when hearing the story of the Wise Men. Then one of the figures said to the other, "God is calling upon your spirit to once again illuminate the earth."

Then, turning to the third one, he said, "And your spirit will soon follow." They all paused for a while, looking eastward, as if contemplating the momentous events that lay ahead.

This third one looked toward James. He seemed overjoyed to find someone who was searching. And into James' mind came the words *"Other sheep I have, which are not of this fold: them also I must bring, and they shall hear my voice; and there shall be one fold, and one shepherd."*

James recalled these words from the tenth chapter of John. He realized that bringing the sheep together into one fold was not a matter of converting Muslims and Zoroastrians to Christianity, for Christianity, too, was one of the many folds.

Instead, it meant something much deeper. He realized that each religion was going to have to give up much of the man-made orthodoxy and dogma it had developed over the centuries. Deep, deep down there was common, solid bedrock of truth. But the damaged structures of many ages would have to be cleared away before they could, together, start to build anew.

He glanced at the ruined structures on the hilltop around him—they seemed to be a metaphor of what had happened among the religions. Structures built to the glory of God lay in ruins because of man's misunderstanding of the true nature of the religions that had inspired them. He felt that he was reaching a deeper level of understanding about all of these religions.

The luminous figures seemed pleased that James was reaching this understanding. Then the words *"I have yet many things to say unto you..."* came to James' thoughts. He immediately recognized this statement from Jesus, which John had recorded in chapter 16 of his gospel. He knew the rest of the statement by heart: *"...but ye cannot bear them now."* However, the luminous figure paused and looked directly into James' eyes with great intensity while the following words flooded into his mind: "NOW...ye can bear them!"

This statement was so powerful that James' whole body shook. And in that instant, he felt himself lying on the rocky ground of the mountaintop; he was no longer dreaming. The sun was just beginning to send its rays out from the eastern horizon. James arose to watch, to ponder the events of his dream, and to give thanks to his wife and son and to Jesus and to God, for he felt certain that someone had answered his prayers.

When Zach and Youssef awoke a little later, James excitedly explained all that had happened—both his prayers and his dream.

"Well," said Zach with a sigh, "if your vision was true, it might have implications regarding what we have been thinking about and wondering about ever since we discovered back on the ship that 1844 AD was the same as 1260 AH. Could it be that somewhere, way back in the seventh century AD, someone made a horrible mistake in deciding that the revelation of Muhammad was somehow 'evil'? And both religions have been living according to that mistake ever since."

James replied, "Alas, Eastern Orthodox Christendom—by far the largest branch of Christianity at that time—was in the habit of declaring as heretical anything that didn't agree with the clergy's narrow interpretation of Christ's teachings. They were attempting to force their views on others even within the Christian domain. So it was very easy for them to turn away from Muhammad without giving it a second thought."

"That sad decision," said Zach, "may have enabled the priests to keep their positions and to preserve their access to the donations that were flowing into their coffers, but it has condemned both religions to more than a thousand years of fighting—and cost untold thousands of lives lost over the centuries, on both sides. The thought of the wasted lives, the wasted treasures, and the wasted opportunities is almost unbearable."

"*Almost* unbearable," James echoed. And then, recalling the final words he had heard in his dream, he reminded them, "'*but NOW you can bear them.*'

"Learning about the mistakes that our ancestors have made over the centuries is indeed difficult to bear. But if we are all sheep of different folds

193

that will be gathered into one fold, then each fold will need to let go of some of its cherished orthodoxies and traditions as well as some of its hatreds of things past. It is the only way we can become a single fold following the good Shepherd."

Youssef smiled and nearly shouted, "God is the most great!" then said, "As long as you are in the Muslim world, this new understanding, which God has now revealed to you, will be a wondrous benefit."

Then he added, "You saw the Light rising in the East. Persia is the next nation to our east."

James replied, "Shaykh Hakim told us that we should travel to Persia. I wonder, what makes him think that the Promised One would come from there?"

Youssef answered, "No doubt he explained some of the traditions about how the return of Husayn will come from there. But in addition, the Quran itself warns Muhammad's Arabic followers that if they turned away from the true Path, God would substitute another people in their stead. When someone later asked Muhammad who this people might be, He pointed to His only Persian follower and said, 'This man and his people.'[17]

"So among those of us who expect the Promised One to appear in a conventional manner, as taught by those great teachers of Karbila, Shaykh Ahmad and Siyyid Kazim, it is not surprising that we should expect that He will come from Persia. For I fear that most of the Arabs as well as the Turks, following their Sunni Caliphs, have all too often turned away from the true Path, just as the glorious Quran foresaw. They have shed the blood of the divinely guided Imams and led us down a path guided by their own corrupt desires."

Zach and James were pleased to hear Youssef's frank acknowledgement that not all of the blame for the enmity that existed between Christianity and Islam should fall on the Christian side.

After breakfast they broke their camp, loaded the donkeys, and headed down the mountain and from thence down the gently descending plain into the Jordan Valley on their way to Jerusalem.

They reached the Jordan River by the end of the day and enjoyed a refreshing immersion in its cleansing waters, which flowed southward from the Sea of Galilee. It was somewhere very near here, along these banks, that John had been calling the Jewish people, preparing them for the coming of Jesus. Somewhere near here, Jesus Himself came forward to be baptized by John. The Gospel of John stated that it took place near Salim, and they had passed Tel Salim just a half hour before they reached the river.

They had descended almost 3,000 feet from the previous night's perch on Mt. Tabor to the bottom of the Jordan Valley and found the climate to be noticeably warmer, a welcome change as they were moving toward the cooler winter months. They rested comfortably that night.

The next morning, as they waited to join a passing caravan heading southward toward Jerusalem, Zach found himself still thinking about how to explain all he had learned to his friends back home.

"Our friends at home will remind us that Jesus is the *only begotten Son* of God according to John 3," he said. "So how does Muhammad fit in?"

Youssef said, "God does not beget children nor was He begotten. It says so in one of the very last chapters of the Quran. This was an idea of the ancient Greeks—all kinds of gods matching up and begetting new child gods. No one who believes in a single God can accept the idea that there are any child gods."

"Yes," acknowledged James, "this is a point that Christians and Muslims have disputed for many centuries. I looked into this question when I was in Egypt, and I think we are sitting near the very spot that holds the answer to this dilemma."

"What do you mean?" replied Zach.

"The answer lies in the original meaning of the term 'begotten.' Naturally, we associate the word with physically creating a child, as prospective parents normally do. And the Quran states God did not create Jesus as a physical 'son' in this manner."

Youssef nodded in agreement.

James continued, "But the intention of the original word in the Bible was different. That word meant 'to generate' or 'to send forth.' So in creating children, we are sending them forth into the world. Certainly, God sent Jesus forth into the world, much as a father, who has raised a son, sends his son out into the world.

"But this does not mean the infinite God of the universe was the physical father of Jesus. And while both Christians and Muslims, and even the Zoroastrians, accept that there was some miracle associated with the virgin birth, to suggest that the eternal, unseen, limitless God of the universe would somehow confine Himself into a material form in order to become the physical father of a child makes no theological sense at all. That kind of thinking is more like Greek mythology, as Youssef said."

Youssef agreed, noting that the Quran recognized that Mary was a righteous woman and was a virgin at the time of Jesus' birth. "God caused a miracle of some sort to occur that enabled Mary to conceive and bear the child, Jesus, without the participation of any man. But God was not His physical father."

"So the reason our current location is significant," continued James, "is this: When Jesus was baptized somewhere close by, it is recorded in Luke 3 that the Holy Spirit descended on Him, and a voice came from heaven, which said, '*Thou art my beloved Son; in thee I am well pleased.*'"

"However, in place of the last phrase, other translators who carefully studied the ancient texts used the phrase '*today I have begotten thee.*'

"Now, if Jesus was *begotten* on the day of His baptism, and not on the day of His earthly birth, then clearly 'begotten' in this case means 'sending forth' rather than physically creating a child.

"So Jesus was 'begotten' in the sense that His spirit—the Holy Spirit that had descended upon Him—was 'sent forth' into the world. And it happened here, in this river, where He was baptized. Now, Youssef, is this sense of 'begotten' in keeping with the Quran's verse?"

"Yes indeed," Youssef replied, "and perhaps that is why Muhammad often referred to Jesus as the *Spirit* of God rather than the Son of God—it connotes closeness without suggesting multiple gods."

"This exact term 'begotten,'" continued James," is found again in Psalm 2:7 and even in Acts 13:33. And similar usages are found in I Corinthians 4:15 and in I Peter 1:3, as I recall. In all of them, it is used in the sense of sending forth rather than in the sense of causing a physical birth."

"That is fascinating," commented Zach. "It makes a lot of sense and seems to be in keeping with both a Christian understanding and a Muslim one. I'm beginning to see how much of the animosity between these religions began with small misunderstandings of language between people who were, perhaps, unwilling to try to find common ground."

"Yes," James noted, "to the clergy, agreement with the teachings of Muhammad would have meant the loss of their position of privilege. In the same way, the scribes and the Pharisees of Jesus' time could not accept His new explanations either."

"No doubt true," replied Zach, "but I still have one question: Aside from the 'begotten' part, was Jesus God's *only* son or not? Moreover, there are other places in the gospel where Jesus seems to say that He is the only Messenger."

"Claims of Christian exclusivity," James started, "can be found in various parts of the New Testament. But then, claims of Jewish exclusivity can be found in various part of the Old Testament, such as Moses' statement that no man could change the Law of God and indications that the Jews were God's 'chosen ones.'"

"In Islam," Youssef added, "there are similar claims. They do not negate the religions of the past, but sometimes they are taken to mean no prophet will come again. Indeed, some have interpreted a Quranic reference to Muhammad as the 'Seal of the Prophets,' implying that no other Prophet should ever appear. Yet at the same time, they believe that the Qaim or the Mahdi will appear. It is rather confusing."

"I have contemplated the confusion of these exclusivity claims deeply," replied James. "I think they arise from the fact that the Messengers must protect their teachings from the corruption of false prophets, who, after witnessing the spreading power of the new teachings, wish to exalt themselves by pretending to have their own authority, like the Messenger. There were many such counterfeit prophets among the early Christians, but eventually they were weeded out."

"Likewise among Islam," Youssef noted, "there were several, including *Musaylimah*, even during the Prophet's lifetime."[18]

"And so these statements of exclusivity," James continued, "while helpful—even essential—during the spring and summer seasons of each religion's growth, get carried over into the autumn and winter seasons and become obstacles when the springtime of the new Messenger appears."

Zach mulled this over and then said, "So when Jesus said in John 14 that *'no man cometh to the Father, but by me,'* He was only referring to the Christian age?"

"Well, He certainly was not referring to the pre-Christian age," James replied, "since the biblical prophets and many of the Jewish people obviously came 'to the Father' before Jesus ever appeared."

"Perhaps a similar limitation," Youssef offered, "also applies to a post-Christian age, that is, after the appearance of Muhammad, since many non-Christian people came to understand the teaching of the oneness of God, and the truth of all the Prophets, through Muhammad."

"That is an interesting thought," James replied. "I have another one. Both of the quotes that Zach cited are from the Gospel of John. More than any other writer of the gospels, John wrote in spiritual terms, not in physical ones. For instance, his description of the coming of Jesus ignored Jesus' birth entirely and spoke instead of how the Word of God came into the world.

"So when John quotes Jesus here, perhaps He is speaking of the eternal Christ—that Spirit that existed *'before Abraham was,'* as he noted in John 8:58—rather than the person of Jesus, who appeared and taught for only a few years.

"If, in addition to Jesus, this eternal Spirit was also found in Abraham and Moses, and perhaps even in Zoroaster and Muhammad, then we could understand this statement to mean we cannot find our way to God simply by our own efforts alone. We must receive our knowledge of Him through one of these great Beings, these Messengers of God. This kind of an understanding does not place any one of Them above the Others. Indeed, it suggests that we can understand all of Them as a single Voice or Spirit."

"Yes," Youssef added, "if we could soar above the realm of names for a moment and look instead at fundamental spiritual realities, we would realize all of the Prophets are a single Spirit. Muhammad Himself said, 'I am all the Prophets.'

"All that we know of God and the world of the spirit comes through this Prophet, who has appeared with many names and in various places and ages to teach us. No man can truly approach God unless he comes by the way of the teachings of this Prophet. God gives us these teachings by His grace, but then it is up to us to do the work of following in His way. Man cannot find an independent way."

"My goodness!" Zach leaned back. "Those are some challenging thoughts!"

"Yes," acknowledged James, "but thinking back on my dream and how the prophecies of these religions seem to interconnect them all, it forces me to consider how all of this is coming from a single Divine Source."

Zach's head felt stretched. But it was not throbbing this time. He was beginning to become accustomed to the barrage of new ideas.

A caravan was approaching, so they moved out to join it. After some time to reflect on the thoughts James and Youssef had shared, Zach spoke. "The explanations you two have offered might provide an answer to a question I've often wondered about concerning the name of the One who will return. Some of the biblical references speak of Jesus' return as if it will be the same being with the same name. But others indicate a new name.

"For instance, in Acts 4, Peter said, '*There is none other name under heaven given among men, whereby we must be saved*,' and yet, in Revelation 2 and 3, Jesus says that He will write a '*new name*' in the future. So perhaps the former referred particularly to the time of Jesus, while the latter refers to the name of a future Messenger animated by the same Spirit."

"It is true," acknowledged James, "that Jesus also spoke of the coming of the next revelation, often in terms of His own return but sometimes in terms of another name.

"For instance, in chapters 14 through 16 of John, Jesus speaks of how He will send a '*Comforter*' or '*the Spirit of truth*.' Some of the quotes describe Him as the Holy Ghost, but others sound quite like a real person who is distinct from Jesus and who will '*reprove the world of sin*' and who '*shall not speak of Himself; but whatsoever He shall hear, that shall He speak*' and who will '*glorify*' Jesus."

Youssef replied, "Muhammad reproved the world of sin and did not assert any of His own ideas but only spoke what the angel Gabriel revealed to

Him. He also praised and glorified Jesus and testified to His truth. Thus all three qualifications that John provided are found in the life of Muhammad.

"Moreover, I've read that the name '*Comforter*' comes from the word '*Paraclete*' in the original Greek Bible. But in fact, this is a mis-transcription of the word '*Periclyte*,' that is, 'Illustrious.' And Illustrious (Ahmad) was one of the five names of Muhammad. So we believe that this must refer to Him."[19]

"That's a fascinating interpretation," replied Zach.

"But we must not get lost in the realm of names," cautioned James. "Names can lead, but they can also mislead. Isaiah 7:14 prophesied the name of the virgin's son would be 'Immanuel.' Yet this name was never used for Jesus. Instead, the intent of the prophecy was the spiritual reality of the name 'God with us,' as mentioned in the first chapter of Matthew.

"Likewise, as we look toward the future, Muslims, Christians, and Jews all speak of the return of the Messiah. He is one reality even if we have different names for Him."

*   *   *

THAT EVENING WHILE THEY shared a meal at the caravanserai, James recalled Shaykh Hakim's explanation of the Shia beliefs concerning the return of the Twelfth Imam, the Qaim.

"Since the Sunni branch of Islam does not accept the authority of the Imams," James asked Youssef, "what do the Sunnis believe about the coming of the next Messenger?"

"They believe in the 'Day of Judgment' and the 'Last Day,' which is generally understood to be the end of the world, when all the believers will be taken to paradise."

"Do they anticipate a certain year?"

"They speak of many signs, but I haven't heard of any consensus on a single year."

"And who will return? Will Muhammad come back?"

"No," replied Youssef. "After the Mahdi arises, they believe that Jesus will return."

"Jesus? Really?" said Zach incredulously. "Why would they believe in the return of Jesus instead of the return of Muhammad?"

Youssef shrugged. "It is their understanding, which is based on their interpretations of the Quran as well as the *Hadith*, that is, the traditionally reported sayings and actions of the Prophet, which were not revealed directly from Gabriel as the Quran was."

"So do they believe that Jesus will come down from the sky to save both the Christians and the Muslims?"

"Well," replied Youssef, "He will save the *true* Christians."

"And which denomination of Christianity is that?" asked Zach, wondering whether the Muslims favored the Catholics, the Protestants, or the Orthodox branch of Christianity.

"The true Christians are the Muslims," replied Youssef without hesitation. "For anyone who truly understood the spiritual essence of Jesus' teaching would have seen that same essence in the teachings of Muhammad, and he would have become a Muslim. And indeed, many Christians have become Muslims, especially in the early centuries."

"That is an astounding thought," replied James. "I can imagine many of my Christian friends would be shocked at the idea of seeing Christ descending from the sky only to save the Muslims while leaving the Christians behind!"

James and Zach both chuckled at the notion.

"Is it really so strange?" replied Youssef. "Did you not say that the Christians await the coming of the Messiah? Yet isn't this the same term for the Promised One that the Jews use?

"And when the Messiah comes, don't the Christians expect that He will save them while leaving the Jewish people behind? Isn't this because the Christians regard themselves as the true followers of Abraham and Moses? Do they not also teach that any Jew who truly understood the spiritual essence of Moses' teachings would have recognized that same essence in Jesus' teachings and would have become a Christian?"

James and Zach had to acknowledge these views were commonly held among many Christians. Once again, they were learning to see things from a new perspective.

"If you ever have any trouble understanding the Muslim relationship to the earlier religions, the first thing you should do is to consider the

Christian relationship to the Jewish religion. There are many, many parallels," concluded Youssef.

*   *   *

CONTINUING ALONG THE JORDAN River the following day, it occurred to Zach that he had not inquired about Youssef's connections in Jerusalem.

"My uncle, Shaykh Suleiman (Solomon) conducts trade between all of the Upper Galilee and Jerusalem," Youssef explained. "He comes south each year from Mays al-Jabal, a town north of the Sea of Galilee, to trade the things made in that area for things from Jerusalem. He is, of course, Shiite, and has a similar interest in the teachings of Shaykh Ahmad and Siyyid Kazim of Karbila.

"He also comes to pray at the holy Mosque of Al Aqsa in Jerusalem and to visit the Dome of the Rock. As you may know, Jerusalem is the most holy city to Muslims after Mecca and Medina—the cities of the Prophet."

Zach admitted he did not realize it had such significance to Islam.

"Yes," continued Youssef, "Muslims all over the world recognize Jerusalem not simply because of its association with the earlier Prophets but also because Muhammad Himself traveled there from Mecca in a single night on a flying horse, as bidden by the angel Gabriel. There they prayed, together with the earlier Prophets, on the rock where Abraham had almost sacrificed His son, and from there, Muhammad and Gabriel ascended into the highest heaven. There He again met the earlier Messengers. And there He received the law of daily prayer from God."

"Muhammad ascended into heaven?" Zach was surprised to hear this.

"Yes, like Jesus, He ascended from Jerusalem into heaven. But unlike Jesus, it was not at the end of His earthly life. After His ascent, He returned with Gabriel to Jerusalem and then to Mecca, all in a single night."

"That seems like a rather tall tale," Zach offered skeptically.

"But He could prove it!" Youssef insisted. "While returning, He could see all of the caravans with their goods heading southward to Medina, and He told His followers details about each, which no one could have known without seeing them. As the caravans arrived over the following days and weeks, it turned

202

out that His knowledge about them was accurate in every respect."

Zach thought about the Old Testament story of Elijah's ascent into heaven in a whirlwind and the chariot and horses of fire. He thought also about the Christian belief of Jesus' ascent into heaven and especially about Reverend Bush's explanation of how it could refer to Jesus' spirit rather than His body.

So he asked, "Was it Muhammad's body that flew to Jerusalem and then ascended to heaven and returned, or was it His spirit that did these things?"

"Ah," Youssef smiled, "you have asked a vital question!

"For many centuries, nearly all Muslim leaders have taught that Muhammad made His amazing 'Night Journey' in bodily form. But Shaykh Ahmad—that great teacher in Karbila—taught us that this journey was a journey of His spirit. Many leading Islamic preachers denounced the shaykh for teaching such a revolutionary idea and would have branded him a heretic except that the Shah of Persia was favorably inclined toward his teachings."

Zach replied, "Do you know that we have the very same contention in the West? Many Christians believe Jesus' body ascended to heaven after His crucifixion and that it is—even to this day—floating around somewhere in the clouds.

"To suggest otherwise is a terrible heresy in many quarters. It can result in their congregation closing off all association with anyone who holds such a belief. Yet there are a few of us who understand it was His spirit that ascended into heaven, not His body.

"It still amazes me," Zach continued after a reflective pause, "to learn just how similar the condition of Islam is when compared to the condition of Christianity"

"Yes," Youssef agreed, "and I fear the large majority of those in both faiths will have difficulties relearning the teachings of their own religion from a spiritual perspective."

"How sad," thought Zach. "The peoples of both religions have become so focused on material things that they even see the stories from their own religions in material terms. And how," he wondered, "can they be awakened from such a deep spiritual slumber?"

Zach and James were grateful to be following the Jordan River, with access to fresh water and frequent places where they could pass beneath the shade of trees, which grew near its banks. The hills beyond the river's plain looked dry and barren.

They had nearly reached the Dead Sea when the caravan turned to the right, away from the river, and started a gradual ascent from this, the lowest spot on the face of the earth. A few miles ahead was their destination for the day: the ancient city of Jericho, near the spot where Joshua led the Jewish people into the Promised Land, bringing to an end their forty years of wandering in the desert after their exodus from Egypt.

Zach wondered how long it would be before their own wandering in search of the Promised One would come to an end.

Chapter 15

THE SEARCH IN JERUSALEM

AFTER AN EXHAUSTING CLIMB from Jericho up a narrow winding gully, or *wadi*, that cut through the hills, they came out of the Jordan Valley and reached the ancient walled city of Jerusalem.

Jerusalem!

It was the focus of so much attention from the Western world that Christian maps were formerly oriented with Jerusalem and the East at the top. Hence, "to orient" oneself became synonymous with facing eastward.

Passing through the massive Damascus Gate, Youssef guided them along the winding passageways of the Muslim Quarter until they reached a walled compound. Zach and James were surprised to see its size and opulence, which were much greater than either of them had expected.

The muscular guard who stood at the entrance gate recognized Youssef immediately and bowed slightly as he bade them to enter. They left their animals in the care of the stable keeper, and after washing off the dust of travel in the nearby fountain, they climbed the marble steps. Passing through the portico with its granite columns, they entered the magnificently decorated house. Leaving their shoes behind, they crossed the main hall, which was covered with beautiful Persian carpets. Youssef bade them be seated on the soft cushions on the floor. Servants soon brought in an ornate samovar and a silver tray with fine china teacups. Several platters of delicious food followed.

Suleiman arrived presently. He appeared to be about fifty years of age and walked with a distinguished bearing. He wore a green turban like Youssef's, with a similar family insignia. Zach realized the family had connections to some significant wealth, and the other Arabs they'd encountered would have known it was wise to avoid fighting with a family of such stature. Thus, their protection during their travels was assured.

Youssef provided introductions and explained he hoped to remain a couple of weeks to take care of some business matters while his friends explored the city. Suleiman was pleased to have the company, and James and Zach thanked him profusely for his warm hospitality.

After some talk about their journey, James said, "In Akka, we spoke with Shaykh Hakim, who has recommended that we meet you. We were keenly interested to learn from him of certain connections in the realm of prophecy concerning the coming of the Promised One that are common to both Islam and Christianity."

He proceeded to explain their understanding of the prophecies of Daniel and how they matched exactly the Shia belief concerning the year 1260 AH—both in the upcoming year.

"In the same way that the accuracy of the Magi's prophecy concerning the birth of Jesus compels us to recognize their Zoroastrian religion must have come from the same Divine Source as the Judeo-Christian religion, I am finding that the accuracy of these matching dates of the Christian and Muslim prophecies has forced me to the daunting conclusion that the revelation of Muhammad must also have come from this same Divine Source."

The shaykh smiled wryly. "A very difficult conclusion for you, no doubt," he said. "But for Muslims, we have, from the beginning, regarded the revelations to Abraham, Moses, Jesus, and Muhammad as having come from a single Divine Source. Even the Zoroastrian people, though little-mentioned in the Quran, were generally considered 'people of the Book.'"

"May I venture to suggest," James responded, "that you have, perhaps, little idea of just how difficult—indeed, how nearly impossible—it will be for us to advance this view when we return to our home countries? The vast majority of the people there have, for centuries, regarded the Founder of Islam as being somewhere between a misguided Arabic nomad and, if you will forgive the expression, a manifestation of Satan himself."

The shaykh looked saddened to hear this truth expressed so bluntly.

He sighed and said, "We have no illusions about how the Christian world regards Islam. Two centuries of Christian occupation of the Holy Land, including this very city," he said as he gestured toward his surroundings, "made that perfectly clear.

"What is not as clear," the shaykh suggested diplomatically, "is whether these great differences arose from the teachings of Jesus Himself or whether they arose as a result of the interpretations that later generations of Christians added to Christ's message.

"As to your people, who love Jesus so much that they claim He is clearly superior to Muhammad and also to any of *my* people who may be inclined to rank Muhammad above Jesus, I would ask that you relate to them the following tale that they might understand the truth of the matter:

"Once upon a time, there were two young children among those who attended the school of the good King's royal court. This was the school that trained all of the children of the royal family and the children of the King's most important advisors.

"One day, these two children got into an argument concerning which of their teachers was more knowledgeable. The younger child insisted his teacher must be greater since his teacher was the first one to teach the children and he taught the fundamentals of reading and mathematics, which is the very basis for all other learning. 'This is so important,' he insisted, 'that surely they must assign the best and most knowledgeable teacher to this first class.'

"But the slightly older child said, 'No! My teacher teaches us greater things, such as multiplication and division. Your teacher can teach only adding and subtracting. My teacher teaches fine writing of whole words. Your teacher teaches only the printing of the letters. Clearly my teacher knows more than your teacher. That is why he is able to teach us more.'

"The arguing went back and forth, growing louder each time.

"As it happened, the King was passing by and heard the children arguing. He stopped and asked the children what they were squabbling about. After hearing their arguments, the King smiled kindly and explained:

"'Children, you should know that both of your teachers have studied for many years. Both of them know *many, many* things of which you have never heard—nay, things that you cannot even imagine. Why, in the realm of mathematics alone, they both know far more than adding, subtracting, multiplying, and dividing. They both know of exponents and square roots, of algebra and geometry, of trigonometry and calculus. Do you have any idea what these things are?'

"The boys shook their heads, saying, 'No.'

"'Moreover,' the King continued, 'they have both learned all of these things from the same royal academy and from the same royal library. Their knowledge comes from one common source.'

"'But,' he continued, 'they cannot teach you *all* that they know. You are not ready for most of these things. Gradually, step by step, you will grow in your knowledge. What you learn this year will make it possible for you to learn more next year. But each year, the teachers will teach you only those things that you are capable of learning.'

"The two boys fell silent as they reflected, in light of the King's explanation, on how foolish their arguments had been.

"That day, the children learned an important lesson about the nature of their teachers and why they appeared to have different degrees of knowledge even though they both came from the same royal academy.

"Now, when all of us, as children in the school of the Spirit, realize all of the Divine Teachers have a knowledge that is vastly beyond what any man on Earth can imagine, and when we understand these Teachers will always limit Their message to the capacity of the people They are teaching, then perhaps we will realize how foolish it is to argue about which Divine Teacher was better than the other."

After a thoughtful pause, James said cautiously, "I suppose, perhaps, if we can help people step back from their own situation—from their particular favorite teacher—and see the whole picture, then they might begin to understand this better. Eventually, we will all come to see the unity between these Messengers of God more clearly."

Zach agreed it was a profound lesson and tried to envision occasions at home when he could use it. He would keep it ready for what he felt sure would be a wave of rejection by his American countrymen unless he explained things delicately, helping them to see how the return of the Promised One would save both Christians and Muslims.

That evening, Zach mentioned to James that he would like to read an English translation of the Quran but was unsure whether they could find one. James said they would likely find a copy at the British Consulate.

"The British have a consular office here?" asked Zach with surprise.

"We established it five years ago," replied James calmly, well aware of the British Empire's reach around the globe.

Zach smiled. He was once again grateful to be traveling with a citizen of a global empire.

The following day, they found the consulate, where James enjoyed some proper English tea and a temporary return to all of the pleasant manners of his home country.

In 1734 George Sale, a British orientalist, completed the only direct translation of the Quran from Arabic to English. A copy was available here, which they gladly purchased. It was copiously annotated, with a large introductory section explaining many of the particulars of the Muslim world; Zach found it to be exactly what he had hoped for.

They enjoyed the most wonderful meals with Suleiman each evening as they discussed the events or thoughts of the day. One evening after they finished eating, Suleiman's cat came in and sat next to him. He petted her lovingly.

"This cat," remarked Suleiman, "once taught me one of the most important lessons I have ever learned about God's Messengers."

"Do tell," urged James with raised eyebrows.

"Once, as I was seated at this very spot," he replied, pointing to the carpeted floor on which they sat, "I was reading one of the masterful works of the mystic Persian poet *Rumi*. As I was reading, my cat came by, purring and wanting my attention. But I was too engrossed in my reading.

"At length, I noticed the cat looking up at me and then looking at the pages, as if to ask why I was spending so much time staring at this pile of papers with all of the ink markings on it. Finally, my cat simply laid down on the book, forcing me to pay some attention to her.

"Later, in reflecting on the episode from my cat's perspective, I realized that she has no concept of reading nor has she any knowledge of the worlds of wisdom that leap from the pages of a book into my head. My behavior of staring at the pages for long periods must have seemed extremely odd, even nonsensical, to her."

"Yes," said James, "but what does this have to do with God's Messengers?"

"It is simply this: The Messengers live in a realm that is somewhere between us and God. It is as far removed from our realm as ours is removed from my cat's realm.

"Sometimes God's Messengers may say or do things that are difficult for His followers to understand at the time. Whether it was Moses' killing of the Egyptian, Jesus overturning the money tables in the Temple area, or Muhammad's prayer when He ceased facing Jerusalem and started facing Mecca, or other things. These may seem rash or even nonsensical at the time, especially if we are thinking of God's Messenger as just an intelligent man. But when we understand that He is living in a world far above ours, seeing things from a perspective and with a depth of knowledge that we could not possibly understand, then we can more easily follow, and we will attain a wonderful degree of steadfastness in our faith."

After a moment of quiet reflection, Zach simply said, "Thank you. That is indeed a most valuable lesson and something we should keep in mind as we learn more about Muhammad and, if we are so blessed, when we find the Promised One."

James and Zach felt honored when Suleiman invited them to join Youssef and him on a visit to the "Noble Sanctuary," as it was called—the Al Aqsa Mosque and the Dome of the Rock—on the upcoming Friday, the Muslim holy day. These were located on the plaza on which the Jewish Temple had stood, prior to its destruction by the Romans in 70 AD.

From the outside, the Al Aqsa Mosque appeared to be simply a large stone structure and, while carefully carved, not particularly dramatic.

Its beauty was on the inside, where colored stone arches, stained glass windows, polished granite columns, richly decorated walls and ceilings, and a floor covered with expensive prayer mats all combined to testify to the countless hours of dedicated effort that went into producing a site of such exquisite beauty.

James and Zach had been watching the Muslims pray for several weeks now, so it no longer felt strange. They therefore found it relatively easy to join their Muslim friends in the public prayers in the mosque, and no one outside of their little band saw it as anything unusual.

Afterward, they toured the magnificent Dome of the Rock. Decorated in brilliant turquoise-, emerald-, and gold-colored tiles and surmounted with a large dome, it was clearly the most visible jewel in all of the Holy City. The inside had, again, ornately decorated walls and ceilings. But there was no room for a large prayer hall here, for the entire central area was a bare slab of rock.

"Here," declared Youssef, "is where Abraham demonstrated his obedience to God by being willing to sacrifice his firstborn son, Ishmael."

Zach politely corrected, "As I recall, it was Isaac whom He was called upon to sacrifice."

James interjected, "I, uh, know this has been a dispute between the Jews and the Muslims since the Quran first appeared. For although Genesis 22 says it was Isaac, some of my Egyptian coworkers once told me that chapter 37 of the Quran clearly implies that it was Abraham's firstborn, that is, Ishmael."

But Suleiman shook his head. "Alas, how few have stopped to ponder the true meaning of Abraham's sacrifice! He—who had been unable to have a child until an advanced age—cherished His son greatly. Yet when God called upon him to give up the one thing he cherished most, he was willing to do so. His son, as the Quran notes, willingly accepted God's command.

"To the Jewish people, the thing that was most dear to Abraham would have been Isaac. But to the Arabs, as the descendants of Ishmael, it would certainly have been Ishmael. So you see, both of these Holy Books convey the same spiritual teaching, although their details are adjusted to suit the people to whom they are revealed.

"If we wish to follow the example of our forefather, Abraham, we must be willing to sacrifice those things which we cherish most of all. This willingness to submit to God's will was the true basis for His covenant with Abraham."

"Wisely spoken," said James. "I can see why you are named Solomon the Wise. Similarly, after Abraham, in order to remain true to God's covenant, the Jews of Moses' time had to give up their known life in Egypt for the uncertain life in the wilderness of the Sinai.

"At the time of Jesus, the Jews had to sacrifice their expectation of a kingly Messiah who would slay their Roman overlords and free Jerusalem from the empire's yoke. They also had to be willing to let go of some of the laws of the dispensation of Moses. And they had to sacrifice the opinions of friends and family in order to follow the Messiah. Many successfully made this sacrifice and became Christians, although many others did not."

"And to follow Muhammad," Youssef added, "the Christians of that time had to let go of some of their beliefs, including the belief that Jesus was a part of God or that God could only send His Messengers to the Christian world. And so gradually, many, although not all, of the Christians from northern Africa, Syria, Mesopotamia, and elsewhere were able to make this transition and became Muslims."

"Yes," Suleiman summarized, "in each age, severe tests have been given to separate the wheat from the chaff or the sheep that are willing to follow God's new Messenger from the stubborn goats. And the people of that age are faced with that timeless question: Are you willing to sacrifice some of your old beliefs, some of those things that are most dear to you, in order to remain true to God's holy covenant? Can you follow the example of Abraham's willingness to sacrifice that which was most dear to Him?"

"So the question for us today," Zach added ominously, "is, which old ideas will we be called upon to sacrifice when the Messiah returns?"

"I have reflected much upon that very question," offered James. "In John 10, Christ said that upon His return, He will gather together the many folds of God's followers. Since these folds now include not only a host of Christian denominations but many Jewish interpretations of theological matters as well as the people of the Zoroastrian faith, and—as I'm coming to understand—the vast number of Islamic schools of thought, it will be absolutely necessary for each one of them to place some parts of their understandings, interpretations, and manmade doctrines on the altar of sacrifice in order to come together into the single fold.

"Many will, no doubt, refuse to give up anything. These will be the goats of the new age, known for their stubbornness. But others will hear the eternal spiritual truths of the Promised One, and they will recognize this as the same Spirit—the same Voice—that originally animated their own religion, just as Jesus had explained when describing the voice of the Good Shepherd in verses 3 and 4 of that same chapter of John.

"And they will be willing to sacrifice some of their former beliefs and dogma because, like Abraham, they want to be true to the Covenant of God."

"I suppose," Zach said tentatively, "that giving up our past misunderstanding of the nature of other faiths will be one of the biggest sacrifices that our friends back home will be called upon to make. It has been a challenge for me."

"Yes indeed. We can only hope that, like Abraham, they will be willing to sacrifice some of the things they love the most," concluded James.

They departed from the Dome of the Rock with a much deeper understanding of the lesson gleaned from the sacrifice Abraham had been willing to make at that place several millennia ago.

As they wandered on the plaza along the east wall and looked toward the Mount of Olives, Zach noticed a large gate that was filled in with stone. He saw an older Jewish gentleman standing with his back toward the gate, eyes closed, as if quietly praying. When he at last opened his eyes, Zach asked him what he was doing.

"I am praying to the Lord as I face the Temple."

Zach looked westward across the empty northern section of the plaza and asked, "What temple?"

"You do not see it today," replied the old man, "but I see what stood on this spot 2,000 years ago."

"How do you know it was right here?" Zach asked.

213

"The Temple faced the Sha'ar HaRachamim—the Gate of Mercy, or *the Golden Gate* as the Christians would say, but formerly known as the Shushan Gate," he replied, nodding toward the stone gate behind him.

The mention of Shushan caught Zach's attention for he knew it was the city where Daniel had seen his vision with the amazing prophecies that had led them here.

"So the Temple and this gate and the whole eastern wall of the city all face toward Shushan, in Persia?"

"Is it so surprising?" the old man asked. "When the kings of Persia released my people from their captivity to return to rebuild our holy city, the people were grateful. The Holy Land was still a part of the Persian Empire at that time.

"Perhaps they oriented their city walls toward the Shushan capital to honor this; perhaps also in remembrance of Esther, who became the queen there; or perhaps in remembrance of the vision of the prophet Daniel. But most likely in anticipation of the fulfillment of the verses from the prophet Yechezkel."

"Which verses?" inquired Zach, recognizing now the Hebrew term for Ezekiel.

"You may recall that after he described the Temple, he wrote in chapter 43 that the Lord '*brought me to the gate, even the gate that looketh toward the east; and, behold, the glory of the God of Israel came from the way of the east; and His voice was like the sound of many waters; and the earth did shine with His glory.*'"

After a thoughtful pause, Zach asked, "Do you believe that the Messiah will come from the east?"

"Yes," was the man's reply, "this is why the Temple and its gate look toward the east."

Zach thought for a moment and then replied, "Then why do you face the Temple but turn your back to the gate and the east?"

The man stopped as if he had never thought about this question. Then he said, "I suppose...it is because I am looking toward the past, not toward the future."

He then picked up his things and started walking with them as they continued their conversation.

"Where are you going?" he asked Zach.

"We are returning to our host's home and from there northward and possibly to the east—possibly even to Shushan," replied Zach as he began again to contemplate the possibility of making the "Great Crossing" eastward that Shaykh Hakim had described.

"If you go to Shushan, you must say a prayer for me at the tomb of the prophet Daniel."

"Daniel's tomb is in Shushan?" inquired Zach.

"Yes, it has been there since ancient times, according to my friends from that region," replied the gentleman.

Zach responded, "I would like to visit it, if we travel that far." Then he added, "And where are you going?"

"I am going over to the Western Wall, where I can pray facing east, toward *both* the Temple and the gate, toward the past and the future."

Zach thanked the old gentleman much for sharing his thoughts, and they parted.

*　　　*　　　*

THEY HAD A FEW days to visit significant sites in the city. They continued to inquire whether anyone had heard of a child born in recent years with innate knowledge. But the response was always the same as it had been elsewhere.

They walked the Via Dolorosa, with the fourteen stations at which Christian pilgrims had, for centuries, recalled the events that occurred on Jesus' final journey on Earth. It seemed odd to find the place of His crucifixion at its end, enclosed in the rather dark church and surrounded with statues and candles, since Zach had correctly envisioned it as having been outside.

James explained how, over centuries of veneration, the Church of the Holy Sepulcher had been built to enclose this formerly open space and the walls of the city had been expanded to enclose an area that was formerly outside of the city.

The next day they set out from the city with Youssef to visit both the Mount of Olives and Bethlehem. It was not a great distance to the former,

215

but James and Zach felt as if they were walking through the valley of death since much of the area was filled with graves.

"It is because so many Jews and Christians, and even some Muslims, wish to be buried here, thinking they will be the first to see the Messiah when the great resurrection takes place," explained Youssef.

"A mute testimony to man's misunderstanding of the spiritual message of the Scriptures," noted Zach.

"Yes," James added, "I recall Matthew's statement that after Jesus was crucified, many of the saints who had died arose and went into Jerusalem. If it was taken literally, I believe this amazing event would certainly have been recorded by all the historians at the time—how much more so by the other writers of the Gospels.

"The fact that they are all silent leads me to believe Matthew is likely trying to describe a spiritual reality, saying the saints witnessed Jesus' sacrifice from the spiritual world and were able to have a great effect from that realm on many of those who were living."

The Mount of Olives was the last place where Jesus' disciples saw their visions of Him, as noted in the first chapter of the Book of the Acts of the Apostles. The only structure commemorating this was a small domed chapel-mosque owned and maintained by the Muslim community that recognized that Jesus' ascension was significant to the Christians at least.‡‡

But for Zach and James, their interest in the Mount of Olives was their remembrance of Jesus' most prophetic teaching—His last major talk, as recorded in Matthew 24 and 25.

"Here was the spot from whence Jesus so clearly forecast the destruction of the Temple in Jerusalem, which came to pass less than forty years later," said Zach with a sigh. "How many people, do you suppose, remembered His prophecy when it was fulfilled?"

"I don't know," replied James. "I only know that the persecution the early followers endured at the hands of the Jews turned out to be a blessing in disguise because it caused many of them to spread away from Jerusalem. So the final devastation that occurred here did not affect them as drastically."

---

‡‡ Although there are currently several Christian structures on the Mount of Olives, none of these were in existence at the time of our story.

216

"Here, also," Zach added, "He gave us the two greatest signs of the end to watch for, which have brought us here today. Firstly, He taught that the carrying of the gospel to all of the nations would mark the end of the age and, secondly, that we should then look to the prophecies of Daniel to understand the timing."

"And I would add a third," said James. "We should look to the east when searching for Him."

This last point had weighed on Zach's thoughts.

They spent a while in silent contemplation here at the top of the Mount as they looked over the city of such historic significance and considered how many steps in the spiritual development of Western civilization had occurred within the spaces they could see from this very spot.

They continued onward to Bethlehem—the city where King David had been anointed by the prophet Samuel. Here, they were grateful to be able to find a room in an inn.

*　　*　　*

THE NEXT MORNING, UPON visiting the Church of the Nativity, Zach and James were surprised to find it in rather poor condition.

"*The Jerusalem earthquake*," explained Youssef, "struck here nine years ago. Much of the damage, especially in Christian holy places, has not yet been repaired."

Nevertheless, a Greek monk greeted them outside and showed them the site, which had been identified by Saint Helena, the mother of Constantine, in the early 300s. He explained it had been rebuilt in 565 AD and had remained essentially in its same form ever since. It escaped destruction during the Persian invasion in 614 AD. The Persian commander, *Shahrbaraz,* gazed upon the mosaic and, noting that it depicted people in Persian clothes, he ordered it to be left unharmed.

They stayed a long time at the grotto that had once housed the manger where Jesus lay. Here, in this humble spot, was the place where the shepherds had worshipped the infant Jesus. And in this vicinity, the Wise Men had finally found the King of the Jews.

Zach wanted to speak directly to some Zoroastrians and learn from them whatever he could about the search the Wise Men conducted long ago. If the Zoroastrian Magi had successfully found Jesus, maybe today's Zoroastrians would have some clues about where to look for His return.

Years before, he had read *The Travels of Marco Polo,* including Marco's description of visiting the tomb of the Wise Men, which he and his uncles had seen while traveling through northern Persia. It was, according to Marco, in the town of Saveh. Zach had found Saveh on a map of Persia along the ancient Silk Road between Baghdad and the Persian capital, Tehran.

Zach also thought about all of the other evidence pointing them to the east: the recognition that Daniel's vision had been revealed in Persia and how this might indicate it would be fulfilled in Persia; Jesus' reference in Matthew 24 to the coming of the Son of man from the east and shining to the west; the prophecies in Ezekiel; and the fact that the Temple faced toward Shushan—one of the Persian capitals *and* the city of Daniel's vision of the 2,300 years.

And, as he now knew, even among Muslims, there seemed to be some indications He would arise in Persia. Added to all this, he wanted to meet with this insightful teacher, Siyyid Kazim, whose teachings about the nature of the fulfillment of Islamic prophecies were surprisingly parallel to his own ideas about the nature of the return of Christ. Siyyid Kazim and his immediate followers were in Karbila, south of Baghdad, which was most of the way to Persia.

But Zach was worried that James might not be willing to undertake such a journey. He had convinced him to travel to the Holy Land. Extending the journey all the way to Persia was clearly beyond the scope of the original plan.

So, after much meditation, as they came forth from this holy place, Zach simply said he had decided to push onward toward Karbila and Persia.

"I have no right to ask you to prolong your journey with me," he explained to James that evening. "In London, you agreed only to come as far as the Holy Land. I did not realize then that I might need to go farther east. And so I will go.

"Yet your presence has been so wonderful, and your knowledge so helpful, that I cannot imagine continuing on without you."

"Nonsense!" James exclaimed. "Of course I will travel with you to Persia!" Zach's eyes lit up with joy.

James continued, "Don't you remember my dream while we were on Mt. Tabor? How I saw the light of the Wise Men coming from the northeast and the light of Islam coming from the southeast? And how, after that, I saw a new star rising on the eastern horizon? Those luminous figures were looking toward it and acknowledged that they must soon return. I knew from that moment that we, too, would have to travel to the East if we wanted to find the One for whom we are searching."

"Then," said Zach, as he rose and spoke in a triumphant tone, "our next destination is Karbila—and the presence of Siyyid Kazim. And from there, we go onward into Persia!" Together they now felt the spirit of adventure and discovery coursing through their veins.

*   *   *

ONCE BACK IN JERUSALEM, they discussed the question of how best to reach Karbila. Zach, being inclined toward sailing, suggested booking passage from Jaffa to Port Said, a 90-mile overland trip to Suez, thence south by ship around Arabia and into the Persian Gulf, and finally up the Euphrates River to Karbila.

But Suleiman pointed out that the prevailing winds in the Red Sea made southbound travel nearly impossible at this time of year. He suggested traveling with the caravans heading up to Damascus and beyond to Aleppo.

"Near there, you can find a boat traveling down the Euphrates River that goes all the way to Karbila. The overland section is a little longer, but the sailing distance is much less. And on the river, you are not exposed to the perils of a long sea voyage."

Although Zach did not worry much about the perils of sea travel, he recalled how the Euphrates route was the same one Abraham traveled on His journey after His banishment from Ur. It may also have been the route the Wise Men used when traveling to the Holy Land. He found the notion of following their path to be reassuring.

Youssef noted he had other obligations in Akka and could not join them in their long journey.

But Suleiman mentioned he had a friend in Tiberias, by the name of Musa (Moses), who wanted to make the pilgrimage to Karbila—one of the holy cities of Shia Islam—but could not afford to do so.

"I'm certain that Musa would be happy to assist you on your journey if you can help him with his expenses along the way."

Zach readily agreed. "It is a small price for having such a service."

And so the plan was set. Youssef would continue to travel with them north to Tiberias, on the western shore of the Sea of Galilee. Here, they would meet with Musa and prepare for the journey to Karbila while Youssef returned to Akka.

Suleiman dispatched a fast rider with a message to Musa so he might prepare for the journey. That evening, Zach penned a long letter to his family back home, explaining briefly what they had found and their decision to press onward to the Euphrates and Persia. He assured his sister that they were taking precautions for their safety by traveling with a local guide and almost always in caravans. He explained how he had heard that the safe travel season would begin soon, although he was not quite sure yet what this meant.

In the morning, he and James took the letter to the British consulate, paid for its postage to America, and started their preparations for the long journey ahead.

Chapter 16

ON THE ROAD TO DAMASCUS

THE EARLY NOVEMBER NIGHTS in Jerusalem were becoming chilly, so the traveling trio was pleased to descend back down to Jericho and the Jordan Valley, where the earth and sky were warmer. The recent rains had left a sheen of green scrub-grass on the parched landscape they had seen just a few weeks earlier. Bedouin encampments, with their flocks of sheep and goats grazing on the new growth, dotted the region.

On their third day out, Zach posed a question that had been on his mind.

"We have talked much about the Wise Men who found Jesus following the prophecies of their scriptures. And now we seek His return based on prophecies of the Old Testament, the New Testament, and perhaps even the Quran.

"But I was wondering: Why weren't there any prophecies about the coming of Muhammad that led people to him?"

Youssef replied, "Oh, but there were! There are five that I know of. Four of the seekers found Muhammad through Christian prophetic clues, including two Christians of Bosra, an Arab who had become a Christian in Mecca, and a Zoroastrian who had become a Christian. The fifth was a Jew from Syria who moved to Medina in search of the coming of the Prophet."

"Do tell us of each," requested Zach, curious to hear of these stories.

"Certainly. It is interesting that you should ask that question while we are here since some of the most amazing prophecies came via a Christian monk who lived in Bosra in a solitary cell just a couple of days' journey from here." He nodded toward the northeast.

"A Christian monk?" asked Zach, raising an eyebrow.

"Indeed so. The Jewish Bible and the Christian Bible provide some clues about the coming of a Prophet to the peoples of Arabia. But the most specific prophecies were recorded in sources that were *not* included among the books and letters that were later assembled into the Christian Bible.

"When the Roman armies came to destroy Jerusalem about 35 years after Jesus' crucifixion, many of the early Jewish Christians fled eastward into the hills beyond the Jordan River. They carried with them some of the earliest Christian writings. Several of these ancient works were preserved there for centuries, recopied carefully by dedicated Christian monks, especially among the Nestorian branch, which was later persecuted almost to extermination by the Roman Christians. But the Nestorians survived amongst the Zoroastrians in Persia and the East as well as in pockets in Syria—including the one in Bosra.

"And thus it was that *Bahira*, a monk who occupied a small and austere room, which had been used by many generations of monks before him, knew several details about the coming of a Prophet to the Arabian peoples. He knew that the time had drawn nigh.

"When Muhammad's uncle and guardian brought Muhammad, as a young boy of perhaps ten years, with them on a caravan journey to Syria, the caravan stopped in Bosra. It was here that Bahira recognized the Prophet-to-be, based on certain specific physical traits as well as His uncanny ability to answer all the questions that Bahira posed."[20]

James and Zach found it fascinating that the trait of innate knowledge, ascribed so clearly to Jesus, was also found in the stories of Muhammad's childhood.

"Surely it is a trait of a true Prophet—the first trait we have been seeking," replied James. "Even as a child, He has a knowledge that comes from no human source."

"So like the story of the Wise Men of Jesus' time, there was someone who recognized Muhammad even before He had grown to adulthood and before revelations started to come to Him?" Zach inquired.

"Yes," added Youssef, "and Bahira provided a warning to Muhammad's uncle to protect Him from those religious leaders—whether Christian or Jewish—who might wish to do Him harm. It was something similar to the warnings that the angels provided to both Mary and the Wise Men, which protected Jesus from Herod in those days."

"That is fascinating," replied Zach, his eyes now opened to some history seldom mentioned in the West. "But tell me also of the others."

"*Waraka*, son of Nawfal, was one of the few people in the Mecca area who believed in the oneness of God and the truth of Abraham during the days of idolatry, that is, before Muhammad's revelation. He was a first cousin of Khadija, the woman who would become Muhammad's wife.

"He became a Christian and studied the Bible extensively, including the prophecies of Jesus from the Gospel of John. He was also aware of prophecies from several other sources that indicated a Prophet was expected to appear in Arabia in the near future.

"One of those sources was another monk, named *Nestor*, again from Bosra, who had seen Muhammad during another caravan journey, some fifteen years after the episode with Bahira. That monk, too, recognized Muhammad as the Prophet. When word of this and other incidents reached Waraka, he was the first local person to believe Muhammad was the expected Prophet—about fifteen years before the revelations started.

"And from the Jewish side, there was a fourth seeker, known simply as *Ibn al-Hayyaban*. I do not know exactly what writings convinced him to move from Syria to Medina. Perhaps it was from the Bible, in the prayer of Habakkuk, in chapter 3, in which we read, '*God came from Teman*'—that is, the south—'*and the Holy One from Mount Paran. Selah.*'

"Paran is the wilderness of western Arabia, the mountain of Paran is near Mecca, and Sela is the Arabic name for a mountain by Medina. Or perhaps it was from chapter 18 of the Book of Deuteronomy, in which Moses tells His people that God will raise up a Prophet from amongst 'thy brethren.' The Jewish people, as descendants of Isaac, are 'brethren' to the Arab descendants of Ishmael since the two men were brothers.

"So perhaps Ibn al-Hayyaban was expecting a Prophet to arise from amongst the people of Ishmael, that is, from the people of western

Arabia. Perhaps this is why he moved there, fully expecting to find the new Prophet. Alas, he died a little before Muhammad appeared. Still, his teachings influenced some of the local Jews, who embraced Islam after the Prophet's arrival.

"But the last of these wise men, and the greatest in my mind, was *Salman*, who was originally a Zoroastrian from Persia. Although he was training to become a Zoroastrian priest, at age 19 he met a group of Nestorian Christians who impressed him so greatly that he decided to become a Christian in spite of much resistance from his family.

"Salman traveled for 35 years, learning more about the truth of Christianity from various monks, scholars, and priests throughout Mesopotamia and Syria. He also learned about the expectations these Christians had of a new Prophet who would appear in Arabia, including some particular characteristics to look for. The last of these scholars, on his deathbed, told Salman to go to the Hejaz and search for the new Prophet there.

"Salman no doubt prayed for guidance, which came in an interesting way: While en route to Arabia, he was captured and sold into slavery. His new master took him to his home in Medina—the very town where Muhammad would arrive as governor a few years later. Salman recognized Muhammad almost immediately upon seeing Him, and before long, the companions of the Prophet bought Salman out of his slavery. He became a valiant supporter and provided the critical strategy to defend the community against the attacking armies from Mecca in what became known as the Battle of the Trench. He was the first Persian Muslim and the first of Zoroastrian background.

"I mentioned him back at Mt. Tabor, if you remember. He was the one to whom Muhammad had pointed when asked where God's favors would go if the Arabs proved unworthy."

"This is all truly amazing!" exclaimed Zach. "Not only were there wise men of the Zoroastrians who were able to follow the prophecies of their ancient religion to find Jesus at the right time but there were more wise men—Christian, Jewish, and Zoroastrian—who were able to find Muhammad through some of the hidden prophecies of their religions."

"Yes," said Youssef, "God and His Messengers have always left some clues for us to follow."

"And so we search today," replied James. "I hope we will meet with similar success."

"I hope so too," said Youssef. "You will not fail to let us know what you have discovered when you return, will you?"

James and Zach gave Youssef their assurances that they would let him know.

They traveled onward, pondering the many people who had passed through this very valley, or within a few miles of it, in search of the Promised One for their age.

*　　*　　*

AT LENGTH, THEY REACHED the south shore of the Sea of Galilee—that beautiful gem of freshwater in an arid land, around which so many of the episodes of Jesus' teachings had occurred. The Jordan Valley widened here, with steep hills, eroded gullies, and cliffs still rising up on each side.

The greenery of the landscape during this rainy season was beautiful on the hills, while the blue of this great lake was a joy to behold. They continued up its western shore until they came to the hot baths outside of the ancient Roman town of Tiberias. After the long journey from Jerusalem, they greatly enjoyed a few hours spent relaxing in the natural hot springs.

As they continued into Tiberias, Zach commented that it appeared that many of the buildings were cracked or damaged.

"*The Galilee Earthquake,*" explained Youssef, "almost seven years ago, killed 600 here and caused much damage. Since the Ottomans took over the area in 1839, little has been done to repair the town."

"Interesting," said James, "but I think one of the greatest earthquakes of all time took place just a bit north of here."

"What do you mean?" asked Zach.

James pointed northward up the coast and across the western section of the lake to a point between the two sides of the valley. "Unless I miss my guess, Capernaum would be over there—and beyond it, the Mount of the Beatitudes, upon which Jesus gave His first and most famous sermon."

"I recall the sermon," replied Zach, "but not an earthquake."

"It was a spiritual earthquake for the people who heard His sermon," James continued. "For more than 1,200 years prior to that, the Jewish people regarded the Law of Moses as firmly fixed and unchanging—as surely as you believe that the land beneath your feet is firmly fixed and unchanging. Moses said clearly that no man would ever have the authority to change the Law.

"But the theme of Jesus' sermon was changes to the Law of Moses. Clearly he was either a heretical man or He was not a man at all but a Messenger of God. And thus, He shook the old Jewish order to pieces and established a new order. So when I read references in the Bible to earthquakes, I am inclined to consider whether perhaps these might be spiritual earthquakes instead of physical ones."

*   *   *

THEY FOUND MUSA AS planned. He was eager for the upcoming journey. As soon as he had received the message from Suleiman, he started an early harvest of his olive orchard, as necessitated by his departure. He told them he would be ready to leave in three days. After getting to know Musa, they again spent some time in the town and mosque searching for stories of children with innate knowledge. But as before, no luck.

James said he wanted to spend some time up ahead at Capernaum— that fishing village mentioned many times in the story of Jesus. Zach and Youssef agreed to accompany him there. Zach and James would then join Musa after the caravan left Tiberias, as it passed through Capernaum.

The village of Capernaum, as it turned out, had mostly disappeared over the centuries. They were interested to learn that an American archeologist had started some explorations there five years earlier and had uncovered remains of a synagogue that had once been the focal point of Jewish life.

They climbed the "mount"—more like a broad hillside—leading away from the shore and then turned back to gaze on a beautiful and peaceful scene. From here the entire sweep of the shores of the Sea of Galilee and the hills beyond in every direction could be easily seen. The sky was clear and crisp, the sun was pleasantly warm on their skin, and the fields of grass waved in the gentle breeze. A short distance below, they could see a shepherd leading his flock with a staff in hand. It was so idyllic that they just sat for a long time to drink it all in.

"You know," said Zach at last, "this place seems little changed since the time of Jesus. More so than Jerusalem or Nazareth, or any place I've seen so far, I can feel His presence here."

"Yes," agreed James. "Big scenery sometimes encourages big thinking. It puts our smaller, day-to-day cares into perspective. When I think of the teachings that He uttered here and the impact these have had on humanity over the centuries, I am just struck with wonder."

They remained there for a long time, thinking about the Beatitudes of the Bible and the great significance of the teachings Jesus first gave in this peaceful place.

Finally, James stood up and said, "You know, if I were ever to die in the Holy Land, I would not want to be buried in Jerusalem or even in Nazareth or any of the other places we have visited. I would prefer to be buried right here." Zach agreed that it would be a beautiful final rest. "Seriously," James continued, "I have no close relatives to visit my grave. I could just as easily be buried here."

They spent some time roving the hills and reviewing the biblical verses from the Sermon on the Mount. *"Blessed are the poor in spirit"*— Zach thought of the humble people of this fishing village and especially those humble disciples who did not allow the teachings of the religious leaders of their day to cloud their vision—*"for theirs is the kingdom of heaven."*

Indeed, he thought of their own search up to this point and prayed they would remain humble in spirit and ready to see things from new perspectives, as the disciples had.

The next morning, they ascended the road to the northeast, to the point where it turned west toward Akka. They bid a fond farewell to Youssef, thanking him profusely for all that they had learned while traveling with him. They set up a small camp that afternoon and thought about the significance of the place.

"The task of changing the Law of Moses must have been overwhelming," said James, "given Moses' strict prohibition against adding to or subtracting from the Law, as was recorded in Deuteronomy 4 and again at the end of chapter 12. And yet changes to the Law of Moses were really the essence of the sermon Jesus gave here."

Echoing Matthew 5:17, Zach replied, "He made it clear He did not come to destroy the Law of Moses but to fulfill it."

"True," replied James, and then, after pondering a bit, he added, "And I hope that if the Promised One appears and makes adjustments to the laws of God as we have known them, we will all be able to recognize the validity of that distinction."

That evening, alone on one of the hilltops, they enjoyed the dazzling spectacle of the starry canopy stretched over the placid lake. In the morning, the caravan departing from Tiberias was easily spotted from their perch, and they had no problem finding Musa among the cameleers.

* * *

TOGETHER NOW, THE TRIO continued across the north end of the Sea of Galilee and then started their long ascent out of the lowland and up to the Golan area, passing along the upper edges of the wadies that cut deeply into the sloping land. Before long, the peak of Mt. Hermon was in view, now topped with a smattering of snow. It would guide them on the rest of the route to Damascus.

"Was it not somewhere along this road that Saul was blinded by the light of Jesus," Zach asked, "which led to his conversion and the changing of his name to Paul?"

"Yes indeed," James replied, "a stunning reversal in the persecution of the early Christians resulted from two visions—not only that of Saul but also of Ananias, the Christian whom Jesus instructed on how to find Saul in Damascus and how to heal his blindness."

"A fascinating story," added Musa, who had been listening. "Alas, in Shia history, Damascus does not have such positive associations, for it was the seat of the Umayyad caliphs, who moved the Islamic capital outside of Arabia and away from its spiritual heart in Mecca and Medina.

"You may hear Sunni Muslims speak of the first four caliphs as the 'rightly guided caliphs.' Well, *Muawiyah*, who started the Umayyad dynasty, was the *fifth* caliph. He was concerned only with his own power. He paid little heed to the religious teachings of Islam. He was largely responsible for starting the practice of persecuting and killing the descendants of Muhammad—the Imams of Shia Islam.

"At the beginning, Muawiyah promised that the leadership of Islam would not follow the practice of dynastic succession. But he broke that promise, appointed his son, and started a dynasty that ruled Islam for 90 years, which killed four of the first five Shiite Imams. Even today, the Shia remain few in number here in Damascus. But we can stay on the south side of the city, where we will be more welcome."

As they approached the city, they could see a huge caravan leaving it. "Why, there must be several thousand people with their animals, all heading south!" Zach exclaimed. "What could be so big as to create a caravan of that size?"

"Only one thing," Musa replied. "These are the faithful, bound for Mecca to participate in the pilgrimage. About 6,000 people gather at this time each year in Damascus from all over the region and head south as one large caravan at the beginning of the sacred months."

"The sacred months?" asked Zach.

"For three months warfare is strictly forbidden between any of the tribes so that the pilgrims may travel in safety to Mecca, participate in the pilgrimage rituals, and then safely return. And yes, that period begins today—the new moon appeared last evening. We are fortunate that our outbound travel should be at this time of year. It reduces the risk of an attack."

James added, "The pilgrimage month is the last month of the year on the Muslim calendar. And then..." He paused while contemplating.

"And then the year 1260 begins," Zach finished the thought solemnly. "Foreseen by Daniel, predicted in Revelation, and alluded to in the Quran."

It filled them with a sense of awe and an urgency to move forward, beyond the bounds of this Holy Land, pressing onward into eastern lands unknown to either of them and relying more than ever on their guide, Musa—and on God.

To be continued . . .

End Notes

1   Early Eastern Christians wrote "The First Gospel of the Infancy of Jesus Christ" (also known as the "Syriac Infancy Gospel"), which noted that the Wise Men came to Jerusalem "according to the prophecy of Zoradascht [Zoroaster]." This was first translated and published in English in 1697 and republished as part of *The Apocryphal Books of the New Testament* by William Hone in 1820. (An 1890 edition is available online.)

2   See *God's Strange Work—William Miller and the End of the World* by David L. Rowe, p. 169

3   Historical Note: It is documented that such a visit did in fact occur. See *Commonalities* by Serge van Neck, pp. 24 & 269

4   See William Miller, *Evidence from Scripture and History of the Second Coming of Christ*, Lecture VII, p. 104

5   Ibid., Introduction (1st page)

6   Ibid., Chapter VIII, p. 121. It is not clear whether this was originally Miller's own idea. At least one earlier writer offered similar thoughts. See Edward Bishop Elliot's *Horae Apocalypticae* (Hours of the Apocalypse), Volume 1.

7   Shaykh Muhyi ad-Din ibn Al-'Arabi, quoted in *Islam and the Baha'i Faith* by Moojan Momen, p. 127

8   Cited in *The Epistle to the Son of the Wolf*, by Baha'u'llah, p. 178

9   See *Early Quakers and Islam*, page 57. Quaker views of Islam as early as the late 17th century were remarkably tolerant. Some acknowledged

231

that Quakers who had been taken captive by Islamic (Barbary) pirates experienced greater freedom of religion while in captivity there than they had in their home country of England at that time.

10 See the *Zohar* Torah portion Vayeira, section 117. See also http://www.yivoencyclopedia.org/article.aspx/Tarniks for a general discussion of Jewish understanding of the significance of this time period.

11 See *Hastening Redemption—Messianism and the Resettlement of the Land of Israel* by Arie Morgenstern (Oxford University Press, 2006) for a detailed account of the early 19th century movement of Jewish people returning to the Holy Land, including the specific quotation from the Zohar (page 24) upon which this movement was founded.

12 *The Quran* (Pickthall translation), Chapter 2, v 256

13 See *The War of the Three Gods* by Peter Crawford for a very detailed explanation of the interactions between Christian Byzantium, Zoroastrian Persia, and the emerging force of Islam during this period.

14 See *Muhammad: His Life Based on the Earliest Sources* by Martin Ling pp. 268–269

15 *The Quran* (Sales translation), Chap. 2, v. 136

16 See *The Lands of the Saracen* by Bayard Taylor, chapter 7, for a description of a visit to Mt. Tabor in May 1852.

17 *The Quran* (Sales translation), Chap. 47, v. 38 (last verse of the chapter) and footnote "d"

18 See *Muhammad—His Life Based on the Earliest Sources* by Martin Lings, page 352.

19 *The Quran* (Sales translation), Chap. 61 and footnote "t"

20 Stories of those who recognized Muhammad through prophecy come primarily from *Muhammad: His Life Based on the Earliest Sources* by Martin Ling, pp. 29–30, 16–17, 34–35, 58, 229 & 238. See also *Salman al-Farsi* by Muhammad 'ali Al-Quth.

Bibliography

CHRISTIAN TOPICS

The Bible (King James Version). Note that this was the main English version of the Bible in use during the time period in which the story takes place.

The Apocryphal Books of the New Testament edited by William Hone, 1890. Note that the *Syriac Infancy Gospel* can also be found in *The Suppressed Gospels and Epistles of the Original New Testament of Jesus Christ, Vol. 3, Infancy of Jesus Christ* by William Wake, Aeterna Publishing, 2010.

The Rich History of Quakerism by Walter R. Williams, Barclay Press, Newberg, Oregon, 1987.

Early Quakers and Islam by Justin J. Meggitt, Wipf & Stock Publishers, Eugene, Oregon, 2013.

God's Strange Work: William Miller and the End of the World, by David L. Rowe, William B. Eerdsmans Publishing, 2008.

Evidence from Scripture and History of the Second Coming of Christ, by William Miller, 1840, reprinted by Isha Books, New Delhi, 2013.

Commonalities—A Positive Look at the Latter-day Saints from a Baha'i Perspective by Serge van Neck, George Ronald Publisher, Oxford, England, 2009.

The Resurrection of Christ; in Answer to the Question, Whether He Rose in a Spiritual and Celestial, or in a Material and Earthly Body, by

BIBLIOGRAPHY

George Bush, Prof. of Hebrew, New York City University, New York: J.S. Redfield, Clinton Hall, 1845.

The Prophecies of Jesus by Michael Sours, One World Publications, Ltd, Oxford, England, 1991.

The Story of Christianity by Jean-Pierre Isbouts, National Geographic, Washington, DC, 2014.

Ultimate Things—An Orthodox Christian Perspective on the End Times by Dennis E Engleman, Conciliar Press, Ben Lomond, California, 1995.

A Second Look at the Second Coming, by T.L. Frazier, Ben Lomond, California, 1999.

ZOROASTRIANISM/MAGI

The Magi: From Zoroaster to the "Three Wise Men" by Ken R. Vincent, BIBAL Press/D&F Scott Publishing, North Richland Hills, Texas, 1999.

The Man Who Sent the Magi, by Douglas Roper Krotz, Intermedia Publishing Group, Peoria, AZ, 2011.

The Journey of the Magi, by Paul William Roberts, Tauris Parke Paperbacks, New York, NY, 2006.

In Search of Zarathustra, by Paul Kriwaczek, Vintage Books, New York, 2002.

History of Iran: An Empire of the Mind, by Michael Axworthy, Basic Books, New York, NY, 2008.

The Travels of Marco Polo, Ronald Lantham translation, New York, NY, Penguin Books, 1958.

See also *The Apocryphal Books of the New Testament* listed in the Christian section above for the historic link between these two religions.

ISLAM

The Quran as translated by George Sales in 1734. Note that this version was generally used because it was the main English version of the Quran available during the time period in which the story takes place. Occasionally, the Picktall translation was used.

Muhammad: His Life Based on the Earliest Sources by Martin Lings, Inner Traditions, Rochester, Vermont, 2006.

Salman al Farsi by Muhammad 'Ali-Qutb, Ta-Ha Publishers Ltd, London, 1994.

The Last Day by Wahlied Jassat, George Ronald Publishers, Oxford, 2012.

An Introduction to Shi'i Islam, by Moojan Momen, George Ronald Publishers, Oxford, 1985.

Islam and the Baha'i Faith by Moojan Momen, George Ronald Publisher, Oxford, 2000.

Muhammad and the Course of Islam by H. M. Balyuzi, George Ronald Publisher, Oxford, 1976.

The House of Wisdom—How Arabic Science Saved Ancient Knowledge and Gave Us the Renaissance by Jim al-Khalili, Penguin Press, NY, 2011.

JUDAISM

Hastening Redemption: Messianism and the Resettlement of the Land of Israel 1st Edition by Arie Morgenstern (Author), Joel A. Linsider (Translator), Oxford Univ. Press, 2006.

Zohar, the book of Jewish mysticism, is available from many sources.

RELIGIOUS HISTORY (MULTIPLE RELIGIONS)

Persia and the Bible by Edwin M. Yamauchi, Baker Book House, Grand Rapids, MI ,1990.

Evolution of Human Spirituality, a lecture series by Dr. Ron Hershel, Menucha, Oregon, 2002.

Founders of Faith by Harold Rosen, Baha'i Publishing Trust, Wilmette, IL, 2010.

The War of the Three Gods by Peter Crawford, Skyhorse Publishing, 2014.

1844—Convergence in Prophecy for Judaism, Christianity, Islam and the Baha'i Faith by Eileen Maddocks, Jewel Press, Burlington, Vermont, 2018.

BIBLIOGRAPHY

GENERAL

Rough Passage to London by Robin Lloyd, Sheridan House, Lanham, Maryland, 2013.

The Land of Israel: A Journal of Travels in Palestine by H. B. Tristram, Society for Promoting Christian Knowledge, 1865.

The Lands of the Saracen by Bayard Taylor, NY, 1863.

The Land and the Book by William McClure Thomson, Harper & Brothers Publishers, NY, 1876.

WEBSITES

Wikipedia, for checking all sorts of miscellaneous historical items.

Google Earth: For topography, it is virtually as good as being there.

The Wilmette Institute provided several short courses with much helpful background material.

Great Comet of 1843: http://cometography.com/lcomets/1843d1.html

Prophecy Fulfilled (prophecies from all religions that point to a universal fulfillment in the nineteenth century): http://prophecy-fulfilled.com

Note that many other websites have been reviewed briefly on various topics.

AUDIO LECTURES

"The Apocalypse: Controversies and Meaning in Western History" by Craig R. Koester of Luther Seminary, The Great Courses, Chantilly, Virginia, 2011.

"Turning Points in Middle Eastern History" by Eamonn Gearon of Johns Hopkins University, The Great Courses, Chantilly, Virginia, 2016.

"The Rise and Fall of the British Empire" by Patrick N. Allitt of Emory University, The Great Courses, Chantilly, Virginia, 2009.

"The Industrial Revolution" by Patrick N. Allitt of Emory University, The Great Courses, Chantilly, Virginia, 2014.

"The Ottoman Empire" by Kenneth W. Harl of Tulane University, The Great Courses, Chantilly, Virginia, 2017.

"The Persian Empire" by John W. I. Lee, University of California at Santa Barbara, The Great Courses, Chantilly, Virginia, 2012.

"Sacred Text of the World" by Grant Hardy, University of North Carolina at Asheville, 2014.

About the Author

JAY TYSON grew up outside of Detroit, Michigan, and graduated from Princeton University with a degree in civil engineering in 1976. Shortly thereafter, he married Eileen Cregge. They spent four years in Liberia, where Jay worked on road construction projects. They also spent seven years in Haifa, Israel, where he assisted with historic restoration at the Baha'i World Center. They returned to New Jersey in 1989, where they raised two daughters and Jay continued his career in civil engineering.

Raised in a Presbyterian household, Jay was apt from an early age to deeply ponder spiritual matters. The suicides of three men in his upper-middle-class neighborhood over the course of a few years caused him to question the idea that material success holds the key to fulfillment and happiness.

He became a member of the Baha'i Faith in 1970 and has long observed a daily regime of reading scriptures or books on religion and religious history. *The Wise Men of the West* is his first novel and reflects his commitment to studying religion, history, and geography. His years in the Holy Land also gave him the opportunity to travel to many of the locations in which this story is set.

Jay may be reached at Jay.Tyson@SOOPLLC.com.

www.ingramcontent.com/pod-product-compliance
Lightning Source LLC
Chambersburg PA
CBHW032040080426
42733CB00006B/146